CAPITAL
FINANCING
STRATEGIES
for Local Governments

Capital Financing Strategies for Local Governments

The International City Management Association is the professional and educational organization for chief appointed management executives in local government. The purposes of ICMA are to strengthen the quality of urban government through professional management and to develop and disseminate new approaches to management through training programs, information services, and publications.

Managers, carrying a wide range of titles, serve cities, towns, counties, and councils of governments in all parts of the United States and Canada. These managers serve at the direction of elected councils and governing boards. ICMA serves these managers and local governments through many programs that aim at improving the manager's professional competence and strengthening the quality of all local governments.

The International City Management Association was founded in 1914; adopted its City Management Code of Ethics in 1924; and established its Institute for Training in Municipal Administration in 1934. The Institute, in turn, provided the basis for the Municipal Management Series, generally termed the "ICMA Green Books."

ICMA's interests and activities include public management education; standards of ethics for members; the *Municipal Year Book* and other data services; urban research; and newsletters, a monthly magazine, *Public Management,* and other publications. ICMA's efforts for the improvement of local government management—as represented by this book—are offered for all local governments and educational institutions.

CAPITAL FINANCING STRATEGIES

for Local Governments

Edited by
John Matzer, Jr.

International
City
Management
Association

PRACTICAL MANAGEMENT SERIES
Barbara H. Moore, Editor

Capital Financing Strategies for Local Governments
Telecommunications for Local Government

Library of Congress Cataloging in Publication Data
Main entry under title:
Capital financing strategies for local governments.
    (Practical management series)
    Bibliography: p.
    1. Municipal finance—Addresses, essays, lectures.
2. Municipal finance—United States—Addresses, essays,
lectures. I. Matzer, John, 1934-   . II. Series.
HJ9129.C36   1983   336′.014   83-47
ISBN 0-87326-037-6

Printed in the United States of America.
12345 • 89888786858483

Foreword

Financing capital improvements and equipment is of pressing concern in local governments. High interest rates, tax-exempt issues that compete with municipal bonds, and federal cutbacks all hinder local government efforts to obtain the funds they need.

Capital Financing Strategies for Local Governments describes what cities and counties can do and have done in response to these pressures—implementing innovative financing techniques and turning to such alternatives as leasing arrangements. It also presents ideas for increasing the marketability of municipal securities and enticing investors who have been lured by other opportunities.

This is the second book in ICMA's Practical Management Series, devoted to serving local officials' needs for timely information on current issues and problems. The editor has drawn on current literature to bring a wealth of material to the reader's hands.

We are grateful to John Matzer, Jr., City Administrator of San Bernardino, California, for undertaking this project, and to the organizations that granted ICMA permission to reprint their material. David S. Arnold, Editor, Municipal Management Series, was of great help in planning for this book and the entire Practical Management Series.

Mark E. Keane
Executive Director
International City
    Management Association

About the Editor

John Matzer, Jr., is City Administrator, San Bernardino, California. He was previously Distinguished Visiting Professor, California State University—Long Beach. Mr. Matzer has served as Deputy Assistant Director, U.S. Office of Personnel Management; City Manager, Beverly Hills, California; Village Manager, Skokie, Illinois; and City Administrator, Trenton, New Jersey. He received B.A. and M.A. degrees from Rutgers University, New Brunswick, New Jersey.

Contents

PART 5
Increasing the Marketability of Municipal Bonds

Introduction

John Matzer, Jr.

Local governments are facing a borrowing crunch of unprecedented dimensions. It is becoming more difficult and expensive to raise capital for municipal equipment and infrastructure needs. The volatile tax-exempt bond market has been buffeted by startlingly high interest costs, which have caused many local governments to postpone borrowing or to resort to short-term financing.

Commercial banks and fire and casualty insurance companies, traditionally heavy buyers of tax-exempt bonds, are abandoning the market because of lagging profits, record underwriting losses, and more attractive ways to shelter income. Individual investors are now responsible for buying approximately two-thirds of all tax-exempt issues, but these buyers, too, are being lured by other shelters. Demand for tax-exempt issues has been diluted by the reduction in the maximum marginal federal tax rate from 70 to 50 percent, tax-free All-Savers certificates, accelerated depreciation, leasing arrangements, and increases in the ceilings on annual tax deductible contributions to retirement savings plans.

Municipal borrowers also are faced with a heavy slate of competing tax-exempt issues. This competition—from revenue bonds used to finance industrial development, small business, home loans, hospitals, and pollution control projects—has increased the supply of tax-exempt securities and increased interest rates. Revenue bonds now account for over 70 percent of the issues sold. This has resulted in a depressed market for general obligation bonds.

Another problem confronting local governments is cutbacks in federal aid, which will generate a greater need for local borrowing. Federal funds have been a major source of financing for local capital projects, accounting in some cases for 50 to 75 percent of total project costs. If responsibility for many federal programs is shifted to state and local governments, the result will be increased pressures on already limited resources.

Cash shortfalls, defaults, and statutory revenue limitations have curtailed the ability of local governments to employ traditional capital financing techniques. Cutback management practices such as deferred maintenance and deferred replacement of capital assets are creating considerable pent-up demand for capital funds. The ability of municipal governments to obtain these funds is severely limited by deterioration in credit quality, lower bond ratings, and poor market conditions. These conditions present a challenge to local officials to identify alternative capital financing mechanisms and to improve the marketability of their securities.

The demand for new financing techniques

The uncertainty and instability of the municipal bond market has forced municipal borrowers to experiment with some novel capital financing strategies designed to attract investors and raise sufficient capital at reasonable interest rates. Examples of the new techniques include bond issues with warrants, put bonds, zero coupon bonds, floating interest rate issues, higher call premiums, lines of credit, commercial paper, and a variety of short-term issues. Governmental units are also making extensive use of leasing, industrial and commercial development bonds, and tax increment and special assessment financing.

This collection of articles provides an overview of innovative capital financing techniques and the factors that have led to their creation. The selections describe how many of the techniques work, discuss their advantages and disadvantages, identify major issues, and provide advice on how local governments can make their securities more attractive. The articles are from recent literature. Although some may refer to legislation or cases that are a year or two old, they were selected for their outstanding descriptions of financing techniques and applications.

Part 1, "The Municipal Borrowing Crisis," discusses the factors that have led to a need for innovative capital financing. Eleanor Craig discusses the extent to which federal government actions have imposed restrictions on municipal borrowing, and John Kraft examines the full range of limitations on the ability of local governments to structure tax-exempt financing.

Part 2 describes many of the new approaches to capital financing. Lawrence Shubnell and William Cobbs discuss the fundamental features of innovative capital financing techniques and point out some of the pitfalls in their use. "New Gimmicks in Municipal Finance" describes and gives examples of the use of commercial paper, bonds with warrants, put bonds, super-sinker bonds, and sale-leasebacks. Byron Klapper's article provides an in-depth examination of the background, issuances, and benefits and limitations of municipal commercial paper.

Part 3 focuses on the use of leasing as a flexible and cost-effective option to incurring debt. Lisa Cole and Hamilton Brown review operating leases, lease-purchase agreements, and sale-leaseback arrangements, addressing contractual, legal, and accounting concerns. Edward Dyl and Michael Joehnk explore the economics of lease rate-setting, present a simple lease evaluation model, and introduce the concept of a tax arbitrage lease. Kathryn Grover reports on the mechanics and advantages of equipment lease-purchasing, identifying leasing companies and describing how they operate. In "Oakland Sells the City Jewels," the terms, conditions, and benefits of the sale-leaseback of the Oakland, California, museum and auditorium are described.

Part 4 includes articles on industrial development, tax increment, and property-secured revenue bonds. In the opening article Charles Edmonds and William Lloyd look at the history of industrial bonds, outline the procedure followed in using the bonds, and discuss the advantages and disadvantages of industrial bonds to a user firm. Daniel Laufenberg reviews small-issue and selected-purpose industrial bonds, analyzes the costs and benefits of using industrial development bonds, and examines the controversy surrounding the issuance of the bonds. Next, Sheryl Lincoln discusses efforts to restrict the use of industrial revenue bonds, including policy options set forth in a Congressional Budget Office study on small-issue industrial revenue bonds. Richard Mitchell describes tax increment financing as a strategy for community development and shows how it works. Jack Huddleston compares tax increment financing laws in fourteen states—the nature of the enabling legislation, the receipt and distribution of tax increments, the planning and implementation process, and major project requirements and limitations. Finally, Walter Pudinski reports on the use of property-secured revenue bonds in Rialto, California.

Part 5 includes information that will help local officials improve the marketability of their bonds. L. Mason Neely describes the characteristics and mechanics of issuing small-denomination bonds, thereby expanding the bond market to the small, individual investor. Lauren Miralia examines the marketability of bonds backed by bond insurance. The article outlines the basics of bond insurance and the results of a survey of commercial bankers, which indicates their attraction to insured municipal bonds. Martin Katzman describes the operation of municipal bond banks and the potential benefits of participation in them. His article reviews the characteristics of bond bank participants, the hidden costs associated with banks, and the feasibility of expanding the concept. Martha Wall discusses major factors that affect credit position, describes how cities can rate themselves, and presents valuable tips on how cities can entice investors. Diane Hal Gropper looks at the competitive business of advising tax-exempt issuers on how to raise money and solve other financial problems. She discusses the phenomenal growth in demand for such services, identifies the types of firms serving as advisors, and points out some of the problems.

The book is concluded with a bibliography that directs the reader to further sources of information.

Strategies for using innovative financing

The financing techniques described here are not meant to be a panacea to municipal capital financing problems. Although they are important tools, they must be used with caution, because risks are associated with each one. Some of the techniques complicate and distort financial reporting and analysis of financial condition. Others provide short-term solutions that can result in long-term problems. Short-term debt, for example, creates a need to refinance in the future. Some of the techniques involve segregation and restriction of funds. All of them involve legal issues and public understanding and acceptability. The risks can be minimized if new techniques are employed as part of a comprehensive capital financing strategy. Such a strategy enables policymakers to intelligently evaluate the need for and implications of innovative financing alternatives given the present and long-term financial condition of their governmental unit.

A capital financing strategy should include the following components:

1. A system for assessing the government's fiscal condition. Such a system makes it possible to tailor capital financing programs to the overall financial condition of the governmental unit. (Guidelines for developing a system can be found in *Evaluating Local Government Financial Condition,* a series of five handbooks available from the International City Management Association. One of the handbooks provides step-by-step instructions for establishing a financial trend monitoring system.)

2. A comprehensive financial policy framework that sets forth written fiscal performance goals for capital improvements, debt, revenue, operating budgets, reserves, investments, accounting, and financial reporting. Financial policies facilitate long-term financial planning and preserve the credibility and fiscal integrity of the governmental unit. Financing options should be examined in terms of consistency with established financial policies.

3. A multi-year capital improvements program that identifies capital needs, ranks them in order of priority, and systematically considers alternative financing methods, including innovative ones. Capital programming provides a framework for analyzing the feasibility of financing options in terms of the total capital and operating costs of proposed projects.

4. A capital decision-making system that bases decisions on the time value of money, differing rates of inflation, opportunity costs, and cash flow. Evaluations of alternative methods of financing capital assets should incorporate the technique of discounting to present value—computing the present value of money that will be spent or received in the future. An analysis of the present value of all dollars for such options as debt financing and leasing will more accurately identify the least costly method.

5. A program for keeping bond rating agencies and underwriters informed of financial developments. Current information on audit findings, economic development, and capital and operating budgets is of great interest to investors and can contribute to improved bond ratings and marketability.

6. A system for ensuring the adoption and maintenance of sound financial management practices, including the preparation of annual financial reports that conform to generally accepted accounting principles and earn the Municipal Finance Officers Association (MFOA) Certificate of Conformance. Every effort should be made to avoid the use of financial gimmickry. Official statements prepared for bond sales should comply with the Disclosure Guidelines for Offerings of Securities by States and Local Governments issued by MFOA. Full and fair disclosure of financial information is critical in the case of lease agreements and other innovative financing techniques. The ability of local governments to raise capital at reasonable rates will depend on how much confidence investors have in their financial information.

7. A system for carefully evaluating the potential impact of the full range of conventional and innovative capital financing alternatives. The development of new and complex financing instruments has created a need for a high degree of financial expertise. Therefore it is essential that local officials contemplating the use of such techniques avail themselves of competent financial advisors.

A well-planned and well-executed capital financing strategy can lead to improved credit ratings, increased competition for securities, lower interest rates, and enhanced creditworthiness. By following a systematic approach, local officials can minimize the risks and maximize the potential benefits of newer financing techniques. Careful evaluation and application of financing instruments and better marketing of municipal securities will enable local governments to meet the challenges of the complex and competitive municipal finance market.

The Municipal Borrowing Crisis

Impact of Federal Policies on Municipal Bond Financing

Eleanor D. Craig

The federal government has assumed a very important role with respect to the capital financing options available to state and local governments. That role is frustrating attempts by the municipalities to provide their citizens with sound and stable financial management. In addition, the federal government's position with respect to bond financing has, and probably will continue to be, very volatile.

High rates of inflation, capital spending requirements accompanying federal monies, an expanded definition of what should be a "public purpose," and the shift of certain responsibilities to lower levels of government have caused dramatic increases in the long run borrowing needs of municipal governments. This is the supply side of the market.

Compounding these problems on the demand side, is the diminished ability of financial markets to absorb traditional instruments of long term finance. Excellent investment alternatives have emerged and the portfolio requirements of the major former purchasers have changed. The poor performance of the long term bond market in the past few years, municipal defaults, and municipal tax limits have lowered the appeal of long term bonds.

Many options exist for state and local governments to finance their capital needs. However, all of these seem to be very costly to the municipal governments, and for taxpayers in general.

Inflation

The present and anticipated high rates of inflation are the cause of the heavy interest burdens that municipal borrowers are paying. Interest costs for the average state and local security have risen 450 basis points since 1977 (*Weekly Bond Buyer*, 1981). Thus $50 mil-

Reprinted with permission from *National Tax Journal*, vol. 34, no. 3 (September 1981). Published by the Tax Institute of America.

lion of capital expenditures funded in 1977, would have carried interest costs of $28.9 million; and the same $50 million funded in March 1981 would have carried interest costs of $52.6 million (assuming level debt service payments). These increased debt service costs will impose heavy burdens on the operating budgets of many governmental entities for many years to come.

When interest rates are high, and it is anticipated that they will decline, governments will often postpone sales of long-term securities. Rather they opt to place shorter term instruments in the debt market. To a large extent, this occurred in 1980 when notes constituted 36 percent of the dollar volume of municipal debt sold (Kreps, 1981). Refinancing this short term debt will greatly increase the volume of credit demand in the next year.

The high interest rates accompanying inflation have differential impact on the various sectors of the economy. Purchases which require large outlays are usually debt financed. These are also purchases which can be postponed more easily than the average consumption transaction. Examples of such purchases are houses and automobiles. Thus when interest rates are high, and especially when the height is viewed as temporary, consumers buy fewer of these durables than otherwise would have been the case. If a recession which lowers consumers' incomes is coincident with the high interest rates, the producers of the durables receive a "double whammy." 1980 was a year of both recession and high interest rates, and the government sought to give relief to those sectors which suffered disproportionately. The forms of relief were numerous and included federally-guaranteed loans to an automobile manufacturer and numerous funding programs for public and private housing. Much of this federal involvement placed the government in the credit markets, driving up interest rates, further crowding out private investment, and generating increased inflationary pressures.

The construction industry, another interest-sensitive sector, placed considerable pressure on state and local governments to alleviate the problems in housing. Many state and local governments sold Mortgage Revenue Bonds which provided tax-exempt money to local banks. These banks in turn, loaned the relatively inexpensive funds to home buyers. To assure the eligibility of this funding device for tax-exempt status, most municipalities placed income and locational restrictions on the borrowers. Nevertheless, these financing devices played a significant role in many local housing markets. In Delaware, for example, 65 percent of the value of new housing mortgages in 1980 was funded by these tax-exempt monies (Delaware State Housing Authority, 1981). Housing bonds represented 3 percent of all long-term tax-exempt financing in 1970, and 32 percent in 1980 (*Weekly Bond Buyer*, 1980). These funding devices for owner-occupied residences are being phased out through 1984 under federal legislation called the Ullman Bill, in honor of the sponsor.

The most serious impact that inflation has upon the municipal governments is that it raises the nominal costs of capital projects. The estimates for the construction of the Louisiana Offshore Oil Port were less than $100 million in 1974. Today, as the Port is about to receive its first oil shipments, the construction costs have exceeded $600 million (Louisiana Offshore Terminal Authority, 1980). Financing these, and other construction projects has put tremendous pressure on the markets for long-term securities.

Federal mandates

Many of the programs that the federal government funds are geared to specific state and local needs and are administered and provided at the appropriate municipal level. Most of these programs tie the availability of federal funds to the willingness of the lower level of government to "match" a portion of the federal money. Many of these projects involve capital expenditures and therefore are funded at the local level through the bond market. Muller and Fix (1980) have studied the cost burden of complying with the requirements for federal grants on municipal finances. Direct federal grants to state and local governments amounted to 22 percent of state and local revenues in 1979, up from 17 percent in 1970 (U.S. Dept. of Commerce). Although there was a wide variation in the costs of compliance between the cities studied, Muller and Fix found that the incremental capital costs for complying with the federal mandates averaged exactly the size of the federal grant. Thus, the intergovernmental transfer of funds has necessitated extensive borrowing by state and local governments.

Many of the federal programs require expenditures that vary with the economic health of the recipient. Unemployment insurance programs cost more to states with high rates of unemployment than those with little unemployment. Achieving the same level of pollution abatement and safety standards is far more expensive in cities with aged capital structures, than where the machines and equipment are relatively new or under construction.

Defining public purpose

As economic growth faltered in the mid and late 1970's, the federal government tried desperately to compensate for the lack of economic progress by designing policies to encourage more growth. Increases in the monetary base that exceeded output growth were supposed to soften the impact of higher energy prices. Access to tax-free monies was supposed to aid industrial development, particularly in those regions where economic distress was most evident. Mandates on pollution control were supposed to be less onerous when the monies were available on a tax-exempt basis.

The net result of federal involvement to ease the blow of economic stagnation was more stagnation, accompanied by higher inflation and interest rates. Molchan (1980) points to the "newly perceived public responsibility in the areas of housing, pollution control and hospitals as generating 43 percent of the value of new municipal securities in 1979, in comparison with almost none in 1972." These projects had largely been the concern of the private sector ten years ago. Industrial revenue bonds are a good example of how the concept of a "public purpose" has shifted in line with decreases in overall economic progress and high inflation rates. Congress has become increasingly alarmed at the loss of tax revenue from these issues. A study by the Congressional Budget Office indicates that the volume of this financing was $8.4 billion in 1980 (15 percent of the tax-free markets) compared with $1.3 billion five years before (4 percent of the same market) (*Wall Street Journal*, 1981). There is a $10 million cap on each financing for every separate location. The intention of the limit is to restrict the use of this financing tool to relatively small projects for geographical areas or industrial needs which suit the definition of "benefits to the public as a whole" (Molchan, 1980). However, relatively large corporations have also used this financing option. K-Mart used $220 million in tax-exempt bonds to open 96 stores in 19 states between 1975 and 1980. McDonalds financed the opening of 32 restaurants with IDB's in 1979. Tax-exempt bond financing of these establishments only lowers the price of capital to the firms using this option, allocating capital to firms whose activity is "favored" by a government unit, and away from "unfavored" and potentially more productive firms. Taxpayers are financing some of the costs of capital, rather than the users of the products sold, and creating allocative inefficiencies in the economy.

The higher the interest rates, the greater the absolute spread between the taxable and tax-exempt financing, and thus the more attractive the tax-free sources become for business. Most of these issues are privately placed at local banks, the municipality merely becoming the conduit for the tax exempt status. The Congressional Budget Office study cites the possibility of sales reaching $35 billion by 1985. The local banks are not unhappy with these "bonds," since the "bonds" don't count under the normally constraining legal requirements for specific loan to deposit ratios. In addition, these higher risk bonds carry higher yields than other tax-exempt offerings (Hersh, 1980).

Interstate, intrastate, and interregional competition for economic development has probably also been significant in encouraging the use of IDB's. Since 47 states allow these bonds, the interstate competitive benefits of this financing tool may cancel out. In a parochial sense, IDB's may be an aid to economic development even if they actually have little impact. That is to say, sometimes the perception of tax or cost differentials between various communities acts to stimulate business interest. The availability of IDB's may indicate a community's interest in business expansion or willingness to offer other concessions.

Many have argued that any tax exempt financing mechanism imposes efficiency costs on an economy (Hersh, 1980; Molchan, 1980; and Mussa, 1978). In a technical sense, the budgetary efficiency losses are measured by comparing the loss of tax revenue due to the tax exempt status of the bonds with the costs of a direct subsidy to the recipient of the tax exempt money. Since the marginal tax rate of the bond purchasers exceeds the difference in interest costs between the taxable and tax-free financing options, this represents an inefficient means of providing incentives. Thus, if the marginal tax rate of the purchaser was 40 percent and the taxable bond's yield exceeded that of the tax-exempt bond by 30 percent, it would be cheaper for the federal government to grant a direct subsidy to K-Mart, or whomever, equal to the differential yield and have K-Mart borrow in the private capital markets along with all other users of available investment funds.

Intergovernmental role shifting

The relative centralization of governmental services at the federal level may have peaked, and a reversal of that trend may have begun. President Reagan's fiscal austerity program includes the redirection of many of the federal government's programs to the local levels. Federal expenditures increased from 20.8 percent of GNP in mid-1979 to 23.4 percent by the end of 1980. This upward trend had begun in 1965, but has accelerated rapidly in the past few years. State and local spending, in contrast, has risen at the same rate as GNP since 1973, slowing down from more rapid growth rates in the late sixties and early 1970's (Federal Reserve Bank of St. Louis, 1981).

Assuming the successful implementation of Reagan's programs, much future funding of spending at the state and local level that was federally funded in the past, will now have to be financed locally. The magnitude of this shift is impossible to predict, but the direction of change is clear, and the impact will provide a substantial increase in the need for long-term financing for municipal governments.

Traditional purchasers

The demand side of the market also poses serious problems. As state and local government needs for long term capital are mushrooming, the historical buyers of municipal debt are turning to alternative investment opportunities, for at least six reasons.

First, profits in America in the past year have been low. The tax exempt feature of a bond is only attractive to the extent that there is positive taxable income. In a recession, the levels of taxable income are lower than they would have been in periods of economic expansion.

Second, the proposed reduction in tax rates for corporations and individuals will further reduce the relative desirability of the tax-exempt feature of a potential investment.

A third reason is the relatively poor performance of the municipal bond market in the past few years. Commercial banks were badly hurt by the paper (and real) losses in their long-term bond portfolios that occurred when interest rates rose and bond prices fell. Most banks are now following an active policy of shortening the average maturities of their fixed income accounts. This policy shift will give investment managers more flexibility in actively buying and selling their municipal securities in the event of another long and steady increase in interest rates.

Fourth, there are many alternative excellent investment options available today that didn't exist ten years ago. Tax shelters have been offered to numerous other forms of financing, such as the intricate leasing arrangements which have been developed. The traditional twenty- or thirty-year general obligation bond has lost its relatively exclusive status as a tax shelter.

A fifth reason that purchasers are less interested in long-term bond investments is that there have been some defaults in the municipal market. The February 1975 default of the New York Urban Development Corporation made the default possibility a realistic option in municipal finance. The impact on the bond market was severe, and particularly hard on the poorer credit risks. The average spread between the yields on Aaa and Baa municipals doubled from 10 percent at the end of 1974 to 20 percent one year later (Molchan, 1980).

Finally, the state and local budgetary position, and thus the backing for long term debt, has been eroded. Inflation has directly driven up the cost of the services that these governments provide, yet their revenues have been less responsive to the "inflation-induced bonus" than have federal revenues. Proposition 13 and the other tax limitations imposed by governments in thirty-two states have placed permanent ceilings on the taxing capacity of those governments. The value of the "full faith and credit" pledge on the long term bond has been weakened by the public's distaste for high and rising government spending. Benson (1980) sees evidence of this in the reduction of the spread between interest costs of revenue issues compared with general obligation bonds carrying the same maturities. Voters can't disrupt the revenue flow from a project—a LOOP, a public power station, or a toll road; whereas the electorate can choose to decrease the general tax revenue available to its government.

The deterioration of the budgetary position of municipal governments will have serious long term consequences on the capital structures of these entities. Petersen (1979) suggests that a relatively easy way to reduce expenditures when faced with budgetary squeezes is to postpone capital improvements, replacements and maintenance. He says "foregone repairs and routine replacement will produce a wasting disease on the stock of public facilities, accelerating their deterioration and requiring more expensive remedies—as any New Yorker can readily attest" (p. 21). The results of the deteriorating capital structure are not immediately evident, and thus more politically palatable than would be similar budgetary savings involving welfare payments or class sizes in the schools. The levels of expenditure for noncapital expenditures are much more likely to be legislatively mandated and to result from campaign promises.

As a practical matter, budgetary problems, regardless of source, will make it more difficult for municipals to issue debt, more expensive when it is issued, will reduce its marketability and the value of its backing, and require more extensive capital expenditures in the future.

Options

The tremendous needs for tax-exempt credit, partially generated by the federal government's failures with macroeconomic policy, face-to-face with a reduction in investor interest in buying state and local long term debt have created a very serious situation for the financial community. The market test is probably the best indicator of the seriousness of the problem. A measure of the extent to which state and local governments have been crowded out of capital markets is the ratio of tax exempt yields to those in the private capital markets. An increase in that ratio, would indicate a relative decrease in the demand for, and/or an increase in the supply of, municipal credit. All things will sell at some price; in this case the relative cost is becoming very high. In early 1980, the average yield of the 20 municipal bonds was 59.3 percent of the yield on a corporate bond of comparable quality. In early 1981, the relative position of the state and local securities had deteriorated, such that the ratio has consistently exceeded 75 percent (Federal Reserve Bank of St. Louis).

Municipal finance will be forced to be far more creative in the future. Bonds with "put" features giving investors a means to recoup their money if interest rates rise, issues with warrants which are convertible into bonds with more complex call features, deep discount and floating rate issues will all probably be more commonplace.

The taxable bond option, whereby the municipality will be able to choose whether it wants to sell in the tax-exempt or taxable market, and receive a direct subsidy if it sells in the taxable market, is another alternative.

Federal formulas for funding and mandates for programs will have to become increasingly flexible. When the costs of compliance vary with the fiscal capacity of the government, funding levels will have to be tied to some measure of fiscal distress.

In addition, state and local governments will have to reassess their functions with respect to their citizens. Reducing levels of service, greater use of fees and charges for those functions whose purpose is not to redistribute income, and spinning off some responsibilities to the private sector, all must be investigated.

The picture is grim. The federal government has imposed serious constraints on traditional municipal bonding financing. To the extent that these constraints can be removed through increases in economic health, the municipal market will gain some relief. However, I believe that a much more active policy is necessary to reserve the tax-exempt market for those projects which cannot be financed privately, and not to use it as an escape vehicle from high interest rates.

Benson, Earl D., "Municipal Bond Interest Cost, Issue Purpose and Proposition 13," *Governmental Finance*, Municipal Finance Officers Association, Sept. 1980.

Delaware State Housing Authority, *Quarterly Review of Housing in Delaware*, Winter 1981.

Federal Reserve Bank of St. Louis, "National Economic Trends," Feb. 27, 1981.

Federal Reserve Bank of St. Louis, "U.S. Financial Data," various issues.

Fischer, Philip J., Ronald Forbes and John E. Petersen, "Risk and Return in the Choice of Revenue Bond Financing," *Governmental Finance*, Sept. 1980.

Galper, Harvey and Eric Toder, "Modelling Revenue and Allocation Effects of the Use of Tax Exempt Bonds for Private Purposes," Office of Tax Analysis, Dept. of Treasury, Dec. 1980.

Hersh, Arlene, "The Controversy Over Industrial Revenue Bonds Heats Up Again," *Dun's Review*, Sept. 1980.

Kreps, Matthew J., "Decline in Tax Exempt Volume Predicted by Most Observers," *Weekly Bond Buyer*, Jan. 12, 1981.

Louisiana Offshore Terminal Authority, *Official Statement*, Deepwater Port Revenue Bonds, April 11, 1980.

Mentz, J. Roger, Mitchell E. Menaker and Emil G. Pesiri, "Leveraged Leasing and Tax-Exempt Financing of Major U.S. Projects," *Taxes*, August 1980.

Molchan, Thomas M., "Reform of the Municipal Bond Market: Alternatives to Tax Exempt Financing," *Columbia Journal of Law and Social Problems*, Vol. 15, #3, 1980.

Morner, Aimee, "Long-term Bonds with New Lures," *Fortune*, March 9, 1981.

Muller, Thomas and Michael Fix, "Federal Solicitude: The Impact of Federal Regulation on Municipal Finances," *Regulation*, American Enterprise Institute, July/August 1980.

Mussa, M., "The Taxable Bond Option: Appraisal of its Economic Effects," *Weekly Bond Buyer*, May 15, 1978.

Petersen, John E., "Close-Up on the Post-13 Bond Market," *Taxing and Spending*, Winter 1979.

U.S. Dept. of Commerce, Bureau of the Census, *Governmental Finances*, various issues.

Wall Street Journal, "Firms' Wider Use of Tax-Exempt Bonds Sparks Renewed Concern in Congress," April 2, 1981.

Weekly Bond Buyer, "The Bond Buyer Index," March 2, 1981.

Weekly Bond Buyer, "Use of Revenue Bond Financing Seen Overtaking GO's in 1970's," Dec. 22, 1979.

Weekly Bond Buyer, Dec. 12, 1980.

Winders, John J., "Misuse of IDB's Will Spur Changes, But Federal Action Should be Avoided," *Weekly Bond Buyer*, Dec. 1, 1980.

Control of Tax-Exempt Financing: Is Local Policy Initiative Preempted?

————————————————— John L. Kraft

The Reagan Administration entered office with several economic mandates, including federal budget and tax cuts. The reduction of federal outlays involves many programs which have direct impacts on state and local governments. The shrinking federal budget is designed to, among other things, lessen federal control over state policy and return discretion to local government. This "new federalism" will adjust the balance of power between the national and state levels.

Despite these broad goals, some actions of the federal government in recent years threaten the ability of the states to implement their public policies. State and local governments have seen their prerogatives chipped away, particularly in the area of tax-exempt financing. The impending blockage of federal funding for various programs makes the states' ability to structure their own financing packages all the more important. An examination of recent and proposed federal actions affecting municipal finance illustrates how the federal government has interfered with local initiative regarding important public policy objectives.

The Reagan economic game plan strikes at federal fiscal policy on two levels—income tax reductions and budget cuts. The ultimate impact on state and local entities is at this time uncertain. Certain broad effects, however, are apparent.

The tax cut has important consequences for state and local governments. The Reagan tax bill calls for the reduction of federal income tax brackets by 25 percent over the next three years. Another important component of the tax bill is the reduction of the maximum marginal tax rate from 70 percent to 50 percent on January 1, 1982. The bill also provides for indexing of tax rates to offset "bracket

Reprinted with permission from *National Civic Review*, October 1981.

creep" due to inflation. Special deductions for charitable contributions are now available to taxpayers that do not itemize. These tax cuts and the other provisions reduce the advantage of tax-exempt obligations for the individual investor. For example, a 1980 investor will have a 25 percent reduction in the tax rate over the next three years. For a tax-free bond to keep pace with its current yield equivalent to taxable obligations, interest rates paid by state and local governments must rise. A person with the same income in 1984 would need a higher tax-free rate to achieve the same effective after-tax yield equivalent as in 1980.

A second consequence of federal tax reduction hits states which "piggyback" their individual income tax rates to percentages of federal rates (i.e., Rhode Island, Vermont).

A reduction of the federal tax rates automatically reduces revenues in these states. Without an adjustment of their formulas, these states stand to suffer a loss of revenue.

The Administration is increasing depreciation allowances for business assets. Forty-five states currently impose corporate income taxes. The shorter write-off time will reduce corporate tax receipts for these states. One estimate is that this aspect of the tax bill could reduce state corporate tax levies by $700 million.

Direct competition with tax-exempt municipals is also in the offing with the enactment of the All-Savers Act. Despite strong opposition from various organizations representing municipal issuers, both the Reagan bill and the Democratic counterproposal contained a version of this act designed to preserve the thrift industry. The basic provisions that were enacted allow financial institutions to issue federally insured, tax-exempt, one-year savings certificates beginning October 1, 1981. The law limits the interest on these certificates to 70 percent of the yield on a one-year Treasury bill, or about 10 percent tax free at current rates. It also limits the cumulative tax benefit to $1,000 per individual and $2,000 per joint return. The direct competition with municipal tax-exempt issues comes at a time when the individual investor has grown to about 20 percent of the municipal market.

The budget cuts have a more direct impact on state and local government. Eighty-three major programs and 200 smaller ones are targeted for cutbacks. These cuts are concentrated in those areas of the federal budget involving direct payments to individuals, programs targeted to local governments and local capital projects, since defense spending is scheduled to increase and certain other areas cannot, by law, be reduced. State and local governments will be faced with the choice of reducing their level of services or increasing their expenditures. Increasing expenditures means raising taxes and borrowing at the state and local levels.

Despite dire predictions of immediate danger to state and local governmental units, the picture is not quite that bleak. If the Reagan program achieves its overall goals, there will be increased productivity and investment, lower inflation and increased economic growth. State and local governments will share the benefits. The ability of the states to survive the initial impact of the program will depend in part on their ability to structure financing to accomplish essential policy objectives.

An important tool of state and local governments is the power to borrow. Borrowing for capital improvements helps maintain a stable tax system. Many believe it is more equitable to pay for the capital cost of a facility over its life, rather than have current taxpayers foot the entire bill when the facility is built. Finally, few local governments can afford "pay as you go" capital facilities, just as few individuals can afford to pay cash for a home.

In entering the credit market, governmental borrowers have an important advantage: their obligations are tax exempt. Several important justifications have been advanced for this exemption. One is that the exemption is mandated by the Constitution of the United States. Another is that the exemption promotes fiscal independence of the local units and thereby helps preserve our system of federalism. Both are closely rooted in the argument that local units are in the best position to determine their own public policies and should be allowed to use tax-exempt financing to pursue those goals.

There is substantial opinion available to support a constitutional basis for tax exemption for municipal obligations. This premise is grounded on the doctrine of "reciprocal immunity." While this position is by no means unanimous, a convincing case can be made in its support. The federal government, however, never has accepted this proposition. The current statutory tax exemption, codified in Section 103 of the Internal Revenue Code, places severe limits on what was once a relatively unhampered power of state and local governments to borrow at tax-free rates.

Prior to the passage of the Sixteenth Amendment, the federal government had made sporadic attempts to tax municipal obligations. The U.S. Supreme Court consistently rejected those attempts, relying on the reciprocal immunity doctrine. The enactment of the Sixteenth Amendment allowed Congress to "lay and collect taxes on incomes, from whatever source derived, without apportionment among the several states, and without regard to any census or enumeration." Proponents of constitutional tax immunity for state and local obligations maintain that this amendment does not abolish reciprocal immunity, but merely removes the apportionment requirement. Opponents focus on the phrases "from whatever source derived" and claim federal ability to tax any income, including that derived from municipal obligations.

The federalism argument also has constitutional overtones. The states' ability to determine and implement public policy on a local level is an important component of the federal system. Of course, there is no question that the federal government can override state determination of public policy in certain areas, such as defense, interstate commerce, etc. Nevertheless, the Supreme Court has recognized that certain activities and attributes of state and local governments are protected by the Tenth Amendment, which provides that, "The powers not delegated to the United States by the Constitution, nor prohibited by it to the States, are reserved to the States respectively, or to the people." The court has held in *National League of Cities* v. *Usery* that Congress cannot "impair the States' ability to function effectively within a federal system."

The states must be given wide latitude to determine issues of public policy because they are in the best position to diagnose local needs. The states must also be given leeway to define and revise their concepts of public purpose, because as one state supreme court said:

A slide-rule definition to determine public purpose for all time cannot be formulated; the concept expands with the population, economy, scientific knowledge, and changing conditions. As people are brought closer together, . . . the public welfare requires governmental operation of facilities which were once considered exclusively private enterprises . . . and necessitates expenditures . . . for purposes which, in an earlier day, were not classified as public. Often public and private interests are so commingled that it is difficult to determine which predominates. (*Mitchell* v. *North Carolina Industrial Development Finance Authority*, 273 N.C. 137, 144, 159 S.E.2d 745, 750, 1968.)

This North Carolina case was chosen to illustrate a point. A taxpayer challenged the North Carolina Industrial Development Finance Authority Act as not being in the public interest. Despite the broad statement of public purpose quoted above, the North Carolina Supreme Court struck down the statute as a violation of the state constitution. The court found that one of the powers of the finance authority, acquiring sites and constructing and equipping facilities for private industry, would not serve a valid public purpose. Subsequently, the state passed a provisional statute that became effective on the approval of an amendment to the state constitution by the electorate in March 1976. This history illustrates the exact point made by the court—"public policy" is not a concept etched in stone. It evolves with the needs of the public.

Congress, despite some occasional but significant lapses, generally has recognized the value of exempting state and local obligations from taxation. Since 1913, the Internal Revenue Code has excluded the interest on municipal obligations from gross income. Opponents of tax exemption have refined their strategy to an attack on specific areas of exemption. Thus, over the past 15 years, several major limits have been placed on municipal governments' freedom to structure tax-exempt financing. These include arbitrage limitations, limits on industrial development bonds and restrictions on housing bonds. In addition to limits on issuers, there have been limits placed on purchasers. For example, the Glass-Steagall Act prohibits commercial banks from underwriting many municipal revenue bonds. Another example was promulgation by the IRS of Revenue Procedure 80-55 which barred banks from deducting interest they pay on negotiated public time deposits secured by tax-exempt obligations. This procedure was withdrawn only after an intense lobbying effort by the banks and the local units which saw this as a serious threat to their ability to market their securities.

The promulgation of Revenue Procedure 80-55 illustrates a further problem for municipal issuers. While Congress paints its statutes with a broad, general brush, the IRS has been filling in the details with a collection of regulations, private rulings and procedural releases. And while Congress has given the IRS the ability to fill in the gaps in the statute, the IRS has exceeded the congressional intent in some areas and gone beyond the statutory limits.

The enactment of the arbitrage provision of Section 103 in 1969 and the subsequent regulations promulgated thereunder was preceded by IRS Technical Information Release 840 (August 11, 1966). Therein, the IRS announced that it would no longer give favorable rulings on the tax-exempt status of municipal obligations in certain "arbitrage" situations. The Tax Reform Act of 1969 codified the denial of exempt status to arbitrage bonds. The Treasury regulations promulgated under the arbitrage code provisions now prohibit a variety of practices of municipal issuers whereby proceeds of exempt obligations might be used to acquire obligations with a materially higher yield.

The arbitrage provisions particularly restrict the freedom of municipal issuers to pursue public policies. For example, refunding of outstanding issues has now become exceedingly complicated. This has happened despite the fact that there are valid public purposes behind certain refunding decisions, such as the desire to avoid prohibitive covenants or the need to restructure debt. The regulations have gone so far as to make it impossible to even earn the cost of restructuring debt through investment of bond proceeds.

Other regulations promulgated by the IRS have raised serious questions. In several areas, the IRS may have overstepped the statutory intent and even its own regulations in its pronouncements. As an example, the IRS has defined "materially higher" in refunding situations as zero. Another example can be found in Revenue Ruling 80-328, which discusses the arbitrage consequences of a contemporaneous issuance of notes and bonds. Despite the language of the regulations allowing for certain temporary investment periods, the IRS has disallowed a practice which is not only commonly used in construction financing, but which also produces no more arbitrage than that normally allowed under the regulations. In a current illustration of this problem, Washington State has filed suit in the tax court against the commissioner of taxation seeking to decide whether discount and administrative expenses can be taken into account for the purpose of computing yield.

Prior to 1968, there were no federal limits on the issue of industrial development bonds (IDBs). IDBs, which are issued by governmental units and backed by private credit, were first used in 1936 in Mississippi. The authorizing law was challenged in the Mississippi Supreme Court in 1938. That court held that the construction and leasing of a factory to private industry by a municipality satisfied a valid public purpose. The United States Supreme Court had ruled in 1914 that it would not review decisions of state courts delineating a state's definition of "public purpose." Thus, it is up to the individual states to determine their own public purposes. Once having made that decision, the issuance of tax-exempt obligations requires only the enactment of enabling legislation.

By 1960, 17 states had enacted such legislation, and the annual volume of reported sales of IDBs reached approximately $100 million. By 1968, when 40 states permitted IDBs, the volume of reported sales reached over $1.5 billion, which represented almost 10 percent of all municipal issues.

Restrictions on IDBs were enacted by Congress in the Revenue and Expenditure Control Act of 1968. With certain important exceptions, the tax exemption was removed from IDBs. Those exceptions are basically two-fold. First, certain types of facilities are completely excepted, such as airports, docks and wharves, and mass commuting facilities. No dollar limit is placed on financing involving these exempt facilities. The second exception, commonly called the small issue exemption, places a dollar limit on all other IDBs. Any project for $1 million or less can be financed. In addition, the original legislation allowed up to $5 million of IDBs to be issued with certain capital expenditure limitations on the recipient of the funds. Subsequently, the $5-million small issue exemption has been raised to $10 million.

Following the enactment of the Revenue and Expenditure Control Act, the volume of IDBs issued plummeted from over $1.5 billion in 1968 to $24,020,000 in 1969. The volume of IDBs has increased since, reaching a reported volume of $570,076,000 in 1978.

The Administration and Congress are currently reviewing the use of IDBs, a review that had its original impetus in the Carter Administration and the Democratic Congress. The current tax bill, however, does not contain IDB legislation. Recent positions regarding their use have run the gamut from proposals to remove all limits to calls for the elimination of IDBs altogether. There is, however, no clear-cut sentiment within the federal government on the revision (if any) of IDB financing.

Congress has expressed conflicting viewpoints. Proposals have been introduced to raise the capital expenditure limit on small-issue IDBs tied to HUD urban development action grants (UDAGs) from $20 million to $50 million, while the House Ways and Means Oversight Subcommittee held hearings on restricting their use in some manner. The Congressional Budget Office has published a study of small-issue IDBs. This study, initiated during the Carter Administration, presents several alternatives. While the study professes to be an aid to congressional deliberation, it frames the issue as: "...whether and, if so, under what circumstances the federal government should incur revenue losses to subsidize the borrowing costs of private industry without exercising any control over these expenditures." The basic premise of this argument is that the federal government has the right and the ability to control IDBs, and that it can do so better from Washington than can the states.

The Administration has adopted a hands-off policy for the time being. The Treasury Department has declined to take a stand. During the hearings before the House Ways and Means Oversight Subcommittee in April [1981], John Chapoton, assistant secretary of the Treasury for tax policy, testified that the Treasury was not at this time ready to set a policy on IDBs. Mr. Chapoton reiterated this sentiment when he stated that revision of IDB legislation is "certainly not a high priority item." However, Dr. Norman B. Ture, Treasury undersecretary for tax and economic affairs and one of the chief architects of the Administration's tax-cut plan, has in the past advocated an increase in the small-issue dollar limit.

Proposals for modification of Section 103 involve federal dictation to the states of the states' own public policy. The options generally combine targeting IDBs to types of business and/or distressed areas. These types of revisions can be relatively passive in that a mere change in legislation could accomplish some of these goals without requiring establishment of a new bureaucracy. Other, more activist, proposals include expansion of SBA, HUD or FmHA programs as a complete substitute for IDBs.

Several basic issues underlie any discussion of revision of Section 103. These issues include the alleged loss of federal tax revenue, competition in the tax-exempt bond market, competition among businesses with and without tax-exempt financing and the ability of state and local governments to determine their own public policies. These issues highlight the interests of the various parties involved—the federal government, the investor, the business community and the municipal governments.

State and local governments look at IDBs as a means of attracting industry to or expanding industry within the community. More jobs, a stronger tax base, aid to development and provision of services are among various public benefits generated. The businesses that take advantage of this type of financing benefit primarily from interest rates below prevailing conventional rates. Investors obtain a tax advantage by holding exempt securities. The federal government sees IDBs as a program to allow the states to allocate resources as they see fit, always subject to the potential for federal control.

Among the states currently issuing IDBs, there is a wide divergence of views as to the public purposes for their issuance. This divergence of views, however, illustrates each state's differing interests and needs. Proposals to revamp IDB use invariably result in more federal regulation. For example, proposals to eliminate IDBs and replace them with SBA direct loans and guarantees would require a complete restructuring of the SBA and a tremendous expansion of its capacity. These types of proposals run counter to the current administration's goals of reducing federal control over local decision making. Other federal programs are being consolidated into block grants, absent federal restrictions. IDBs are one of the few currently existing means by which the states may directly allocate their own resources.

The wide variety of IDB use reflects the extremely liberal criteria used in some states to determine whether a project constitutes a public benefit. Local communities rarely approve bonds that constitute abuses, but sometimes consider inappropriate factors in determining whether to issue IDBs. In order to assure that IDBs provide a net benefit, some states, including New Jersey, restrict their use for projects which would result in employee relocation within the state. The New Jersey Economic Development Authority requires that employees be able to relocate without undue hardship if the project's new location involves extra commuting. Only a small minority of states has established such rigorous criteria, however; other states should follow the examples set by New Jersey to ensure that their use of IDBs complements their concepts of public purpose.

Under current law, states and localities exhibit a great deal of discretion in their use of IDBs: they may choose to combine them with other efforts to promote economic development; they may be entirely under the control of the state, or the state may relinquish all authority to local government; the process for issuing bonds may include public participation, or it may be a routine administrative action that takes place without public knowledge. In a few states, local authorities may issue bonds for projects in other municipalities.

A small minority of states targets IDBs to designated areas. For instance, Massachusetts permits the location of industrial projects anywhere in the state, while other projects are eligible for tax-exempt financing only if they are located in "commercial area revitalization districts." Iowa also limits commercial use of IDBs to urban redevelopment areas. New Jersey restricts IDB-financed commercial projects to areas that include roughly one-third of the state's population. Rhode Island prohibits the use of IDBs for retail establishments but permits their use for office buildings that contribute to downtown redevelopment in older cities.

Targeting is most effective if it is a state policy, and all of the states which impose targeting requirements have agencies that play an active role in issuing IDBs. Some localities require targeting despite the absence of any state requirements. For example, in Erie

County (Buffalo), New York, criteria for the use of IDBs for commercial projects are extremely stringent despite a broad state statute.

The targeting of IDBs to areas in need of redevelopment encourages their use in conjunction with UDAGs. Housing and Urban Development officials estimate that in 1979 roughly 40 percent of UDAG projects were coupled with IDBs.

The elimination of IDBs would particularly hurt older, northeastern communities with eroding tax bases. This result would be not only unfortunate but also extremely ironic. IDBs were originally used in the southern states and have played a major role in the growth of the Sunbelt. Now that the northeastern states have begun to utilize IDBs to upgrade their industrial and commercial base, there is a call for their elimination despite efforts by responsible state officials to revise their programs to reflect changing views of public interest. Despite the failure of IDB opponents to enact restrictions to date, proponents should be aware that the issue has not been finally put to rest.

One of the most fundamental concerns of any local community is housing. Inflation and rising interest rates drive the cost of construction of new housing and rental units higher every year. The federal and state governments have attempted to alleviate these problems and stimulate the housing market in various ways. In 1978, Congress voted over $32 billion for housing programs. Also in 1978, approximately $5 billion of municipal housing revenue bonds were issued. The government has been forced to finance about two-thirds of all new rental units, and in some localities (e.g., New York City) virtually all new rental units are federally financed.

Municipal financing in housing takes a variety of forms. Several types of programs are available on the federal and state levels. These include direct loan programs, mortgage revenue bonds and Section 11(b) bonds. Direct loan programs are generally financed by state housing agencies for multi-unit construction. Mortgage revenue bonds are basically used to finance single-family units by using the bond proceeds to purchase mortgages from lending institutions. Section 11(b) bonds are used to finance low- and moderate-income apartment buildings.

Single-family mortgage revenue bonds have become the target of extensive federal scrutiny. Originally designed to assist low- and moderate-income families to become homeowners, the concept has been extended to include higher-income participants. The so-called "Chicago Plan" involved the use of mortgage revenue bonds to finance upper-class homebuyers. The popularity of this "Chicago Plan" spread outside of Chicago to other cities and resulted in a deluge of such issues. The spread of this type of financing led to fears that eventually all home mortgages would be financed by tax-exempt securities. The original purpose of the Chicago Plan financing was to keep upper- and middle-class homeowners in the central city. The glut of such issues on the market, however, only raises the cost of all other municipal borrowing. Local officials realized this problem and began to limit these issues prior to the federal restrictions.

Various public purposes exist for government involvement in the issuance of mortgage revenue bonds. Government involvement can serve to help low- and middle-income families afford safe and sanitary housing. In addition, urban areas can benefit from targeted aid of this sort. The major criticism of these bonds, however, is that the original public purposes have been shunted aside and the programs have overreached areas better left to private mortgage markets. These abuses are characterized by the Chicago Plan. Congress, reacting to this situation, severely curtailed their use in 1980.

On December 5, 1980, the Omnibus Reconciliation Act of 1980 was signed by President Carter. This contains the Mortgage Subsidy Act of 1980 (the "act") which restricts future single-family and multi-family housing bond issues. Single-family issues have been halted while issuers attempt to assess what will be necessary to comply with the new legislation. Multi-family issues, which qualify as an exempt activity under Section 103, have been limited to rental units. The act amended Section 103 to prevent multi-family projects from being financed under the small-issue exemption.

The act, according to the House bill, was "designed to direct the subsidy from the use of tax-exempt bonds for owner-occupied housing to those individuals who have the greatest need for the subsidy, to increase the efficiency of the subsidy, and to restrict the overall revenue loss from the use of tax-exempt bonds for owner-occupied housing." The act restricts the structure of financing, establishes mortgage eligibility criteria, places a ceiling on the maximum amount of state tax-exempt financing for single-family units, limits the arbitrage available to issuers and makes changes in Section 103 relating to multi-family units. New issues of qualified mortgage bonds are scheduled to lose their exemption at the end of 1983. The effect of the act, however, has been to stop the issuance of single-family housing revenue bonds completely. Pressure on Congress to reexamine the act has been increasing to the point that Representative Barber Conable, ranking Republican on the House Ways and Means Committee, stated that if the act cannot effectively be used in its present format Congress will have to reopen the issue.

Section 11(b) of the Housing and Community Development Act of 1974 authorizes a federal tax exemption for bonds issued to finance housing projects subsidized under the Section 8 program of HUD. This Section 8 program is a rent subsidy for low- or moderate-income families or elderly persons. Section 11(b) financing is available whether the projects are sponsored by profit or nonprofit groups. Bonds are issued by local housing authorities and are backed primarily by the HUD subsidy. HUD estimated that 20,000 to 25,000 Section 8 units were financed via tax-exempt bonds or mortgages in 1978 and 1979. A proposed reduction in Section 8 units, however, will limit the local housing authorities' ability to provide this type of housing.

It is evident that the financial capability of the states to finance housing development has been drastically reduced. At the same time, federal housing programs are undergoing heightened scrutiny. The burden of providing housing has not been eliminated, however, as approximately 1.8 million new households are created each year in the United States. What has been eliminated is the states' initiative to develop bold, innovative programs for developing lower mortgage rates and an expanded housing pool.

One of the more expensive capital improvements a municipality must provide is a sewer system. As communities develop and subdivision continues to spread from central communities, the demand for extension of sewer lines will increase. In 1968, there was more than $1.8 billion of sewer bond financing, while in 1978 there was over $4.4 billion. The ability of a municipality to charge user fees for hookups into the municipal system results in the majority of these financings being revenue bond issues.

Federal involvement in sewer financing is two-fold. First, the federal government has established various environmental standards to which local governments must adhere. Therefore, sewer systems must be constructed or upgraded to meet these federal standards. This federal involvement, along with the tremendous expense involved, results in the second level of federal participation: provision of capital grants to cover up to 75 percent of the total construction costs.

Unlike IDBs and housing bonds, there is at present no clamor for the removal of tax-exempt status from sewer bonds. Instead, the problem comes from proposals to eliminate or limit various grant programs. Typically, state governments provide up to 15 percent of the capital grants, and 75 percent of the cost is covered by federal money. Thus, only about 10 percent of a sewer system's present cost must be financed by a municipal bond issue. Without federal aid the local share is 85 percent or even more. Whether necessary projects will still be built and where the funds will come from are open questions at this time. The effect on user charges and whether the states will have to increase their aid to the local governments also need to be examined. Sewer projects are suspended in a financial limbo. Developers are caught with partially developed tracts of land awaiting hookups into municipal sewer systems that may never come.

The twin-edged federal involvement in sewer financing is an example of a severe problem for state and local governments—the problem of "federally mandated costs." The federal government, through legislation and regulation, mandates expenditures on the part of lower-level government units. The wherewithal to finance these programs is not part of the mandate. The result is a squeeze on local budgets. Where the mandated cost is great, as in sewer financing, the program becomes too much of a burden and cannot be accomplished without corresponding federal aid. A choice must therefore be made to cut the mandated costs along with the funds formerly provided to finance those projects.

The short-term effects of federal budget and tax cuts will require state and local adjustments. In order to make those adjustments, the state and local units must have the freedom to use the tools at their disposal. These tools include the use of tax-exempt obligations and the freedom to determine local public policy. This freedom to decide local public policy at a local level is at the same time the freedom to make mistakes. However, it is also the linchpin of our federal system without which local units cannot survive.

PART 2

Innovative Financing Techniques

Creative Capital Financing: A Primer for State and Local Governments

Lawrence D. Shubnell and William W. Cobbs

The creation of creative financing

Webster defines "creative" as, among other things, having the power "to invest with new form." As the word "creative" applies to municipal finance, this meaning is especially appropriate when it comes to raising capital. In recent months, neither the issuer of tax-exempt securities nor the tax-exempt market itself has been able to plod along in a "business-as-usual" fashion. In fact, since 1979, a host of new tax-exempt instruments has been coming to market as the market has shifted from a period of stability and predictability to one of volatility and uncertainty.

Both issuers and buyers of tax-exempt debt instruments are confronted with non-traditional circumstances that have prompted them to respond in non-traditional ways that have been creative. States and local issuers have been faced with historically high interest rates and frequently have been unwilling to commit to long-term obligations that result in interest payments of three times the original amount borrowed. By the same token, buyers are unwilling to lock into fixed returns, feeling uncertain about inflation, tax liabilities, and yield curves in the future. Enter "creative financing": governments still need to borrow, investors still need to earn returns, and creative financing seeks to marry their respective needs to mutual advantage.

Scope of this review

This examination of creative financing is offered as an introduction, or primer, designed to familiarize the reader with the fundamental features of new capital financing instruments in the tax-exempt mar-

Reprinted with permission from *Resources in Review,* May 1982, published by the Government Finance Research Center, Municipal Finance Officers Association.

ket. It does not exhaustively treat each or every of the new techniques from every policy aspect or technical nuance. Nor should the impression be given that the non-traditional debt instruments discussed are recommended for widespread adoption. Indeed, the prudent approach for a state or local issuer is to consider carefully, with a knowledgeable financial advisor, the alternatives. Our point is to illustrate that in this period of budget crunches and tight markets, capital can be raised in a variety of ways, many of them new. This puts a premium on systematically working through the possibilities for innovative debt structuring, the consequence of various approaches, and balancing today's savings against the probability of tomorrow's risk. In sum, designing a tailored capital financing program that will both meet current cash needs and accommodate future borrowing requirements is complex and needs sober analysis. With this caveat, we offer a description of state-of-the-art financing techniques recently employed in the tax-exempt market.

State-of-the-art techniques

Much of what has been dubbed "creative" in the tax-exempt sector is really not brand new, but rather adapted from other markets, including the taxable corporate and European debt markets. One of the most popular creative techniques, commercial paper, is a case in point.

Commercial paper   Issued originally in the corporate sector by merchandising firms to finance seasonal borrowing requirements, especially inventory and accounts receivable, commercial paper is a short-term obligation, usually of 30 to 90 days maturity. Normally issued by a broker for a fee of ⅛ to ¼ of 1% of principal on all trades, depending on the size of the program, tax-exempt commercial paper currently carries interest rates 100 to 200 basis points below the cost of a publicly sold note of similar maturity, even after taking into account the broker's fee, the back-up line of credit, start-up costs and administrative expenses. A bank line of credit is necessary in the event that the commercial paper cannot be "rolled-over" at maturity or otherwise taken out; the cost of a credit line is about ½ of 1% of the unused portion of the backup amount. Start-up expenses consist primarily of legal fees for financial documentation and authorizing opinions. Administrative costs include personnel to oversee frequent roll-overs of short maturities and custodian services.

Tax-exempt commercial paper is unsecured and must be accompanied by a periodic disclosure memorandum to investors. A special commercial paper credit quality rating must be obtained from a nationally recognized credit rating agency. Cash is generally available to the issuer on the same date as the sale date of the commercial paper. The amount of commercial paper outstanding can be raised or lowered as needed once the program is established. This permits an issuer to borrow additional amounts in smaller increments than is customary when using more traditional short-term tax-exempt instruments.

Tax-exempt commercial paper is most adaptable for financing seasonal borrowing needs, or for financing a continuing capital

---

Background: During 1981 the Commonwealth of Kentucky sold six note issues with a total value of $120,600,000. The following compares the estimated total costs incurred by issuing Bond Anticipation Notes with the costs that might have been incurred by issuing Tax-Exempt Commercial Paper.

Costs of issuance
Two-year notes—$120,600,000
    (6 issues)

Fiscal agent fees	$	250,000
Discount (1%)		1,206,000
Total costs		1,456,000

Tax-exempt commercial paper

One-time cost		60,000
Line of credit		603,000
Rollover of paper (every 90 days)		1,206,000
Total costs	$	1,869,000

Interest cost assumptions

Two-year notes sell at 9.5% (actual average on six issues)	$	22,914,000
Commercial paper at 7.0%		16,884,000

Totals

Two-year notes	
Issuance cost	1,456,000
Interest cost	22,914,000
(1) Total costs	24,370,000
CP rollover two years	
Issuance cost	1,869,000
Interest cost	16,884,000
(2) Total costs	18,753,000

Savings with tax-exempt commercial paper (1)−(2)	$	5,617,000

Source: Data from Office of Investment and Debt Management, Commonwealth of Kentucky.

Costs comparison: two-year bond anticipation notes vs. commercial paper financing.

spending program until long-term permanent financing is appropriate or affordable. However, a recurring requirement for sizeable ($20–$25 million minimum) short-term borrowings is necessary to justify the cost of establishing a tax-exempt commercial paper program.

The State of Connecticut was one of the earliest tax-exempt issuers to use commercial paper. The cities of Wilmington, Delaware, and Columbus, Ohio, have issued commercial paper, as have Los Angeles County and Chesterfield County, Virginia, among others. Thus far, 26 issuers have come to market with tax-exempt commercial paper and an estimated $1.7 billion is outstanding.

Floating rate instruments   An adaptation from the Euro-currency markets, the floating rate instrument places the risk of interest rate fluctuations (and inflationary trends) on the borrower rather than on the lender. Thus, the cost of borrowing becomes a variable

---

An inflation-proof bond?

The zero coupon, deep discount, and variable rate bonds approach the concept of an indexed bond. When a bond is indexed the principal (face) value and the coupon (interest) rate are adjusted to changes in some measure of inflation, or some other measure of value such as gold prices.

In contrast to the traditional bond (where investors face the risk of being paid back in cheaper dollars as inflation eats away at the value of principal and the purchasing power of fixed interest payment) an indexed bond protects the investor from erosion in the principal, and inflation would drive up the interest yield. For example, a 3% indexed bond would yield $33 of interest on an original issue of $1000, rather than $30, if inflation after one year were 10% since the principal value would have risen to $1,100. A low coupon is possible on an indexed bond because the investor seeks only his "real" yield for the coupon since the portion of the yield typically required to compensate for inflation is replaced by the indexing. Of course, the issuer is required to pay the entire inflation-driven principal value at maturity. On a 20-year bond at 10% inflation this would amount to a $6000 maturity value on an original $1000 of principal.

The issuer of an indexed bond faces considerable uncertainty in debt service planning, and assumes significant risk exposure in cash availability at maturity dates. Indexed bonds may also raise thorny tax problems dealing with arbitrage allowances if sinking funds equal to the inflation-appreciated principal are established, and as to the tax treatment of the annual increases in the bondholder. Nonetheless, if long term interest rates fail to move lower and federal policies portend longer term inflation, the next "creative" instrument in the municipal market may be the indexed bond.

cost rather than a fixed cost to the issuer, thereby protecting buyers from the loss of market value in the face amount of debt instruments. This shift of the traditional risk-bearing relationships becomes attractive if tax-exempt issuers can attain otherwise lower interest rates than might be possible using a fixed rate security, because it attracts investors that have lost their appetite for long-term fixed-rate debt instruments, primarily as a result of capital erosion. Thus, the issuers of floating rate securities can broaden their market, an especially important consideration for some borrowers, particularly those not enjoying the highest credit ratings.

A variety of floating rate instruments have been used in the tax-exempt market. (See box: *An Inflation-Proof Bond?*) Among them, the following are representative:

1. Flexible Rate General Obligation Certificates of Indebtedness, secured by the full faith and credit of the State of Washington. These were issued as one-year notes, but permit investors either to tender the certificates every 30 days or to roll them over at prevailing interest rates;

2. Floating Rate Collateralized Revenue Bonds, issued by the Ohio Air Quality Development Authority. On these limited obligation 30-year bonds, secured by a pledge of loan payments made by the Cleveland Electric Illuminating Company, interest is payable every six months and calculated by using a formula based upon prevailing rates during the prior six months;

3. Variable Rate Student Loan Revenue Bonds, issued by the South Carolina State Education Assistance Authority as special obligations and secured by insured student loan payments. These 17-year bonds pay interest quarterly, which is calculated at a rate that is geared to that on Treasury bills. Similar issues have been offered by the Virginia Educational Loan Authority and by authorities in Kentucky, Minnesota and Kansas;

4. Floating Rate Monthly Demand Pollution Control Revenue Bonds, issued by the Industrial Development Authority of Apache County, Arizona on behalf of the Tucson Electric Power Company. Interest on these 40-year bonds is payable monthly and determined using a multi-tiered formula that considers numerous interest rates to determine the rate.

Bonds with warrants   Traditionally associated with common stocks, warrants permitting holders to purchase additional bonds were first issued at the end of 1980 in conjunction with a bond sale by the Kingdom of Sweden. The first sale of a tax-exempt bond with warrants was by the Municipal Assistance Corporation for New York City. A warrant entitles the holder to purchase additional bonds at a fixed discount price during a specified period, thereby providing a "reverse call" option on the security. Because the warrants pay no interest, they have no intrinsic value unless the market price of the security rises above the call price. The lack of intrinsic value does not, however, imply a lack of market price because certain investors have always been willing to pay for the right to a call option, since they anticipate the possibility of higher bond prices (and lower interest rates) in the future.

From the issuer's standpoint, the willingness of investors to purchase such an option provides an opportunity to reduce the cost of borrowing. It is estimated that because of the warrant feature the MAC issue carried an interest rate one-half a point lower than would otherwise have prevailed. However, MAC's total debt service costs may be higher than otherwise if interest rates drop sufficiently to prompt holders to exercise the warrants. If rates decline, and the warrants are not exercised, it has been estimated that on this particular sale MAC will have saved about $11 million in interest payments over the life of the issue through the use of warrants.

Put option bonds   This feature is designed to limit capital deterioration due to increasing rates because investors have the option to tender their bonds back to the issuer at par at the end of a specific period (usually 5 to 10 years) after the sale date. In some cases, the put may be made every year thereafter; if so, after the tender period the bonds effectively become one-year debt instruments and should trade at prevailing rates for comparable short-term securities. For issuers, the existence of a put entails a substantial refinancing risk and a back-up source of money to meet the tender, if it is exercised, is a letter of credit agreement from a commercial bank. To provide this back-up, a bank usually charges an annual fee of approximately 100 basis points on the outstanding amount of principal. Market participants state that this arrangement has saved issuers as much as 200–300 basis points in interest costs for an issue.

Refinements and special features   Certain features—both traditional and novel—can be incorporated into various debt financing instruments to provide issuer safeguards, to meet investor preferences, or to create implementation mechanisms. Among the traditional designs, *call features* are frequently found on long-term bonds. The call permits the issuer to redeem or retire the bond after a certain period of time, frequently 10 years, at a premium to par. Such a feature enables the issuer to escape continuing payments of high coupon rates in markets where a refinancing would result in a lower net interest cost to maturity after taking into consideration the call premium.

In a newer vein, some variable rate bonds are issued as "*convertibles*" whereby the lender is permitted, within certain time constraints, to exercise an option which converts the variable rate interest feature to a fixed rate interest coupon for the duration of the term of the security.

Almost all variable rate notes and bonds, except those of the very shortest term or commercial paper, will carry *ceilings and floors* below which the interest rate is guaranteed not to fall (minimum interest rate), and above which interest payments may not go (a maximum rate).

In order to determine the interest on a floating rate debt instrument, various *interest indexes* have been used. It is common to tie the actual interest rate paid to a percentage of an easily identifiable market measure such as U.S. Treasury bonds or notes. For example, a tax-exempt floating rate security with quarterly interest payments might be tied to 13-week Treasury bills at 75% of the effective yield. The interest index ultimately selected, its computational complexity and its accuracy as a measure of prevailing rates, will materially affect the market success of a variable rate instrument.

Many of the new debt instruments are backed by credit arrangements with large, top-rated commercial banks. Frequently, *letters of credit* or *lines of credit* back up issuer obligations and guarantee liquidity. For example, the put option notes incorporating a floating interest rate issued by the State of Washington contained a bank back-up of a noteholder's tender. For a fee (discount) of three-tenths of one percent of the principal amount of the initial issuance, and, in addition, a commitment fee of one-half of one percent on the unused portion of the credit call and a management fee of one-tenth of one percent, the bank stands ready to assure liquidity and manage the note issue. It is usually necessary to have such intermediate credit arrangements because, typically, tax-exempt issuers are not set up to carry out rapid-pace transactions in the credit markets.

Other structuring devices, such as the *zero-coupon bond*, are offered to attract investor attention. These bonds pay no interest prior to maturity. Instead, they are offered at deep discounts to compensate the investor for giving up current interest payments. The investor is willing to accept a lower than market rate return for an extended period because of the guaranteed fixed rate of return. However, the issuer, because of the deep discount, receives much less cash up front than would otherwise be the case with an issuance at par. Explaining to the public why the city has sold $30 million in bonds to raise $7 million cash, for example, may prove difficult, no matter how advantageous the transaction.

Leasing   A variety of leasing options has been employed as a financing technique for the acquisition of assets and as alternatives to the traditional bond issue. Under the right circumstances, leasing can offer advantages to both the public and private sectors in that the private sector is able to use tax benefits which can be passed through to lower the cost of capital to the governmental units.[1]

Leases carry a wide range of labels. A brief recap of the more popular lease forms is presented below:

(a) Operating Lease—An agreement between a user (lessee) and owner (lessor) of an asset for rental of the asset for a specified period of time. (Otherwise known as a true lease.) The lessor usually takes the tax benefits and responsibility for maintenance, insurance, and taxes in return for the payment of a periodic fee.

(b) Capital Lease—A lease of a capital asset that is treated as a sale because certain conditions are met by the lessee which are tantamount to ownership characteristics. Forms of capital leases are lease-purchase or conditional sales leases which render the user/lessee the owner of the property and, thus, permit the lessor exemption of the interest portion of the lease payments from federal income taxes.

(c) Financing Lease—In this case, the lessee negotiates a purchase with a supplier of property and simultaneously arranges for a bank or leasing company to buy the property. The lessee then executes an agreement with the financing institution from which it rents the property.

(d) Sale-Leaseback—An arrangement whereby the owner of an asset sells the asset to a financing entity and then enters a lease for use of the asset with the buyer paying a fee that covers the financing cost of the purchased asset. The lessee (seller) obtains cash from the sale and the lessor (buyer) obtains the tax advantages of asset ownership.

How safe is the "safe-harbor"?

"Under severe budget pressures, many municipalities are exploring ways to cut costs or raise cash by selling the long-neglected tax benefits inherent in their construction projects. And some are finding ways to do this without resorting to 'safe-harbor' tax leasing, which has become politically jeopardized.

"Because of the controversy about huge tax savings for corporations using this feature of the 1981 tax law, Senate Finance Committee Chairman Robert J. Dole (R-Kan.) has proposed that safe-harbor deals be sharply restricted. That has put a damper on leasing arrangements specifically authorized for municipal transit authorities.

"... In Denver, for example, the transit authority had expected seven bids in a safe-harbor lease involving city buses. After Dole's announcement, two bids were received, and even these were later withdrawn. Thus, cities are eagerly turning to traditional sale-leasebacks that pass along depreciation write-offs to syndications of high-income, private investors who can use tax shelter."

Business Week: April 5, 1982, p. 95.

(e) Leveraged Lease—This involves the use of debt and equity capital, with the equity contributor obtaining the tax benefits of ownership and the overall debt financing employing tax-exempt bonds or notes. The idea of leverage comes from the utilization of a small equity (usually 20%) contribution to acquire a larger valued asset by employing debt financing for the balance. The leveraged lease is similar to a sale-leaseback or a financing lease, and may be executed as a safe-harbor lease.

(f) Safe-Harbor Lease—Similar to a financing lease, or sale-leaseback, this is a lease that transfers ownership of an asset to the lessee at the end of the lease term for a nominal fee, while affording the lessor the tax benefits of ownership. Safe-harbor leasing is generally not applicable to governments since a basic criterion for eligibility for this lease form is that the property must be eligible for the investment tax credit (which is generally not available to assets used for governmental purposes). However, under special provisions in the 1981 tax act, certain governmental activities may qualify for safe-harbor leasing, such as mass transit facilities.

The stepped coupon bond

One of the more innovative of the recent debt structuring techniques is the *stepped coupon bond*. First issued by Lee County, Florida (April, 1982), this type of bond features a maturity structure and interest coupon designed to lower the interest cost to the issuer and to protect the principal of the investor. A stepped bond coupon uses a serial maturity schedule with coupon rates that start at lower levels and progressively increase to higher levels. All of the bonds in an issue, regardless of maturity, bear the same rate of interest in any one year, with coupon rate changes from time to time, sometimes as often as each year. All bonds are sold at par. This stands in contrast to the conventional bond where each maturity has a single coupon rate payable over the life of that maturity. For example, the 1990 serial maturity of the Lee County issue carries coupon rates ranging from 8% in 1982 to 14% in 1990. The yield to maturity of this bond is 11.27%.

This increasing coupon feature combines elements of both a short-term and long-term security in terms of rate of return, and cushions the investor from a deterioration in principal. From the issuer's perspective, because of lower early year coupon rates than otherwise attainable under the conventional bond, more bonds may mature in the early years, thereby lowering the average life of the issue. In the case of Lee County, Arch W. Roberts & Co., designers of the stepped coupon concept, estimates that the issuer will save approximately $20 million over the 24-year life of the issue. The net present value savings is about $840,000 on an aggregate issue of $23,900,000. A major benefit of the stepped coupon bonds would be on revenue bonds issued to finance projects requiring capitalized interest.

Although straight leasing is normally more costly in interest notes when compared to general obligation debt, certain forms of leasing, such as the leveraged lease, can result in savings equal to from 100 to 300 basis points when structured properly to capture some portion of the lessor's tax benefits for the lessee. A caveat, however, is important since the fine-tuning of the terms and conditions of a lease will significantly affect the financial benefits available to its different parties. For example, under most leasing arrangements involving a governmental unit as lessee, the investment tax credit is not available.

Because of the newness of many creative leasing arrangements, many are not founded on a well-established body of practice, and some may even be considered on the fringe of the law. An additional uncertainty rests with Congress and the federal agencies (particularly the U.S. Treasury), which show increasing restlessness with respect to some of the leasing opportunities presented by the 1981 Economic Recovery Tax Act. For example, Senate Finance Committee Chairman Robert J. Dole (R-Kan.) has proposed that safe-harbor leasing be sharply restricted (see box). Municipal lessees would be well advised to keep a sharp watch for shifting legislative and regulatory sands and be prepared to move fast.

Perspective on creativity

It is important to approach the tax-exempt market with two objectives in mind: (a) borrowing at the lowest attainable interest rate within the context of future liquidity needs and revenue forecasts, and (b) using an instrument that is attractive to investors yet within the realm of prudence of issuers in the assumption of future risks. Governmental borrowers ought to develop a capital financing program tailored to their overall financial condition and fiscal philosophy.

Creative cautionary

Creative financing opens up new potentials, but provides pitfalls, as well. First, many of the new devices are creating an overhang of short-term debt that will need refinancing in the near future. The more stockpiling of such debt, the more difficult will be refinancing as everybody attempts to come to market at once. Also, creative financing is often associated with off-the-balance-sheet debt and the segregation and restriction of funds. Not only can this impair a unit's fiscal flexibility by tying up monies otherwise available for general purposes, it also makes reporting and understanding a unit's financial condition more difficult. Creative financing, if used simply as an expedient, can be a prescription for trouble, especially in times of financial and economic contraction.

Make no mistake about it, creative financing is a creature of uncertain markets and "hard-to-sell" investors. An issuer should not
jump on the bandwagon of new financing techniques if more conventional approaches are available and acceptable, unless it is satisfied
there is sufficient benefit compared to the risk. Taking advantage of
current market demands through use of creative techniques implies
willingness and ability on the part of issuers to accept and deal with
future market uncertainty, a burden formerly assumed by investors.

In addition to the financial considerations, governmental units
contemplating a creative financing arrangement must also take into
account other practical concerns. These include the political acceptability (and popular explainability) of such arrangements; a unit's
technical ability to manage them; and the laws (local, state and federal) that influence such arrangements. But, while there may be no
"free lunches," careful and knowledgeable scrutiny of the financing
menu may turn up some specials that prove to be real bargains.

1. For an extensive overview of govern-
    mental leasing techniques with ex-
    amples, refer to "Municipal Leasing:
    Opportunities and Precautions for
    Governments," *Resources in Re-
    view*, p. 6, January 1982 [reprinted
    in Part 2 of this volume].

New Gimmicks in Municipal Finance

Even though they are paying record interest rates, the nation's hard-pressed municipalities have found it increasingly difficult to market their bonds, tax-free though they may be. Many investors have been so badly burned in the fixed-income markets, as prices sagged further with each upward rachet of interest rates, that many have foresworn bonds—particularly long-term ones—for all time.

And the financing problems of the nation's municipalities are not likely to get any better, even if interest rates begin to drop later this year [1981]. In the first place, many investors are likely to remain gun-shy about bonds. At the same time, many cities are sure to have even greater need for money as the Reagan budget cuts start to pinch in the fiscal year beginning October 1. Still another deterrent to municipals is the slashing of the top tax rate from 70% to 50%, as well as the cutting of taxes across the board, which is sure to decrease the attractiveness of tax-exempt issues. That's why many municipalities, along with their investment bankers, have developed a wide array of innovative financing techniques to attract investors.

Perhaps the most popular of these is municipal commercial paper. Although introduced in 1974, the concept did not catch on until last year, when the market absorbed about $480 million from five issuers. So far this year, almost $1 billion worth has been sold, and this could soar to $5 billion in a year or so, according to John R. Carhuff, who heads First Boston Corp's public finance department.

Raising money with commercial paper provides a number of advantages to a municipality. "A city with a major construction project may prefer not to issue long-term bonds due to currently high interest rates, but may want to start building before costs escalate," explains John Vincent, public finance expert at John Nuveen & Co., Inc. "The strategy is to borrow short-term and refinance with long-term bonds when interest rates are lower."

That is what the city of Columbus, Ohio, did in June when it issued commercial paper with maturities ranging from seven to seventy days and carrying interest rates between 7% and 7¾%. The alternative was to finance with a one-year note at 9%. The $38 million raised has been turned over a couple of times since then and when interest rates fall, the city plans to float long-term debt.

Connecticut's boon

On the state level, Connecticut this month will be the first to go to the commercial paper market. Raising $115 million with commercial paper bearing an average maturity of thirty days rather than with a one-year note saves the state about two percentage points on that financing.

What makes municipal commercial paper easier to sell than traditional vanilla bonds are the bank credit agreements backing these issues. Even less creditworthy municipalities can secure a letter of credit from a bank, which will directly pay the holder at maturity. Thus the investor need only look at the creditworthiness of the bank, not the municipality.

An innovation in the battered long-term market is "put bonds." These are issues that give the holder the option to sell the bond back to the issuer at par after a specific period of time, usually between five and ten years, and every year thereafter on the put date. Thus, if rates rise, investors can get out of a thirty-year instrument at no penalty after only five or ten years. The put bonds carry a lower than market rate because the investor is getting a greater degree of future flexibility. Since the beginning of the year, about a dozen put bond issues have come to market, most of which were issued by housing authorities and health and educational facilities.

Another innovative technique is bonds with warrants to purchase a bond of equal size and interest rate. So far, only New York's Municipal Assistance Corp. has issued such debt. Big MAC floated two issues that mature in 2007 and 2008 and got its $100 million at 10⅝% rather than at 11¼% because it was willing to give investors the option, through January 1983, of purchasing additional Big MAC bonds at that 10⅝% rate. If interest rates should fall between now and January 1983, investors stand to gain. In the meantime, Big MAC gets its money at a slightly cheaper rate than with a straight vanilla bond, but must cross its fingers until January 1983 that rates do not fall.

The flip side of bonds with warrants are long-term bonds with very short call periods. Here, the investor gets a slightly higher rate but stands to lose if rates drop. The issuer, though paying a higher rate, has the advantage of calling the issue after only a few years and refinancing at lower rates if market conditions allow. Tucson airport issued $65 million of such bonds in May maturing in 2006 and carrying an 11¾% rate versus the going rate of 11½% for such an issue. But come June 1, 1983, the airport can call the bonds and refinance if rates have fallen.

The super-sinker bond is an innovation being used by housing authorities. Though potentially a long-term obligation, most of these issues will be paid off in less than one-third the time of their stated maturity. Most housing bonds are for twenty to thirty years because the mortgages backing those loans are for that time period. But the average life of a mortgage is actually between eight and ten years due to prepayments when homeowners sell their houses.

The super-sinkers pay bondholders a specified amount of money equal to the monthly mortgage receipts as well as any prepayments. Thus, rather than being paid off over twenty or thirty years, the holder receives his investment and interest back in only eight to ten years. These super-sinkers carry a rate less than the thirty-year bond but greater than an eight- to ten-year bond.

The newest wrinkle

Sale/leasebacks are being explored by a number of municipalities. Under such an arrangement, a city would raise tax-exempt money to finance a municipal office building, which would be built by private contractors, who would then purchase the building from the city and lease it back. The city would get a chunk of money up front to pay off the financing and cover the cost of the lease, and the investors would get the depreciation on the building, which is of no use to the city. The new tax law, which provides for more rapid depreciation of buildings, could make sale/leasebacks a very popular gimmick.

Investment bankers expect more widespread use of these innovations as well as the development of others, as cities and states become increasingly hard pressed for money. There should be no diminution of this trend, even if interest rates plunge.   —L.A.

Municipal Commercial Paper

Byron Klapper

After lying dormant for half a dozen years, municipal commercial paper is emerging as a potent new debt instrument in the tax-exempt, short-term market. While U.S. corporations have sold unsecured promissory notes for more than a century, use by public bodies is still in its infancy. Until recently, neither issuers nor investors showed much interest in tax-free commercial paper. Now, however, the concept appears to be gaining momentum. Of several issues offered, or scheduled for sale, institutional investors and tax-exempt funds are creating demand which exceeds the available supply.

Reasons for this are both structural and economic. As inflation and taxes climb, investors seek to keep assets liquid and sheltered. What they find is an acute shortage of tax-free, money market securities in amounts large enough to fill investment portfolios. Borrowers also feel the pinch, as interest rates gyrate more widely than ever. Government agencies financing power plants, educational facilities, housing and other projects need quicker access to the money market and flexibility to tailor debt issues to market conditions.

Wall Street is responding by drawing on the experience of the nation's largest companies. The commercial paper market has been a reliable source of short-term cash for corporate treasurers, even in times of tight credit and volatile interest rates. If a large stockholder-owned utility can issue commercial paper, why not a large public power agency? Since notes and bonds of public authorities are tax-exempt, it follows their commercial paper should be tax-free. Bond lawyers researched the issue, and agreed.

Standard & Poor's, which rates about 900 corporate commercial

Reprinted with permission from *Perspective*, September 17, 1980. Copyright 1980 by Standard & Poor's Corporation. Mr. Klapper is Director, Special Fixed Income Research.

paper issues, assigned a team to the project. Earlier this year [1980], S&P published criteria under which it could rate government units and non-profit issuers seeking municipal commercial paper ratings. The ratings are the same as those for companies offering paper. In doing so, S&P recognizes certain tax-exempt notes as municipal commercial paper.

Background

Municipal commercial paper was first offered in 1974 as dealers adapted sophisticated corporate financing strategies to the tax-exempt sector. Shortly after $20 million was issued for a Virginia utility's pollution project, the concept fell victim to a series of events.

The nation's economy went into a tailspin, producing a severe recession. Interest rates climbed to record levels. A state agency defaulted on notes. New York City's fiscal crisis exposed abuses of short-term debt in the absence of accounting and auditing controls. Credit markets closed entirely to certain local governments and agencies. New York noteholders suffered cuts in interest payments and delays in redeeming notes under a state legislated moratorium.

In succeeding years, changes began to be introduced. A federal bailout averted bankruptcy by the nation's largest city. Controls were put in place to curb fiscal excesses and to monitor operations for the protection of taxpayers and investors. A more disciplined approach to municipal finance was developed. Around the country, fiscal policies became more conservative with respect to reliance on short-term debt.

The latest wave of record interest rates and inflation, plus another recession, again put governments to the test in budgeting and raising capital funds. Simultaneously, demand for tax-exempt, short-term debt increased, due in part to new tax-free money market funds. Use of short-term debt in fund portfolios, and by banks and other investors, is stretching the capacity of the $21 billion municipal note market. This supply-demand imbalance in the note sector reawakened interest in municipal commercial paper.

Bellwether offerings

The following issues of municipal commercial paper, by a state education agency, a public power authority, and a housing agency, are viewed as trend setters in this emerging market.

In June [1980], Illinois Education Facilities Authority received an A-1 rating, S&P's highest, on a $60 million revenue issue for construction at Loyola University of Chicago. Interest rate on the 15- to 98-day paper was 4⅛%, well under comparable tax-exempt bank credit lines. Reports from the dealer indicate demand exceeded the offered amount "by more than 300%." Orders had to be rationed among tax-exempt funds, bank portfolios, trust departments and investment advisers. An even lower 3.60% rate was set when first maturities were rolled over two weeks later, in response to improving market conditions. Lehman Commercial Paper Inc. marketed the issue.

In August, Salt River Project Agricultural Improvement and Power District in Arizona began offering $200 million, the largest issue to date. Of that, $120 million is for capital financing, replacing tax-exempt bank credit lines. The balance will finance fuel inventories. Salt River officials estimate the interest rate savings on the A-1 rated paper, versus other short-term debt, could pare up to $3 million from the utility's annual borrowing costs. The initial $25 million portion had an average life of 38 days and rates ranging from 3⅛% to 3⅝%. Goldman, Sachs & Co. was the dealer.

[In October 1979], South Dakota Housing Development Authority issued paper as part of a $15 million authorization for multi-family housing construction in maturities from 30 to 60 days. The paper ultimately was taken down through an issue of long-term bonds the following spring, according to A. G. Becker Inc., the dealer.

Prior to sales by those agencies, only Government Development Bank for Puerto Rico regularly issued commercial paper, through Lehman.

Planned this year are offerings by Sacramento Municipal Utility District, California, by a municipal utility in Georgia and by the University of Southern California.

Market outlook

Several factors could encourage wider use of commercial paper by tax-exempt issuers. Among them:

1. The paper is a more flexible debt instrument than tax-exempt notes. Maturities are shorter: 15 to 45 days on average, compared to six months to one year on notes. Paper is offered continuously, while notes undergo a more complex underwriting. Proceeds are available almost immediately through transfer of Federal funds, versus a week or more before cash from note sales can be committed. Paper issued for working capital is often repaid from operating revenues, while notes are usually redeemed from bond sales, tax revenues or other funds.
2. Interest rates on commercial paper may be substantially lower than tax-exempt bank credit lines, which average 65% of the prime rate.
3. The paper is suitable for portfolios of tax-exempt money market funds, whose assets exceed $3 billion currently, and for established municipal bond funds which hold short-term debt for redemptions.
4. As investors show preference for certain maturities, to meet tax payments, for example, commercial paper issues can be structured to meet demand.

5.   Issuers of paper maintain a market presence almost daily, which could be an asset when they sell long-term bonds.

Offsetting these advantages are several factors which might inhibit rapid growth of commercial paper. Among them:

1.   Some states restrict use of short-term debt by public agencies. Salt River Project, for example, needed enabling legislation before offering commercial paper. In some regions this may be costly and time consuming.
2.   Abuses of short-term debt were linked to certain municipal fiscal crises. As a result, potential issuers may view the new investment vehicle with caution.
3.   Finance officers may be wary of a new debt instrument which is untested through various interest rate and economic cycles.
4.   Agencies are raising short-term cash in the note market or through bank credit lines and may not need alternative financing.
5.   Establishing a commercial paper program involves legal, financial or political considerations which may vary in different regions.
6.   Excessive use of commercial paper or other short-term debt could be a negative factor in an issuer's bond rating.
7.   At present, it would appear only dealers which make markets in both tax-exempt securities and corporate commercial paper have the capacity in place to set up a municipal commercial paper program.

What is commercial paper?

Commercial paper is negotiable, unsecured promissory notes issued by corporations. Maturing in 365 days or less, it often replaces costlier bank credit lines which require compensating balances. The largest companies, like General Motors Acceptance Corp. or Citicorp, issue the paper directly. Others use dealers to tap the market which exceeds $120 billion currently. The market has provided a ready source of funds for industrial and financial concerns, utilities, manufacturers, insurers, mortgage lenders, communications, transportation and other industries.

Companies issue commercial paper for working capital, interim construction financing, to supplement irregular cash flows, finance receivables and inventories and general corporate purposes.

Although designated as "unsecured" promissory notes, most commercial paper rated by S&P is backed by certain liquid assets. This may consist of securities, pools of funds pledged by a parent company to its subsidiaries, or bank credit lines.

Where issuers get irrevocable bank support through letters of credit, lending agreements or note purchase agreements, S&P may look to the creditworthiness of the bank, rather than the issuer, in assigning ratings. While the issuer's credit isn't central to the rating, S&P is still concerned about what may happen in the legal arena should an issuer become insolvent. S&P seeks to determine that timely payment of commercial paper wouldn't be interrupted or violate federal bankruptcy codes dealing with preferential treatment of creditors.

Municipal commercial paper

Municipal commercial paper is similar to corporate paper in many respects. There is this obvious difference, however. In the opinion of bond counsel, paper issued by state or local government units is exempt from federal income tax. Thus, issuers benefit from the lower interest rates available in the tax-exempt securities markets, and investors receive tax-free income.

As a new concept, the scope and use of municipal commercial paper is still evolving. It appears well suited to large agencies with working capital needs, such as financing fuel inventories by utilities, and for interim construction financing. It is expected that paper will be offered in amounts exceeding $50 million, reflecting, in part, the lower profit margins to dealers on commercial paper versus other debt securities.

In the future, states or cities may consider issuing commercial paper instead of notes, which traditionally are repaid from projected taxes, revenue grants or bond financing.

Since 1977, Government Development Bank for Puerto Rico has been the only regular issuer of tax-exempt commercial paper. The agency, which finances development projects of the Commonwealth, has authorization for up to $75 million of three-month commercial paper outstanding. As paper matures, it is rolled over through its dealer to provide a continuous flow of cash.

The agency's paper is rated A-1, S&P's highest, while the Commonwealth, which guarantees the paper, has a single-A rating on its bonds. The difference reflects certain features which assure holders of full and timely payment of the agency's short-term debt. The paper is payable from any available funds of the agency. In addition, it is backed by a credit facility agreement with Manufacturers Hanover Trust Co. Under the agreement, Manufacturers Hanover shall extend credit to the agency to any extent necessary to assure full payment of the paper.

S&P's rating criteria

In evaluating issuers, S&P considers the conservative use of commercial paper. It analyzes debt strategy, reasons for commercial paper issuance and plans and options to retire the issue. It's expected that paper will be offered primarily to finance seasonal working capital needs, repaid from revenues, or for longer-term programs, refinanced with long-term debt.

"Construction financing" is considered somewhat less credit-worthy than working capital financing because repayment depends on the issuer's ability to enter the bond market at a future date. This may be offset by the financial strength of the issuer to overcome these uncertainties, or the degree to which financing is conservative and minimizes risk.

Ratings by S&P reflect its judgment of the likelihood that investors will receive full and timely repayment. Its four categories, from "A" to "D," are the same as those for paper issued by corporations. Within that range, from the highest, are A-1, A-2 and A-3 showing relative degrees of safety. When credit is tight, and investors seek safe havens for capital, debt with the highest ratings have historically had the easiest market access.

S&P's criteria may also apply to certain taxable commercial paper issued by nonprofit organizations, like hospitals and colleges. In reviewing requests for commercial paper ratings, S&P's analysis is similar to that for long-term bonds. Emphasis is on stability and predictability of revenues, and near-term capacity to repay. Four key areas are assessed: operations, legal, administrative and financial.

Certain structural features should be in place by the time the issuer seeks a commercial paper rating from S&P. Among them are:

1. The issue is supported by certain bank lines, liquid assets or both in amounts to cover all outstanding paper. Issuer agrees to provide this data to S&P at least quarterly.
2. The issuer is independently audited and provides data according to generally accepted accounting principles.
3. The issue will be paid down entirely from revenues at least once a year on paper sold for seasonal working capital.

A full statement of S&P's rating criteria is available on request. For further information, please contact Frank Ingrassia, vice president, municipal bond department, at (212) 248-2594.

The following firms have indicated to S&P an interest in the area of municipal commercial paper:

Bache Halsey Stuart Shields Inc.
(212) 791-3688

Bank of America
(415) 622-6392

Bankers Trust Co.
(212) 775-5813

A. G. Becker Inc.
(312) 630-5388
(212) 747-8934

Blyth Eastman Paine
Webber Inc.
(212) 730-8924

Butcher & Singer Inc.
(215) 985-5566

Chase Manhattan Bank
(212) 552-4177

Citibank
(212) 668-3684

Continental Illinois National Bank & Trust Co. of Chicago
(312) 828-4367

Dillon, Read & Co.
(212) 285-5656

Ehrlich-Bober & Co.
(212) 480-9331

First Boston Corp.
(212) 825-7457

First National Bank of Boston
(617) 434-4802

First National Bank of Chicago
(312) 732-4174

Goldman, Sachs & Co.
(212) 676-3103

E. F. Hutton & Co.
(212) 742-5098

Lazard Freres & Co.
(212) 489-6600

Lehman Commercial Paper Inc.
(212) 558-2152

Merrill Lynch White Weld Capital Markets Group
(212) 637-2670

Salomon Brothers
(212) 747-7082

Shearson Loeb Rhoades Inc.
(212) 577-2865

Smith Barney, Harris Upham & Co.
(212) 399-6354

PART 3

Leasing: An Alternative to Borrowing

Municipal Leasing: Opportunities and Precautions for Governments

—————— Lisa A. Cole and Hamilton Brown

In 1981, Memphis, Tennessee, became the nation's largest user of front yard pick-up sanitation carts. Financed, in part, by a $2.8 million lease-purchase agreement, the 200,000 carts allow for hydraulic pick-up of trash, cutting down substantially the cost and time of refuse collection.

In establishing a publicly owned ambulance service, Kansas City, Missouri, has negotiated a $2.5 million leveraged lease agreement with a local bank. By purchasing the ambulances directly from the manufacturer, the city will pay 17 percent less than a private purchaser in sales and excise taxes, and will finance the vehicles at a 12 percent interest rate from the bank through which the acquisition was financed.

Although leasing in its various forms has both strong supporters and detractors, its use has grown steadily as traditional capital funding sources diminish. Like Kansas City and Memphis, hundreds of cities and towns across the country have used leasing in innovative and beneficial ways. With industry estimates for municipal leasing activity topping the $1 billion mark for 1981, local government officials should be prepared for informed consideration of this financing technique.

Much of the material for this article is drawn from a seminar on municipal leasing held on September 30, 1981, at Chapel Hill, North Carolina. Co-sponsored by the Government Finance Research Center and the Institute of Government at the University of North Caro-

Reprinted with permission from *Resources in Review*, January 1982, published by the Government Finance Research Center, Municipal Finance Officers Association. The authors thank A. John Vogt of the Institute of Government at the University of North Carolina—Chapel Hill for his assistance in the preparation of this article and for his co-sponsorship of and assistance in a Seminar on Municipal Leasing, September 30, 1981.

lina, the seminar brought together state and municipal officials, banking, legal and leasing representatives, and university faculty. Like this article, the seminar was designed to discuss the pros and cons of municipal leasing and not to espouse it as the panacea for the ills currently affecting public capital financing. A manual, based in part on the seminar program, will be published in 1982.[1]

Exactly why leasing has gained such popularity among state and local governments in recent years can be explained by a number of economic and legal factors. These include:

1. A government's inability to enter the bond market because it has reached its legally imposed debt limits;
2. A government's inability or unwillingness to enter the bond market because of high interest rates;
3. Lack of voter approval to enable bond issuance; and
4. Growing demands on the municipal bond market may crowd out bonds for certain capital projects or facilities.

These reasons help explain why governments are interested in leasing in the role of lessee. However, a government also can act as lessor, enabling it to make use of and derive revenues from surplus properties or, perhaps, obtain improvements on existing public properties.[2]

Today, however, the most commonly used forms of leasing by governments relate to the ultimate acquisition of property through a lease-purchase agreement, the temporary use of equipment or facilities through a straight operating lease, or a sale-leaseback arrangement under which public property is sold and a portion leased back for the use of the government.

(The Economic Recovery Tax Act of 1981, signed into law on August 13, 1981, contains a much-heralded provision relating to "safe-harbor" leases. With one exception, that of mass transit, vehicles owned by a public entity, public sector equipment or facilities are not eligible. See the box within this special feature that explains the significance of the Act's provisions.)

In addition to exploring why the public sector is interested in leasing, the role and interests of the private sector actors (vendors, manufacturers and/or financing agents) must also be examined. In leasing property and facilities to the public sector, the private sector benefits not only from the lease payments but from one or more tax benefits as well. These include declaring the interest earned through public sector payments to be tax-exempt and being able to depreciate the leased facilities/property. These opportunities and others will be explored later in this article.

Common definitions

Before a discussion of municipal leasing can take place, a common understanding of terminology is necessary. Although various words or phrases frequently are used to describe the same leasing arrange-

---

**"Safe harbor" leasing provisions of
the economic recovery tax act**

The major impacts of the Economic Recovery Tax Act of 1981 include
reduction in personal income taxes, new opportunities for individual
retirement plans, and a variety of tax incentives addressed toward
business. One of the more newsworthy provisions affecting business
provides an enhanced method of depreciating equipment on an accelerated basis. The accelerated depreciation tied in with the Act's "safe-
harbor" leasing provisions make private capital investments significantly more attractive. Under the "safe-harbor" provisions, businesses
that make capital investments but are unable to take advantage of the
depreciation benefits can "lease" those benefits to another company
that can use them to offset their tax liabilities. The Act contains one
provision that makes the new accelerated depreciation and safe-harbor leasing available for the financing of public mass transit vehicles.

Briefly, the Act enables depreciation deductions (under the new
accelerated cost recovery system) to be "leased" by a public transit
authority (that has bought mass commuting vehicles) to a corporation
which has income it wishes to shelter from taxation. This structure,
under the Act, is called a leveraged lease. This opportunity is available
only if the vehicles are financed in whole or in part with tax-exempt
debt and are placed in service after January 1, 1981. The Act also expands the opportunities for mass transit authorities to issue tax-exempt debt (industrial development bonds) to allow for the leasing
opportunities.

---

ments, the following terms will be used in this article:

Operating lease—the lessee (the governmental unit) acquires
use of an asset and the lease term usually runs for only a fraction of
the asset's useful life. The lessor typically is responsible for maintenance, insurance and taxes. This qualifies under the Internal Revenue Code as a lease and enables the lessor to claim tax benefits of
ownership such as depreciation. The Investment Tax Credit, however, is not available when the lessee is a unit of government.

Lease-purchase agreement—a contract that is called a lease
but which in substance is a purchase or conditional sale. A lease-
purchase agreement establishes periodic payments divided into both
principal and interest and a date on which title to the asset changes
hands. The main advantage of a lease-purchase agreement to state
and local governments is that the interest portion paid to the lessor
may be tax-exempt. To generate tax-exempt interest, a contract
must meet the obligation requirements of the Internal Revenue Code
and, at the same time, avoid being classified as debt by state or local
law. Thus a unit of government may treat the same arrangement as a
sale for tax classification purposes and as a lease for accounting purposes. The Internal Revenue Service has issued Revenue Ruling 55-
540 that lists eight general criteria to distinguish an operating lease

from a sales agreement. The tax-exempt interest paid by government lessees is discussed in the Internal Revenue Code, Section 103.

While classified as a sale by the IRS, municipal lease-purchase agreements typically contain a *fiscal funding* or *non-appropriation clause* to avoid classification as long-term debt for accounting purposes. The fiscal funding clause allows the municipality to terminate, without penalty, a lease for which funds are not appropriated beyond the current annual budget. Vendors protect themselves to a degree from non-appropriation by charging a higher interest rate than for a guaranteed contract term and by including in the contract a *non-substitution clause* that states a municipality cannot lease or purchase replacement equipment within a specified time.

Sale-leaseback—an arrangement in which an owner of property sells the property to a financial institution or another buyer and simultaneously executes an agreement to lease all or part of the property back from the buyer. In a sale-leaseback, the seller-lessee obtains the full purchase price from the buyer-lessor on sale, and the seller-lessee retains use of the property.

The actors and their roles

Municipal leasing agreements may involve a number of political, legal, and financial participants in addition to the lessor and the lessee. While the actors involved and the precise roles that they play are dictated by individual lease conditions, we can review the types of involvement found in typical leasing agreements.

Operating lease arrangements

As the *lessee*, or renter, the municipality has use of the property or asset in return for regularly scheduled rental payments.

The *lessor*, normally a manufacturer or vendor, provides the asset, in return for the agreed upon payments. Depending on the amount of the lease and state and local law, approval by the *elected governing body* and/or the *principal elected official* may also be required. As with any document committing public funds, the lease arrangement should be approved by the municipality's *legal counsel*.

Lease-purchase arrangements

Structuring a lease-purchase arrangement is far more complex than for a straight lease. Payments include both an interest and a principal component, and the contract establishes the terms under which transfer of ownership will take place. The lessor in a lease-purchase arrangement is frequently a *leasing corporation* that has financed the purchase of the asset from the manufacturer.

The principal concern of the municipality, as lessee, is to make certain that the interest portion of its lease payments is tax-exempt. Availability of this tax-shelter benefit by the lessor can substantially reduce the rate of interest to the municipality. The economic conse-

---

Lease purchasing in Memphis

The experience of Memphis, Tennessee, provides a good illustration of a lease-purchase agreement. After considerable cost analysis, the city decided to switch from backyard to frontyard refuse pick-up. In order to do so, the city arranged to purchase 200,000 sanitation carts through a leasing company. Finance officials went before City Council and gained approval to receive bids on two installment sales of $2.8 and $4.6 million, with the first request for proposal issued in January 1981. Backed by the full faith and credit of the city, the lease payments were scheduled semi-annually over 5 years, the guaranteed life of the carts. The lease payments are to be included in the Sanitation Department's operating budget and recorded on the appropriate debt statements.

Memphis' experience illustrates some of the drawbacks to leasing as well. After receiving a number of bids on the first offering, the city returned with a heavily promoted $4.6 million lease-purchase proposal to acquire the remaining carts. Although the city received numerous inquiries, only one bid was received and it was at a rate judged too high to be acceptable. City finance officials attributed the lack of response to a required $95,000 "good faith" deposit that perhaps eliminated some smaller firms and a substantial drop in the bond market on the business day before bids were received. Memphis will now turn to the bond market in early 1982 to finance the purchase of the additional carts, an option that might not be open to a smaller, less fiscally sound municipality.

---

quences dictate far more involvement of the municipality's *legal counsel* than in leases where rent alone is paid. While generally less complicated than bond issues, documentation requirements consist of a lease-purchase contract, evidence of security interest retained by the vendor, compliance with competitive bidding requirements, disclosure documents where required, an escrow or trust agreement, and, on occasion, an arbitrage certificate.

Leveraged lease arrangements involve at least three parties: a lessor, a lessee, and a long-term *lender*. The lending party provides substantial financing (leverage) to the lessor in return for both repayment of the loan and a security interest in the asset being leased out. When the leveraged amount is sizeable, the lending institution (often a bank) will sell certificates of participation in the loan to individual investors who may benefit from the tax exemption.

A large leveraged lease arrangement may involve a municipality as *lessee*, a municipal leasing company as *lessor*, financial institution as third party *lender*, an *underwriting firm* to market the *certificates of participation* and a *trustee* to make scheduled payments to the certificate holders. As with all leasing agreements, the approval of an elected body or official is often required.

The actors involved in various leasing arrangements must take

Kansas City's leveraged leasing

The recent experience of Kansas City, Missouri, illustrates the fiscal advantages offered by leveraged, or third party leases. For a number of years, the city's only ambulance service was provided by five private companies with no consolidated communication system. When responses to a number of disasters prompted media and City Council criticism, the city took a number of steps to improve performance. After subsidizing a city-wide dispatcher system and consolidation of the private firms into a single entity, Kansas City decided to buy out the still inadequate ambulance service. As part of the agreement to establish a non-profit Municipal Ambulance Service Trust, the city agreed to provide 25 new ambulances and several new radio base stations. City Council approved a $2.5 million leasing arrangement scheduled over the five and one-half years. During the examination of its options, the finance department discovered that the city could save 16 percent in excise and sales taxes if the municipality, rather than a private corporation, purchased the vehicles.

Anticipating the purchase, the city structured a $2.5 million master municipal lease (leveraged lease) and advertised for third-party financing. The award was made in June of 1981 to a local bank that offered an attractive 12 percent rate of interest. The lease has been structured so that the interest portion is tax exempt, and the bank has offered certificates of participation to other investors. Once the contract was arranged, the entire borrowed amount was invested in an escrow account yielding 16 percent interest. In November 1981, purchase of the equipment was begun out of the City's working capital fund that, in turn, is being reimbursed by the escrow account as delivery and payment are made. Title to the ambulances has been pledged as a lien to the bank until the 66 monthly payments complete the purchase of the equipment. The ultimate source of payments is from revenues in the Municipal Ambulance Service Trust established as an enterprise fund.

into account several important considerations that center around legal provisions and restrictions, the financing arrangements, and the practical decision of whether to lease or buy.

Contractual and legal concerns

Most leasing arrangements available to governments must be considered in light of the legal provisions and restrictions regarding the acquisition of facilities and equipment and the incurrence of financial obligations. These controls may be exercised by either the state government or local laws. In addition, historic (and perhaps political) practices may hinder or regulate the nature of lease contracts or even the ability to enter into such an arrangement.

While the laws regarding governmental leasing vary from state to state, the general parameters of these laws are similar. In any leasing arrangement other than an operating lease, a major consideration for the lessee, in order to achieve maximum economic benefits, is to make sure that the lease is qualified as a tax-exempt obligation under Section 103(b) of the Internal Revenue Code.

To qualify under the Code, the government unit must be the owner of the leased good or intend to own it. Ultimately, governments should seek an opinion from counsel to ensure that the interest component will be tax exempt. The contract should then include a payment schedule that lists the principal and interest components of all lease payments. This statement is essential to assure the attractive tax exemption.

The impact of the non-appropriation clause (which, as stated earlier, enables a lessor to terminate a contract in the event of the non-appropriation of funds) can be partially offset by a statement in the contract of the lessee's intent to continue to renew for the full term.

In efforts to attract investors, contracts should provide as much "security" as possible. This can include:

1. A statement of the availability of funds and a description of the process for obtaining timely payment.
2. A statement that if a lease agreement is terminated early the jurisdiction will not replace the equipment within a specific period of time.
3. A statement of essentiality of the leased equipment. A piece of equipment that may be viewed as luxurious or not necessary can be considered to be of higher risk to the investor and, without assurance to the contrary, could result in a higher interest rate being charged.
4. A clause allowing the lessor to assign the lease or to sell certificates of participation in the lease. This is particularly important in large lease transactions.
5. A statement that title will remain with lessor in states where transfer of ownership establishes the incurrence of debt on the part of the municipal lessee.
6. Where applicable, a statement of the agreed upon purchase price at the end of the lease. The amount should be nominal (one dollar is frequently used). This clearly indicates that the lessee intends to acquire an equity interest in the property during the term of the entire lease.

An important point for the lessee to remember is that there exists no right of refusal to pay any lease payment if equipment fails to work or if repairs are necessary. These problems frequently are resolved if the lessor, in the contract, requires that the equipment or facility be properly insured. This can at least provide protection in the event of damage or destruction.

Accounting for leases

Private and public sector accounting standards for lease and lease-purchase agreements are drawn from two major sources: *Statement 13* (as amended and interpreted) by the Financial Accounting Standards Board (FASB)[3] and Statement 1 from the National Council on Governmental Accounting (NCGA).[4] While these documents concur at many points, most of the discussion that follows will focus on several important differences. There are two leasing arrangements, however, in which accounting procedures are both straightforward and well established. First, in a straight operating lease without equity or ownership considerations, the rental payments are accounted for as expenses or expenditures in the appropriate fund. Second, in governmental proprietary funds that are operated like commercial enterprises, the criteria provided in the FASB pronouncements apply.

While FASB's *Statement 13* is the principal source of information concerning leasing arrangements, differences between the private and public sectors preclude its full application to governmental type fund accounting for municipalities. *Statement 13* requires that the discounted present value of the future lease obligations (principal only) be capitalized and reported in the annual financial statement. A number of governments argue that with inclusion of the "non-appropriation" clause in a lease contract, capitalized leases do not exist in the public sector. After much discussion, there is consensus that future commitments to lease-purchase agreements should be reported annually on the balance sheets.[5]

A second problem exists in deciding where to record the capitalized lease obligation. Private sector standards require an entry in the individual account group in which the obligation occurs. Accounting standards for governmental fund types do not provide for recording long-term liabilities within individual fund financial statements. The governmental accounting model from *Statement 1* of NCGA and the 1980 edition of *Governmental Accounting, Auditing and Financial Reporting* (GAAFR) both recommend the following solution:

1. The capitalized lease obligation be recorded in the General Long-Term Debt Account Group. (While interest payable in future years is not required to be shown in the statement, it should be fully disclosed in the accompanying notes.); and

2. Annual principal and interest payments be recorded as debt service in the general fund or other appropriate governmental fund.

While municipal lease accounting has become more standard in the last few years, it should be noted that NCGA has recently issued a discussion memorandum seeking comment on appropriate accounting and reporting practices for leases entered into by state and local governments.[6] Resolution of the issues raised in the memorandum can only encourage the further, responsible use of leasing by municipal governments.

The lease or buy decision—practical considerations

Leasing is no longer restricted to furniture and office equipment, nor to municipalities that have reached their debt limit. But as the option to lease has grown, the lease or buy decision has become correspondingly more difficult to make. The final choice is often based on a strict cost analysis, yet a number of practical considerations may determine which is the more viable option before financial comparisons are undertaken. Any one or a combination of the following conditions might support the option to lease or lease-purchase:

1. A jurisdiction's debt limit has been approached or already reached;
2. The chance for a bond referendum to pass is judged unlikely;
3. The useful life of an asset or changing technology makes issuance of long-term bonds an inappropriate financing mechanism;
4. The cost of the asset or property is not large enough to justify bond financing; or
5. Duration of use does not warrant outright purchase.

Other conditions may suggest a preference for issuing bonds:

1. Local laws prohibit or limit lease arrangements;
2. Political opposition exists to leasing as an acquisition procedure;
3. Equity interests dictate the outright ownership of an asset;
4. The jurisdiction lacks expertise to structure leasing arrangements; or
5. The non-substitution clause limits the jurisdiction's flexibility.

While none of these conditions (except state and local laws) dictate one option or the other, careful weighing of these practical considerations may eliminate unnecessary and costly financial analysis. The issues raised in this section approach a number of key concerns for local officials, but each municipality contemplating acquisition of a capital facility must consider its own needs, problems, and capabilities before deciding whether to lease or buy.

The following bibliography lists recent publications and articles that discuss various aspects of leasing.

Baker, C. Richard and Hays, Steven Rich. *Lease Financing.* New York: John Wiley, 1981. (205 pp) Available from John Wiley & Sons, Inc., 605 Third Avenue, New York, NY 10016. (212) 850-6000.

Eden, C. Gregory H. and Bond, Kenneth W., eds. *Tax Exempt Municipal Lease Financing: A Modern Tool for Equipment Financing in the 1980s.* New York: Law Journal Seminars Press, 1980. (694 pp) Contact the Law Journal Seminars Press, 233 Broadway, New York, NY 10279. (212) 964-9400.

Financial Accounting Standards Board. *Accounting for Leases: FASB Statement No. 13 as Amended and Interpreted Through May, 1980.* Stamford, CT: Financial Accounting Standards Board, 1980. (226 pp) Available from FASB, Publications Department, High Ridge Park, Stamford, CT 06905. (203) 329-8401.

Government Finance Research Center. "Governmental Leasing Techniques." *Elements of Financial Management Series.* Washington, DC: GFRC, 1980. (5 pp) Available from the GFRC, 1750 K Street, NW, Suite 650, Washington, DC 20006. (202) 466-2473.

_____ *Municipal Leasing: Options and Opportunities with Emphasis on Surplus School Buildings.* Washington, DC: GFRC, 1980. (approx. 150 pp) Available from the GFRC, 1750 K Street, NW, Suite 650, Washington, DC 20006. (202) 466-2473.

Municipal Finance Officers Association. "General Long-Term Debt Account Group." *Governmental Accounting, Auditing, and Financial Reporting,* 1980. pp. 57–58. Available from the MFOA, 180 N. Michigan Avenue, Chicago, IL 60601. (312) 977-9700.

Nichols, F. Glenn. "Debt Limitations and the Bona Fide Long-Term Lease with an Option to Purchase: Another Look at Lord Coke." *Urban Lawyer,* Spring 1977. pp. 403–420. Contact the American Bar Association, 1155 E. 60th Street, Chicago, IL 60637. (312) 667-4700.

Pritchard, Robert E. and Hindelang, Thomas. *The Lease/Buy Decision.* New York: Amacon, 1980. (276 pp) Available from the American Management Association, 135 W. 50th Street, New York, NY 10020. (212) 586-8100.

Wallison, Frieda K. "Tax Exempt Lease Financing Gains Attention as Economic Conditions Change." *The Daily Bond Buyer—PSA Supplement,* November 3, 1980. (3 pp) Contact *The Bond Buyer,* One State Street Plaza, New York, NY 10004. (212) 943-8200.

1. The seminar and manual were funded in part by a grant to the Government Finance Research Center from the Financial Management Capacity Sharing Program of the Department of Housing and Urban Development. The authors would like to express their gratitude to the panel members and the seminar audience for the valuable information they shared.

2. Government Finance Research Cen-

ter, *Municipal Leasing: Its Role in Community Development with Emphasis on Surplus Schools* (Washington, DC: GFRC, September 1980).

3. Available from Financial Accounting Standards Board, High Ridge Park, Stamford, CT 06905.

4. Available from NCGA, 180 N. Michigan Avenue, Suite 329, Chicago, IL 60601.

5. FASB, NCGA, and GAAFR guidelines, in addition to many individual authorities strictly recommend on balance sheet accounting.

6. *Discussion Memorandum* on Lease-Purchase Agreements, December 8, 1981, available from NCGA, 180 N. Michigan Avenue, Suite 329, Chicago, IL 60601.

Leasing As a Municipal Finance Alternative

Edward A. Dyl and Michael D. Joehnk

In recent years, many state and municipal governments have found it difficult to acquire funds to finance facilities and equipment. Increased competition for the investor's dollar and changes in the perceived risk of most tax-exempt bond issues have caused interest rates in the municipal bond market to rise relative to prevailing rates in other sectors of the bond market. The shortage of public sector financing has been further exacerbated by private corporations issuing tax-exempt industrial development and pollution control bonds, thereby absorbing loanable funds traditionally reserved for municipal borrowers. Given this environment, alternatives to direct borrowing as a means of municipal financing should be explored. This paper examines one such alternative—the financial lease.

Leasing enables the municipality to employ the private sector indirectly as a source of funds, since the lessor provides the resources needed for the acquisition of the facilities. However, although considerable attention has been devoted to leasing in the private sector (see, for example, Van Horne [17] and the references he cites), there is scant literature pertaining to the economics of public sector leasing. For example, in their recent treatise on local government finance, Moak and Hillhouse [12] pay little attention to equipment leasing and leave the reader with the impression that leasing is almost invariably an undesirable course of action for a municipality.

This treatment of municipal leasing apparently reflects the prevailing attitude of most municipal financial officers, who rarely consider leasing as a viable financing method. It is widely believed that leasing is inherently more expensive than other sources of financing (see Snyder [16]). In addition, many municipal financial officers seem to believe that financial leases are not widely available to municipalities. Neither of these beliefs is true. Actually, leasing may have much to offer the municipality that is in need of financing for equipment or facilities. For example, consider the following factors:

1. Leasing may provide the municipality with the opportunity to raise needed capital in situations where local laws prevent direct bank borrowing (which is a comparable intermediate-term alternative);
2. Leasing may provide municipalities which have little or no access to traditional capital markets with the means of obtaining financing for equipment and facilities (see Antieu [1] and Snyder [16]);
3. Leasing is a convenient means of obtaining equipment which, because of size considerations, may be too small an expenditure to warrant a bond issue, yet too large to finance out of current revenues;
4. Leasing may provide municipalities with a means of avoiding cumbersome and costly voter approval and other legal constraints on the capital raising function of municipalities, such as statutes that limit the levy on property (see Magnusson [9];[1] and
5. Leasing may allow the municipality to free up cash and debt capacity for other needs without deferring equipment acquisitions.[2]

In many situations, leasing may also be the least expensive means of equipment financing. In this paper, we focus on the quantitative aspects of municipal lease financing. The section that follows deals with the rate-setting decisions of the lessor and illustrates the economic and institutional factors that may render leasing a viable municipal financing procedure. We then examine leasing decisions by municipalities and present a relatively straightforward approach to lease evaluation by municipal financial managers. We then consider the possible risks (in financial terms) of leasing instead of borrowing and purchasing. Finally, we discuss the tax-arbitrage lease, which combines lease financing with direct investment by the municipality of those funds freed up through leasing. Because our attention throughout is directed toward leasing as a financing technique, we consider purely "financial," rather than "full-service," leases (i.e., leases that merely provide a means of financing as opposed to those that provide both financing and maintenance of the equipment being leased).

Taxes and the economics of leasing
Although the various qualitative factors delineated in the preceding section suggest a number of special situations where municipalities

may find leasing an attractive financing alternative, a major move toward leasing by municipalities will result only if lessors are able to provide such financing on a basis that is price-competitive with the municipal bonds and other sources of municipal debt financing.

The primary economic reason for the existence of the financial lease is related to income taxes; in particular, to tax benefits accruing to the lessor. In the corporate sector, financial leases provide a means of transferring income tax deductions for depreciation and investment tax credits from lessee firms, which are unable to utilize these benefits fully, to lessor firms, which can use the tax deductions to the fullest (see Brigham [4] and [5]). Because municipalities are tax-exempt entities and, therefore, have no use for depreciation tax deductions and investment tax credits, the potential for a similar transfer of tax benefits to lessor firms by public sector lessees clearly exists. Thus, leasing may enable municipalities to reduce their borrowing costs by transferring to the lessor tax benefits which were previously valueless to the municipality.

A brief discussion of the economics of lessor rate-setting will illustrate this point (see Dyl [7] for a more detailed analysis).[3] Assume that a potential lessor (e.g., a commercial bank, a leasing firm, a commercial finance company, or a private investor) requires a 12 per cent pre-tax return on investment and has a marginal income tax rate of 50 per cent, resulting in a 6 per cent after-tax required return. Under what terms will the lessor lease $200,000 worth of depreciable equipment (e.g., garbage trucks, police cars, a computer, or whatever) to a municipality?

Assume that: (1) the equipment may be depreciated over a 10-year life toward a 5 per cent salvage value using the sum-of-the-years digits method, (2) the market value of the equipment at the end of 10

Year	Depre-ciation	Value of depre-ciation tax deduction	Other ownership benefits	Total cash flow	Present value at 6%
1	$36,363.64	$18,181.82	$20,000.00	$38,181.82	$36,020.73
2	32,727.28	16,363.64	0	16,363.64	14,563.64
3	29,090.90	14,545.45	0	14,545.45	12,212.65
4	25,454.54	12,727.27	0	12,727.27	10,081.14
5	21,818.18	10,909.09	0	10,909.01	8,151.93
6	18,181.82	9,090.91	0	9,090.01	6,408.80
7	14,545.46	7,272.73	0	7,272.73	4,836.80
8	10,909.10	5,454.55	0	5,454.55	3,422.24
9	909.10	454.55	0	454.55	269.05
10	0	0	7,000.00	7,000.00	3,908.73
					$99,875.64

Table 1. Ownership benefits to lessor.

years is expected to be $4,000, and (3) the equipment qualifies for an investment tax credit of 10 per cent. With this information, the proportion of the lessor's return that will take the form of ownership benefits (from depreciation, income taxes, and salvage value) can be determined. As we shall see, such benefits effectively reduce the amount that must be recovered from lease payments.

A procedure for computing the value of the ownership benefits realized by the lessor is illustrated in Table 1. The first column shows the annual depreciation of the equipment, using a standard form of accelerated depreciation (i.e., the sum-of-the-years digits method), and the second lists the amount by which the lessor's income taxes will be reduced each year as a result of the tax deduction for depreciation (i.e., the amount of the deduction times the lessor's marginal income tax rate). This reduction in taxes is, of course, essentially a cash inflow to the lessor. The third column in Table 1 shows other cash flows resulting from the lessor's ownership of the equipment. These include the investment tax credit in the year of purchase ($20,000) and the proceeds from liquidating the asset at the end of the lease term ($7,000). The liquidating value in this case includes the $4,000 cash value of the asset and an income tax deduction of $6,000 for book loss on liquidating the equipment (i.e., the difference between the $10,000 book value in year 10 and the $4,000 sale value); the value of this income tax deduction is $3,000, resulting in a total cash flow of $7,000.

The annual cash flows to the lessor from tax benefits and other ownership benefits are shown in the fourth column of Table 1, and the last column shows the present value of these cash flows given in the lessor's required 6 per cent after-tax return. The total present value of $99,875 is the portion of the lessor's original investment recovered from ownership benefits (and, of course, includes a 6 per cent after-tax return). Note that this is before considering any lease payments. Thus, the lessor need only recover $100,125 (i.e., $200,000 minus $99,875), from payments to be made by the lessee. It is interesting to note that, in this case, *half* of the lessor's required return has been generated by income tax and depreciation benefits that are of no real value to the municipal lessee.

The annual after-tax lease proceeds required to recover the balance of the lessor's investment and desired profit can be computed from the following equation:

$$(1) \qquad L_{at} = NC \Big/ \sum_{t=0}^{n-1} (1 + R)^{-t}$$

where L_{at} denotes the required after-tax proceeds, NC is the remaining net cost to be recouped (in this case, $100,125), n is the life of the lease (which for a financial lease, will generally be equivalent to the depreciable life of the equipment being leased—in this case, ten years), and R is the lessor's required after-tax rate of return (i.e., 6 per cent in our example). Note that this equation assumes level lease payments made in advance (i.e., at the beginning of the year), which is the usual practice in the equipment leasing industry.

By using equation (1) we can see that the proceeds required by the lessor in our examples are

$$L_{at} = \$100,125 / 7.8017 = \$12,834$$

However, because the annual lease payments from the lessee will be taxed at the lessor's marginal tax rate, to determine the actual lease payment (i.e., before-tax) required by the lessee, L_{at} must be adjusted as follows:

(2) $L = L_{at} / (1-T)$

where L is the annual lease payment and T is the lessor's marginal tax rate. Thus, the resulting lease payment for our illustration will be

$$L = \$12,834 / .5 = \$25,668$$

What does a lease payment of \$25,668 suggest about the viability of leasing as a municipal financing alternative? A detailed discussion of lease evaluation is provided in the following section, but at this point it is sufficient to note that the lessee is receiving net benefits of \$174,332 (i.e., the \$200,000 worth of equipment less the initial lease payment of \$25,668) in exchange for nine future annual payments of \$25,668. Thus, the effective rate of interest on this lease is essentially 6 per cent, even though the lessor is earning the equivalent of 12 per cent, pre-tax return. As a result of the transfer of tax and other ownership benefits from the municipal lessee to the lessor, financial leases will clearly be competitive with many alternative sources of municipal borrowing. Indeed, recent studies of the municipal bond market suggest that a corporate lessor with a tax rate of 50 per cent could easily offer a finance rate more attractive than the rate available to the municipality by issuing tax-exempt bonds (e.g., see Rosenbloom [15]).

The lease evaluation decision

The preceding discussion has shown a potential economic rationale for municipal leasing. Such insight is, of course, useful to the lessee, if for no other reason than to provide a basis for knowledgeable bargaining in lease negotiations. At the same time, municipal financial officers must have a procedure for assessing the economic desirability of a financial lease. This section of the paper develops a municipal lease decision model and illustrates its application.

The municipal lease evaluation model is similar to widely used corporate procedures. Due to the absence of income tax considerations, however, the technique is considerably less complex. In particular, items such as "lost" depreciation and "lost" investment tax credit can be ignored because they are of no consequence to a tax-exempt lessee. Municipal lease evaluation basically encompasses three items: the annual lease payments to be made by the municipality over the term of the lease (L); the estimated salvage value of the equipment to be realized at the end of the life of the lease (SV_n); and the invoice and installation costs of the equipment to be leased (C).

The annual lease payments (L), which typically commence at $t = 0$, are generally quoted by the lessor. Normally, the lease payments are an annuity, as in the rate-setting example presented above. In some cases, however, a lessor might wish to establish an uneven lease payment pattern; this would have no effect on the lease evaluation procedure described below. The salvage value (SV_n) represents the estimated market value of the equipment at the end of the life of the lease and is an opportunity cost to the lessee. The potential variability of this "cost" is discussed in the following section. Finally, of course, the cost of the equipment, C, is included in the evaluation model as a measure of the gross benefits from leasing.

Municipal leases can be evaluated either by comparing the effective interest rate on the lease to the cost of alternative financing, or by comparing the present value of the lease costs to the benefits resulting from the lease (see Van Horne [17]). We personally prefer the cost-benefit analysis approach, both because of its computational simplicity and because it provides a tangible measure of the (present) dollar benefits of leasing. In addition, while either approach will result in the same accept/reject decision for a given lease, the present value procedure has the added attribute of allowing the decision maker to evaluate competitive lease proposals more accurately.

In the present value procedure for lease evaluation, the various real and opportunity costs of leasing are discounted to determine their present value, and this result is compared to the benefits from the lease. In particular, the present value cost (PVC) of a lease option may be specified as:

$$(3) \qquad PVC = L \sum_{t=0}^{n-1} (1 + i)^{-t} + SV_n (1 + i)^{-n}$$

where i equals the discount rate and the other terms are defined above. The appropriate decision rule is for the municipality to employ the financial lease in lieu of an alternative financing technique whenever $PVC < C$ (i.e., when leasing is less costly than purchasing the equipment).

Before applying equation (3) we should address the question of the appropriate discount rate, i. The time value of money in the public sector is generally thought of in terms of the so-called social rate of discount. A popular definition of the social discount rate is as follows: given that some unidentified alternative use of the resources in question can be expected to produce a rate of return equal to i, the resources should be utilized in the public sector only if they yield a return equal to or greater than i (see Baumol [2] and Marglin [10] for further discussion). The social discount rate, however, is irrelevant in the present case since it is not the alternative uses of public funds that are of concern, but rather alternative financing techniques. Thus, because in evaluating leases the municipality is narrowly concerned with evaluating a specific debt management alternative, we aver that the municipality's borrowing rate is the appropriate definition of the alternative cost of acquiring resources in this case: thus, it is the proper discount rate.

To illustrate briefly the application of the proposed lease evaluation procedure, consider the example developed earlier in connection with the lessor's rate-setting decision. Recall from that example that the municipality in question was considering a ten year lease to acquire the services of a piece of $200,000 equipment with an estimated salvage value (SV_n) of $4,000 at $t = 10$, and an annual lease payment (L), as proposed by the lessor, of $25,668, to be paid annually from t_0 to t_9. The only other item needed to evaluate this lease is the municipality's current borrowing rate, which we posit to be approximately 7 per cent (true annual interest cost). Using equation (3) it can be seen that

$$PVC = \$25,668 + \$25,668 \, (6.5152) + \$4,000 \, (.50835) = \$194,926$$

Since the value of PVC is $5,074 *less* than C, it follows that there is considerable economic justification for undertaking the proposed lease in lieu of the borrow-and-purchase alternative. In effect, the municipality is obtaining the services of a $200,000 piece of equipment (C) for a present value cost of $194,926—thereby generating a (present value) savings of $5,074 over what it would cost to purchase and finance the equipment at a 7 per cent borrowing rate. Such savings, of course, occur because of the municipality's ability to transfer ownership benefits to the lessor, which in turn leads to a difference in the effective costs of borrowing vs. leasing (i.e., 7 per cent for the former as opposed to approximately 6¼ per cent for the leasing alternative).

Evaluating risk

Our evaluation of a municipal lease has thus far proceeded on the premise that the decision is free of any risk to the lessee. While we have noted some of the uncertainties that the lessor must consider in the rate setting process, it should be clear that the lessee, likewise, must evaluate the risk in undertaking the lease. The municipal lessee, of course, is subject to the usual operating risks to which any entity would be exposed when making investment decisions—such as the continued economic justification for the asset, the possibility of obsolescence, the ability to generate sufficient cash flow to service debt requirements. However, these risks are not unique to lease evaluations. In the context of this article, the primary concern is with the risk exposure of the municipality when it undertakes a lease in lieu of purchase of the asset. Such risk exposure basically emanates from a single variable—the salvage value of the asset.

Variability in the salvage value can affect the decision in one of two ways: (1) if the lease is acceptable, then the risk to the municipality is that the realized salvage value may turn out to be greater than the expected amount used in the lease evaluation; or, (2) if the lease is deemed unacceptable, the risk is that the cash proceeds from the salvage value at a time of liquidation will fall short of the estimated amount. In either case, changes in salvage value may be sufficient to reverse the decision to undertake (or reject) the lease alternative. Very simply, the lessee can assess the extent of salvage value risk exposure by determining the SV_n necessary to reverse the decision. That is, the lessee computes how large the salvage value must be before leasing is no longer attractive (i.e., where PVC becomes greater than C). The municipality can then estimate the probability of the revised salvage value actually occurring.

The adjusted salvage value required to reverse the decision (which we will denote as SV^*_n) can be defined as:

$$(4) \qquad SV^*_n = [C - 1 \sum_{t=0}^{n-1} (1 + i)^{-t}] (1 + i)^n$$

where all the terms are as defined above. In any condition where $SV^*_n \geq 0$, the probability of such a salvage value occurring must be determined. Assuming a normal distribution of possible salvage values, the standard normal deviate (Z) necessary to bring about the indicated change can be computed. Once this Z-value has been determined, the probability of occurrence can be measured by consulting a table of areas under the normal curve. The standard normal deviate (Z) is defined as:

$$(5) \qquad Z = \frac{SV^*_n - SV_n}{\sigma_n}$$

where σ_n is the standard deviation of the expected SV_n and the other terms are as defined above.

To apply this risk evaluation procedure, the only additional piece of information required is the standard deviation of the estimated salvage value. Assume that, in our example, the estimated standard deviation is $3500. Using equation (4), we can determine the adjusted salvage value (SV^*_n) required to reverse the decision (made in equation (3)) to proceed with the lease. For our illustration, SV^*_n would equal:

$$SV^*_n = [\$200,000 - (\$25,668 + 25,668 (6.5152))] (1.9672) = \$13,967$$

Thus, if the salvage value were greater than $13,967, the municipality would be better advised to forego the lease.

Of course, after this revised salvage has been computed, the probability that the actual salvage value will be $\geq SV^*_n$ must be determined. To do this, the Z-value is computed according to equation (5); for our illustration

$$Z = \$13,967 - \$4,000/\$3,500 = 2.85$$

Given a Z-value of 2.85, the probability of actually realizing the adjusted salvage value can be found by referring to a table of areas under the normal curve. In this example $P(Z > 2.85) = .0022$; in other words, there is a less than 1 per cent chance that the salvage value will be great enough to reverse the decision to lease. In this case, the risk analysis merely reaffirms the decision indicated by the PVC analysis—i.e., there is better than a 99 per cent chance that leasing is superior to the purchase alternative.

The tax arbitrage lease

Thus far, only leasing as an alternative to other forms of *external* financing has been considered. However, due to the tax exempt status of municipalities, lease financing may also be beneficial to municipalities as an alternative to *internal* financing (i.e., paying cash for equipment). In particular, the use of lease financing may permit the municipality to arbitrage between the taxable and tax-exempt sectors of the capital markets. The municipality may acquire low-cost lease financing by passing on tax benefits to the lessor while, in turn, investing the freed-up cash (i.e., funds not expended on the leased asset) in high-yield, fully taxable instruments—e.g., term certificates of deposit or Treasury securities. This "leasing instead of spending" procedure may be referred to as tax arbitrage leasing. In effect, the municipality may wish to use a lease as a financing vehicle, not because it lacks the funds to finance the acquisition from its general fund, but, rather, because the municipality may be better off by using its available cash in some investment outlet other than ownership of its own facilities and equipment. Although there are a number of restrictions upon a municipality's issuing tax exempt bonds and investing the proceeds in taxable obligations (see Ritter [13] and [14]), the alternative of "leasing instead of spending" to accomplish the objective remains available.

The evaluation of a tax arbitrage lease is essentially identical to the evaluation of a general municipal lease, except that the relevant discount rate is the investment rate that can be earned on the investment of excess funds by the municipality instead of the alternative finance rate. For example, in our illustration, assume that the municipality now has the $200,000 in cash required to purchase the equipment, and that it can invest its cash at an annual return of 9 per cent. The municipality is now considering leasing the equipment for cash (i.e., a tax arbitrage lease). Given a level lease payment, the PVC of such a tax arbitrage lease can be computed as follows:

$$(6) \quad PVC = L \sum_{t=0}^{n-1} (1 + i^*)^{-t} + SV_n (1 + i^*)^{-n}$$

where i^* is the investment rate and the other terms are as defined above. Thus, using a 9 per cent rate, the PVC for this lease is

$$PVC = \$25,668 + \$25,668 (5.9952) + \$4,000 (.46043) = \$180,981$$

If the municipality leases the equipment and invests the funds thus freed up at a 9 per cent rate, the present value of the savings from leasing instead of purchasing the asset will be $19,019 (i.e., $200,000 minus $180,981). The source of these savings is, of course, the combination of a relatively favorable lease payment (due to the tax benefits passed on to the taxable lessor) and the relatively high, and taxless, investment by the municipality.

The fact that the savings on the tax arbitrage lease amounts to $19,019, versus only $5,074 when the lease was compared to the traditional debt financing alternative, results from the difference between the municipality's investment rate (assumed to be 9 per cent) and its borrowing rate (assumed to be 7 per cent). Because investment rates are usually greater than borrowing rates, tax arbitrage leases will frequently be desirable even in situations where equipment leasing would not otherwise be a viable *financing* alternative (presuming, of course, that the municipality has the available cash to begin with). To date, neither lessors nor municipalities have shown any inclination to avail themselves of the benefits of tax arbitrage leasing on a large scale. However, doubtless this situation will change as the mutual benefits of this unregulated tax artifice become apparent.

Conclusion

This paper has examined the viability of leasing as a municipal finance alternative. The discussion of the economics of leasing demonstrates that tax benefits that are normally valueless to a municipality will, in effect, reduce the payments required by lessors. Thus, a financial lease may often be competitive with a municipality's other (and tax-exempt) financing alternatives. We then presented a lease evaluation procedure for municipal financial managers to use in comparing leasing with other sources of financing. It is evident that the present value approach is a simple algorithm, which requires little sophistication on the part of the user. Even the evaluation of the "risk" of foregoing substantial salvage values on leased assets is relatively straightforward. Finally, we noted the possibility of tax arbitrage leasing, where the financing lease is an alternative to spending cash rather than to borrowing. The tax arbitrage lease is perhaps the most intriguing aspect of our discussion in that it permits municipalities to exploit their tax exempt status to reduce their operating costs.

Notes

1. Of course, municipal managers may also have ulterior or, at least questionable motives for avoiding citizen scrutiny of capital expenditures.
2. However, the effect of leasing on residual debt capacity is probably modest. See Miller and Upton [11] and Lewellen, et al., [8].
3. In the interest of simplicity, we ignore the possibility of the lessor's using leverage to finance the purchase of the asset. Leverage leasing provides additional income tax benefits to the lessor, because his interest payments are tax deductible, but the analysis of leveraged leases is computationally complex (see Bierman [3], Childs and Gridley [6] and Wiar [18].

References

1. Antieu, C.J., *Municipal Corporation Law*, Volume 2, New York: Matthew Bender, 1973, pp. 15.82-15.86.
2. Baumol, William J., "On the Discount Rate for Public Projects," in R.H. Haveman & J. Margolis, editors, *Public Expenditures and Policy Analysis*, Chicago: Markham Publishing, 1970, pp. 273-290.
3. Bierman, Harold, Jr., "Leveraged Leasing: An Alternative Analysis," *The Bankers Magazine*, 157 (Summer 1974), pp. 62-65.
4. Brigham, Eugene F., "Equipment Lease Financing," *The Bankers Magazine*, 149 (Winter 1966), pp. 65-75.
5. Brigham, Eugene F., "The Impact of Bank Entry on Market Conditions in the Equipment Leasing Industry: Reply and Correction," *National Banking Review*, 2 (March 1965), pp. 421-424.
6. Childs, C. Roger, Jr., and William G. Gridley, Jr., "Leveraged Leasing and the Reinvestment Rate Fallacy," *The Bankers Magazine*, 156 (Winter 1973), pp. 53-61.
7. Dyl, Edward A., "Leasing Instead of Lending—An Approach to Lessor Rate-Setting," *Journal of Commercial Bank Lending*, 59 (November 1976), pp. 41-48.
8. Lewellen, Wilbur G., Michael S. Long and John J. McConnell, "Asset Leasing in Competitive Capital Markets," *Journal of Finance*, XXXI (June 1976), pp. 787-798.
9. Magnusson, Jon, "Lease-Financing by Municipal Corporations as a Way Around Debt Limitations," *George Washington Law Review*, March 1957, pp. 377-396.
10. Marglin, Stephen A., "The Opportunity Costs of Public Investments," *Quarterly Journal of Economics*, May 1963, pp. 274-289.
11. Miller, Merton H., and Charles W. Upton, "Leasing, Buying and the Cost of Capital Services," *Journal of Finance*, XXXI (June 1976), pp. 761-786.
12. Moak, Lennox L. and Albert M. Hillhouse, *Concepts and Practices in Local Government Finance*, Municipal Finance Officers Association, 1975, pp. 235-238.
13. Ritter, Wallis C., "An Analysis of the New Proposed Regs on Arbitrage Bonds Under Section 103(d)," *Journal of Taxation* (September 1973), pp. 164-168.
14. Ritter, Wallis C., "Working with Treasury's Reproposed Regs on Arbitrage Bonds Under Section 103(d)," *Journal of Taxation* (September 1973), pp. 130-134.
15. Rosenbloom, Richard H., "A Review of the Municipal Bond Market," *Economic Review of the Federal Reserve Bank of Richmond*, 62 (March/April 1976), pp. 10-19.
16. Snyder, Gerald L., "Making Leasing Attractive for Municipal Financing," *The Bankers Magazine*, 154 (Winter 1971), pp. 102-105.
17. Van Horne, James C., *Financial Management and Policy*, 4th Ed., New York: Prentice-Hall (1974), Chapter 19.
18. Wiar, Robert C., "Economic Implications of Multiple Rates of Return in the Leveraged Lease Context," *Journal of Finance*, XXVII (December 1973), pp. 1275-1286.

Equipment Leasing: The Newest Boom in Government Purchasing

Kathryn Grover

The local government marketplace is one which grows from the political necessity to respond to public demand. To a large extent, it is populated by industries whose real and potential fortune springs from the misfortunes of cities and counties. Saddled, for example, with a federal mandate to clean up local waters, air and land, local governments have helped build the pollution control equipment industry into a healthy, lucrative enterprise.

But there is at least one industry that's begun to gain a foothold in the marketplace whose profits do not travel a one-way street. That industry is equipment leasing, a practice virtually unheard of in cities and counties a decade ago.

Most municipal statutes that deal with capital equipment acquisition are mute on the subject of leasing. And, often that very silence has been taken as a prohibition by municipal officials. In 1958, the International City Management Association found only 32 of 77 cities it surveyed were leasing any type of equipment at all.

But the leasing picture has changed drastically in just the past few years. Although statistics documenting leasing activity by local governments are not available (such deals are marketed on a private-placement basis), the growth of that activity is evident from the fact that at least seven companies have been created in the last seven years that deal exclusively or in part in the local government market. It is further evidenced in these companies' own phenomenal rates of growth.

Leasing itself is a $50–$100-billion industry with a projected 15% annual growth—about twice the rate of growth in the Gross National Product. The Milwaukee-based American Association of

Reprinted with permission from the May, 1979, issue of *American City & County* Magazine.

Equipment Lessors says that leasing accounted for about 15% of all capital outlays in 1975. And, judging from what lessors have told *American City & County*, leasing will figure prominently in municipal equipment purchases, which have begun to rebound after three years of double-digit growth slowed to less than three percent growth in 1975-76.

Just as the pollution control industry capitalized on a sullied environment, the leasing industry is turning a profit on municipal capital shortages, an increasingly tight-fisted voter and searing inflation in equipment costs (the American Public Works Association says some heavy-duty equipment costs have increased three- and four-fold over the past several years). But equipment leasing—particularly lease-purchasing, the chief area of growth—offers numerous advantages to local governments, regardless of size and fiscal capacity.

For one thing, the lease-purchase conserves working capital. Because most lease-purchase contracts include a "fiscal funding" clause, governments can budget yearly lease payments as they do other appropriations, and such payments do not apply to the debt ceiling. There is no need to seek voter approval to float bonds for equipment purchases. And there is no need for managers to try to build up capital improvement project (CIP) funds until an outright purchase is possible, all the while watching inflation stay one or two steps ahead of their purchasing power.

Most lease-purchase contracts require only an initial installment to put the equipment in the municipality's hands. Down-

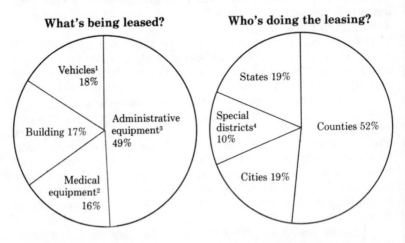

| What's being leased? | Who's doing the leasing? |

Vehicles[1] 18%
Building 17%
Administrative equipment[3] 49%
Medical equipment[2] 16%

States 19%
Special districts[4] 10%
Counties 52%
Cities 19%

Source: Municipal Funding Corporation analysis of 231 current leases.
1. Road and street maintenance, fire, ambulances, police.
2. X-ray, scanners, EKG.
3. Computers, telephone systems, office equipment, printing.
4. Hospitals, fire, sewer.

Who's leasing what and where.

payments are rare. And because the equipment is on the premises almost instantly, cities and counties can save current operations and maintenance funds expended in the effort to keep obsolete equipment functional. In a lease-purchase arrangement, too, the government is constantly building equity in the equipment. Terms of the lease-purchase contract—the term itself, the amount of the installment, the frequency of installment—are very flexible. In addition, depending somewhat on which lessor company a local government contracts with, you can lease-purchase just about anything you would normally buy.

Most lessors agree that the real boom in equipment leasing by local governments has only occurred in the last three years. Previously, the chief impediment was the extreme variability in local statutes on the matter of capital equipment buying; how can a city arrange to buy a fire truck over five years' time when it can legally only budget from year to year? It's only been in the past five years that contracts have been refined to the point that they comply with municipal funding authority. Now it is simply a matter of local counsel issuing opinions which attest the legality of this funding arrangement, and of generally educating city and county officials about the availability and legitimacy of the option.

At the present time, even the Internal Revenue Service supports these arrangements. Lessors are regulated under Section 103 of the 1954 IRS Code, which, though it does not mention lease-purchase specifically, allows lessors to accumulate tax-free interest income. As a result, the interest rates on lease-purchase financing are typically comparable to those in the municipal bond market. Usually, they are slightly higher because of the higher risk involved should a government be unable to appropriate the lease payment from year to year. If a leasing company issues a penalty against an entity guilty of so-called "non-appropriation," the interest rate will be a little lower than if the lessor enacts no penalty.

Most in the field do not penalize governments for non-appropriation and are similarly sensitive to the intricacies of municipal capital financing in other respects as well. Most have done remarkable business as a result.

The Municipal Funding Corporation, one of two that began exclusively with local government leasing, did $500,000 worth of business in 1972 after its incorporation the year before. By 1978, MUFCOA was doing an $18–$20 million business, and it expects to do twice that this year. Moreover, says Operations Manager Ellen Swoverland, "We're expecting business to double for the next three to five years." Federal Leasing (whose name conceals the fact that 80% of its business is state, county and municipal) has financed over $200 million of equipment since its creation in 1974. And Dallas-based First Continental Leasing Corporation, which began marketing its services to local governments only 18 months ago, says it's done "several million dollars worth of transactions" since then.

Because of the intensely competitive nature of the new industry, other firms—Spectrum Leasing in Vienna, Va., First Municipal Leasing Corporation in Denver, New York City's Commercial Funding Corporation and the major car and truck rental companies—will not divulge figures on their growth. "Our participation in such events (as the 1978 APWA equipment show in Boston) reflects our continually aggressive attitude toward the market. We're devoting quite a bit of attention to it," says Leigh Smith, director of editorial research at the Hertz Corporation. "But we do not like to tell our competition what we're up to. Does Macy's tell Gimbels?"

Most of the companies in the municipal equipment leasing field began with computers, a market for which leasing has always been considered a good financing vehicle, given its rapid technological advance and its corresponding high incidence of equipment obsolescence. But, depending on the company, what can now be financed under a lease-purchase agreement is almost limitless, in response to the myriad capital needs of local governments and the associated pressure of vendors plying their wares in cities and counties across the nation. MUFCOA started out in lease-purchasing with copiers, word processors, dictating equipment, computers and computer peripherals. But Swoverland says that after two years of concentration in that field, the market moved "very heavily" toward rolling stock—fire trucks, ambulances, garbage trucks and all manner of road maintenance equipment. Other companies report a similar movement.

"Our thrust has been in the computer marketplace," says Spectrum Leasing President Michael Wueste, "but it's changing because the municipalities want it to change." Spectrum is now getting involved with rolling stock and the lease-purchase of real property.

Federal Leasing is moving into street sanitation equipment, school buses, real property and—like MUFCOA—environmental systems equipment. With 85% of its business in data processing equipment currently and the rest in construction and hospital equipment, President Daniel Morley says, "Our corporate intent is to have, by 1 August 1981, a favorable mix of non-data processing and data processing equipment." And, with an executive from the environmental systems field on its staff, the firm plans to "actively bid" recycling systems this year.

Generally speaking, the lease-purchase process can be conducted in one of three ways. Some firms, such as MUFCOA, work directly with a municipality that has already chosen the equipment type and vendor it desires. "We don't deal in equipment; we see ourselves as bankers," Swoverland says. "All we want to know is what the bottom line is, and we'll put up the funds for the city. Municipalities want to deal with the local vendors, who can supply them with equipment but can't give them extended financing." Allan Fischer, president of

Commercial Funding Corporation, feels that most lessor financing companies should act as banks rather than as middleman vendors. "We would want to know that we have an asset we can market" in event of repossession (which rarely occurs), but other than that leasing companies, he feels, should remain uninvolved with equipment *per se.* "The equipment risk is the risk of the municipality, and I think that's as it should be," Fischer says. "The leasing company only helps you get that asset."

Other companies take a different approach. First Continental Leasing in Dallas, for example, does its principal transaction with vendors. Typically, the lessor works closely with large, national manufacturers who have reliable product lines. When such manufacturers have sales requiring financing, they contact First Continental Leasing. The lessor will then monitor local statutes before the RFP or the bid, and only after the award will the company enter into a direct contract with the municipality, in order to take advantage of the tax exemption on interest income.

Most other companies do business both ways. First Municipal Leasing gets a great deal of direct business from its public information effort. "We get a lot of repeat business from lessees, and business from agents who seek to lease facilities for public agencies," says President John Lohre. "We also work with manufacturers who sell to local governments but who don't want a lot of their receivables tied up in municipal paper. Vendors bring business to us too. It's a cash sale for them," he points out, "not a term sale."

There is variation, too, in these companies' criteria for entering into such contracts with municipalities. Most commercial leasing companies that have entered the municipal equipment leasing field pay a bit more attention to credit ratings from the municipal bond market than do those firms designed exclusively to lease to public entities. Friedman says First Continental Leasing tries to deal only with "top credit-rated entities"—BAA and above—to minimize risk. Spectrum Leasing's Robert Bowen says, "Someone with a suspect rating you would look twice at. I have a little trouble putting together a deal with New York City, or Cleveland. We structure what we feel are intelligent, quality transactions." And Federal Leasing's Morley

Equipment	Increase	Equipment	Increase
Excavators	+53%	Air compressors	+26%
Scrapers and graders	+56%	Passenger cars	+31%
Pavers	+35%	Trucks	+41%
Tractor-loaders	+54%	Buildings	+39%

Selected equipment price increases, 1974–78.

says, "We've walked away from an awful lot of business. But we can do a Cleveland or a New York under certain strong parameters that protect the investor."

One of the strongest parameters is, of course, rating in the bond market. MUFCOA says it will "evaluate closely" low ratings, but it has financed local governments with poor bond ratings, and some who finance with cash and thus have no ratings at all. And Lohre at First Municipal Leasing says the credit rating judgement varies depending on how tight the money market is. When interest rates are high, the firm is more selective about which entities it signs contracts with, and lower-rated governments will pay comparatively more in lease payment per year.

Other parameters influence the structure of the lease-purchase agreement. Federal Leasing Corporation investigates the equipment type, its useful life, the desired term of the lease, the use to which equipment will be put and the municipality's purchasing history. As do most firms, MUFCOA looks at the equipment type, its cost and its useful life and will structure a term for the lease that approximates its useful life.

What about costs? Aside from out-of-hand, direct purchase of equipment, it would appear that lease-purchase is the cheapest thing around for governments who want to own the asset. It's certainly a better deal than waiting for cash-on-hand: MUFCOA figures that to wait five years to buy a $100,000 piece of equipment at present rates of inflation would cost $149,414 by 1978, while to finance it in 1974 by lease-purchase—even at 11% interest—would cost only $130,454. And, two analysts from Brook Incorporated in Chicago recently did a study showing that, with few exceptions, a lease-purchase will always be cheaper than a bond. Issuing a bond includes the cost of holding a referendum, legal fees, underwriting, printing and advertising costs. The lease has no added expense except the interest rate. And the total expenditure on the lease will be less because of the lease's shorter life, even with the higher interest rate and the higher installment. Lohre says that the terms in lease-purchase agreements are typically four-, six- or eight-year terms; terms of ten years or more are rare. In the bond market, a ten-year term is considered very short. Moreover, the lease-purchase is not a debt. Yet, because it is not and is subject to yearly appropriation, the lease-purchase "deserves a higher yield because it carries a greater risk."

The lease-purchase is not only useful in the "scramble for capital" but is, some analysts say, the appropriate way to buy capital equipment. Its new availability to municipalities not only broadens revenue sources by opening up a new capital market, but it also is well tailored to capital equipment acquisition. That is because the life of the loan is usually matched to the life of the asset. Therefore, it isn't necessary to inundate the long-term bond market with short-term project financing. As Bowen at Spectrum Leasing says, the municipal bond market has typically served higher volumes, longer terms and more construction-oriented projects. "Any user entity that is at all cost-conscious has to look at this type of program, because it's really not feasible in my mind for a municipality to procure all its money on the bond market," he says.

But lease-purchasing can't do everything for you. Most contracts will not allow the lessee to cancel in order to buy similar equipment. In addition, full-service contracts are not usually possible, entailing as they do a heightened risk for the investor. So if you want to buy a piece of equipment and specify as a condition of sale that service will be forthcoming from the vendor, lease-purchase is not the way to go. And most companies will not finance what they term "throwaway items" which depreciate rapidly. Federal Leasing won't, for example, finance small orders of copiers, and many firms don't advise financing short-lived items such as police cars unless it is done as a mass-purchase order on a regular replacement schedule. Federal Leasing says it will fund "anything," even garbage carts, so long as such small items are a bulk purchase and it has even funded cities that pool their resources for a lower unit cost.

Clearly, leasing is not just a last resort that, as Swoverland says, "waves a red flag to the taxpayers" in cities straining at their debt limits and facing an ever more hostile constituency. It presents itself as a viable way to diversify one's ability to finance capital equipment. And no one is more aware of that than the industry that's suddenly sprouted up to provide that money. For example, Smith Barney Harris Upham & Company in New York City, investment bankers for First Municipal Leasing, has done $150 million of business since 1975. "Our business doubles every year," says one banker there, "and we expect to do $75 to $100 million of business in 1979. It's a real gold mine."

How to make lease-purchasing work

The lease-purchase contract need not be limited to the acquisition of a single fire truck or backhoe. If you have something more ambitious in mind than just the purchase of one unit of equipment, chances are you'll be able to finance it by lease-purchase.

The first thing to do is contact one of the lessor financing agencies. That firm's account executives then review your statutory situation and make you aware of the proper route to such an agreement. Normally, your local bond counsel is asked to issue an opinion attesting the legality of lease-purchasing within your regulatory framework. Then the lessor can spell out your payment options, and you can choose the one that suits you best.

Next, specify the equipment you wish to buy and the vendor or manufacturer. Bond counsel and the lessor firm prepare all the necessary documents; the lessor then usually writes up a purchase order, and the customer stipulates the conditions of delivery. At First

Municipal Leasing Corporation, the firm makes the initial payment to the vendor or manufacturer. All other payments are made by the city or county to a designated transfer agent, typically an investment bank. Title is transferred at the end of the lease term unless a local government prefers, or is required by law, to hold title to the equipment upon delivery.

Repeat business is frequent. One Colorado county is putting its entire road mantenance equipment fleet on a lease-purchase basis. Ruidoso, N.M., a town of 7500 persons whose population balloons to 45,000 during the summer tourist season, has bought ten of its 100-unit fleet of road equipment through lease-purchasing. Frank Potter, Ruidoso's assistant administrator, says the town has bought motor graders, garbage trucks and other equipment "as cheap or cheaper" via a MUFCOA lease-purchase than it could if it had floated bonds. Ruidoso just bid a $322,000 hot-mix plant, which it will buy through a lease-purchase contract at an interest rate of 6.6%.

"We would not finance equipment that has a life of from two to five years only," Potter told *American City & County.* "But we'd finance a $58,900 *Caterpillar.* In the next two years, that piece of equipment will be $80,000 and our previous one lasted 18 years."

Lease-purchasing can be a good way to comply with environmental regulations too. In 1974, when Neola, Iowa, renovated its wastewater treatment plant, the Environmental Protection Agency strongly urged the town to control its water usage better by installing water meters. Lacking the capital for this large public works project, Neola went to FMLC to lease-purchase 400 generator remote readout meters, three two-inch meters and one 1.75-inch meter. Neola makes quarterly payments over a five-year term, can prepay the lease at certain specified dates, and has found a "noticeable change in water usage" as a result of the installation. The town insures the meters, and the manufacturer provides maintenance under a separate guarantee program.

You can also take the lease-purchase route in pursuit of innovations. Tinley Park, Ill., had researched the notion of giving patrolmen personal cars. The city's Board of Trustees had approved the $150,000 program, but that money was not available in the city's budget. Tinley Park initially bought 16 cars under the lease-purchase plan and will phase in another seven over the three-year term of the lease. The 25,000 city found the overall crime rate dropped 18% the year after the personal car program was enacted. It also found cars were lasting three years or longer, compared to the six-month life of fleet cars, that traffic accidents dropped slightly, court traffic fines went up 66% and overtime hours for patrolmen dropped 17%. High Point, N.C., bought two garbage trucks, two lifters and some 21,000 mobile refuse carts by lease-purchase as a way to cut the high personnel costs of refuse collection. With the new vehicles, the city cut some

60 workers from the sanitation crew, reduced the number of collection routes from 18 to 11, and saved $400,000 in a year.

Other possible lease-purchase arrangements include master-leasing, which allows the purchase of different types of equipment within the availability of budgeted funds. The lessor can extend the city a line of credit and schedule purchases and retirements of needed equipment without separate review and documentation for each piece of equipment. Or, as Woodland Park, Colo., is doing, you can lease/leaseback. The city had FMLC lease property for a municipal services building, build the structure, and then lease it to the city.

Oakland Sells the City Jewels

While today's cornucopia of tax benefits and investment incentives has stirred the adrenalin of private investors and municipal managers alike, one of the most publicized recent examples of innovative finance in California cities was not significantly influenced by the Economic Recovery Tax Act at all.

There are two major differences between the sale of the city of Oakland's Museum and Auditorium, and more traditional equipment leasing in the private sector: this transaction centered on a municipal facility, and the city used municipal bonds to make it possible for private investors to purchase the buildings.

For investors, the incentives are tax exempt income from lease payments, and the shelter of traditional "straight-line" depreciation on the buildings. The money spent to rehabilitate the Oakland Auditorium, estimated at over $10 million, will also be eligible for accelerated depreciation under the new tax laws.

Background

In February, 1981, the Oakland city council reviewed a staff report which described the condition of the Oakland Auditorium. The report included needed repairs, both immediate and long-range, with an estimated cost of over $10 million. After reviewing the report, the council directed staff to study the various financing alternatives available to the city for the improvement of the Auditorium.

Staff studied various financing strategies and concluded that the only alternative which appeared at all feasible would involve the issu-

Reprinted with permission from the March 1982 issue of *Western City* magazine, the official publication of the League of California Cities. Adapted from the report submitted by city manager Henry L. Gardner to the Oakland city council.

ance of revenue bonds secured through proceeds from the sale of city-owned facilities.

The Oakland city charter provides that the city council may issue revenue bonds for any lawful purpose, and upon such terms and conditions as it establishes by the provisions of a procedural ordinance. The city's bond underwriter maintained that it would be possible for the city to issue bonds to finance the Auditorium improvements if both the Oakland Museum and the rehabilitated Auditorium, to be known as the Oakland Convention Center Extension, were sold to a private investment partnership and leased back to the city.

First, the Museum would be sold and leased back, and the proceeds from this sale would be used to pay back the principal and interest on the Municipal Improvement Revenue Bonds, and to make the initial lease payments to the partnership. The municipal improvement bonds would make cash immediately available to the city, while "mortgage" payments from the investment partnership would be used to retire the bonds.

The Convention Center Extension would then be sold and leased back, and the proceeds from the sale of the Convention Center Extension would be invested. The interest earned would be used to make all the lease payments on the Convention Center Extension and the remaining lease payments on the Oakland Museum. At the end of the lease periods (30 years), both facilities would be repurchased by the city using the remaining invested sales proceeds.

The deal

The following is a summary of the terms and conditions of the financing agreement:

1. *Ownership:* The city will only be selling the Museum and the Auditorium buildings. The city will retain ownership of the land and will, in turn, lease it to the partnership. The city will continue to operate the facilities without any interference from the partnership.
2. *Facilities Lease:* The city will lease the facilities from the partnership for a term of thirty years, with four additional five-year renewal options. At the end of thirty years, the city will have the option to repurchase the facilities or to exercise its first five-year renewal option.
3. *Lease Payments:* Lease payments will be based upon the acquisition of the facilities, estimated costs of rehabilitation, ground rent and real estate taxes. Because the Museum will be open to the public and will not charge admission, it will remain exempt from property taxes.
4. *Construction Contract:* The Auditorium will be rehabilitated according to the plans of the city. The city will be responsible

for the completion of the rehabilitation and will approve all change orders.

5. *Museum Sales Proceeds:* The partnership will pay the city the fair market value of the Museum, which has been determined to be $22 million. The city will receive a cash down-payment and a purchase money mortgage for the balance of the purchase price. The sales proceeds will be used to pay back the principal and interest on the Municipal Improvement Revenue Bonds used to rehabilitate the Auditorium and to make the initial lease payments.

6. *Convention Center Extension Sales Proceeds:* The partnership will pay the city the fair market after-rehab value of the facility which has been estimated to be between $25 and $35 million. The partnership will purchase it with the proceeds from an industrial development bond issued by the city, and the city will invest the proceeds to make the lease payments on both facilities.

7. *Impact on Budget:* The sales proceeds from the Convention Center Extension will be invested in governmental securities or other high yield corporate securities. The interest from these securities will be more than sufficient to pay lease payments for thirty years, with funds remaining to repurchase both facilities. No additional city funds will be required to finance the proposed actions.

A private firm will organize the partnership, to be called Oak Art, to be made up of individual investors whose investment in municipal real property will provide tax-exempt earnings and a useful tax shelter.

The Museum has been sold, and the transaction for the Auditorium will be completed by mid 1982.

Benefits

These tax benefits will actually be shared by the city, because they will be reflected in lower lease payments. In fact, the city's lease payments will be less than the debt service it would have to pay if it were to borrow directly for the funds to rehabilitate the Auditorium. This is because the city will be realizing greater interest income when it invests the proceeds of the Auditorium sale than it will pay in interest on the revenue and industrial development bonds used to finance the sale to private investors.

And what happens after 30 years? A number of provisions effectively guarantee that Oakland's Museum and Auditorium will remain municipal facilities and will revert to the city at a reasonable price. The city retains first right of refusal to purchase the facilities when the lease expires. If the repurchase is not practical in 30 years, the city has another 20 years of options in which to work something out.

The principal from the sale of the Auditorium will not be touched, and will be available to fund the repurchase. The fair market price will be based on an appraisal by the income value method, which determines worth according to income stream. The worth of the facilities to private owners would be questionable, especially since the city retains control of the real property the buildings stand on.

This financing arrangement to rehabilitate the Oakland Auditorium is a creative approach to a long and difficult problem of making substantial and costly repairs to this great municipal facility. This financing technique allows the city to not only make the mandatory repairs to continue operating the auditorium at adequate health and safety standards, but it also allows the city to fully restore the facility to a first class condition. As a result, the Oakland Auditorium can be used with pride as an extension of the City's Convention Center. The best part of all is that under conservative assumptions, no general funds will be required to undertake this major renovation.

PART 4

Economic Development and Redevelopment Financing Techniques

Industrial Development Bond Financing

Charles P. Edmonds and William P. Lloyd

Raising additional capital is one of the most challenging problems of any business operation. In recent months, high interest rates and a general shortage of loanable funds have compounded the problem. The purpose of this article is to discuss a financing alternative that is frequently ignored but that offers significant benefits to both small and large businesses. That alternative is the industrial development bond (IDB). In addition to exploiting increased investor interest in tax-exempt income, IDBs offer:

1. A widening spread between their tax-exempt yields and the yield on regular corporate bonds.
2. Favorable changes in tax laws.
3. Liberalized state regulations on how they may be used.

According to the *Industrial Development and Pollution Control Revenue Bond Financing* brochure, industrial development bonds are "bonds issued by municipalities or municipal agencies . . . for the purpose of providing funds for the purchase of land and the construc-tion and equipping of manufacturing, distribution, and pollution control facilities for lease or sale to responsible companies." As municipal securities, their interest income is exempt from federal in-come taxes. The result is an interest yield substantially below that of regular corporate bonds.

Industrial development bonds are usually issued by an agency of a town or city to provide funds for a private company. The agency retains title to the property financed, but enters into a long-term lease or installment sales contract with the user company. At the end of the lease or contract period, title to the property will transfer to

Reprinted with permission from *Financial Executive*, April 1981.

the company. Sale of the bonds by the municipal agency qualifies the bonds for their tax-exempt status while the earnings power and credit-standing of the user company make the bonds attractive to investors.

History

The first IDBs were sold by the state of Mississippi in 1936. The basic purpose was to attract industry and stimulate employment. Until the 1970s, the bonds were a unique financing device of southern states. During the period of 1959 to 1968, only six states (Alabama, Arkansas, Georgia, Kentucky, Mississippi, and Tennessee) accounted for 87 percent of all issues and 60 percent of the dollar volume. As the usefulness of IDBs became apparent, other states enacted laws permitting their use. They are now used in at least 45 states. The IDBs first issued in Mississippi were general obligation bonds, but most current issues are revenue bonds secured by the income of the property being financed.

Growth and development of IDBs have been influenced by a number of legal rulings, opinions, and legislative changes. It is fair to say that their development in the past has been limited by the uncertainty of their legal status. The U.S. Supreme Court upheld the legality of the Mississippi bonds in 1938, but state courts in Nebraska and Florida ruled that public funds could not be used for private industry. Under such uncertainties, the market for IDBs remained shallow, and few investment bankers were willing to underwrite them. In many cases the market for IDBs was limited to the community in which a plant was built.

After several favorable rulings and increased use of the bonds by large corporations, the volume of IDBs grew rapidly during the 1960s. However, sales plummeted in 1969 as a result of two government actions: the Revenue and Expenditure Control Act of 1968 (P.L. 90–364), which limited the federal income tax exemption on the interest payments of IDBs to issues of $1 million or less, and a Securities and Exchange Commission ruling that IDB issues of more than $300,000 must be registered with the SEC and be subject to all regulations applicable to issues of corporate securities.

According to provisions of P.L. 90–364 *(Commerce Clearing House—Standard Federal Tax Reports)*, a bond is classified as an industrial development bond if:

The obligation is part of an issue, all or a major portion of the proceeds of which is used directly or indirectly in any trade or business of a person other than an exempt person (that is, a governmental unit or a religious, educational or charitable organization exempt from tax under Code Secs. 501(a) and 501(c) (3)).

Payment of the principal or interest on the obligation is, in whole or in major part, (a) secured by an interest in property (such as a factory, land, or equipment and machinery) used in a trade or business or in payments made (such as rent or lease or sales proceeds) in respect of this property, or (b) derived from payments in respect of property or borrowed money that is used (or is to be used) in a trade or business.

In addition to the exemption for bond issues of $1 million or less, regulations exempt interest on IDBs from tax without dollar limit if substantially all of the bond proceeds are used to provide the following facilities:

1. Residential real property for family units. (In this case the emphasis is upon *family* units. Hotels, rest homes, and dormitories do not qualify.)
2. Sports facilities, such as a baseball stadium or swimming pool.
3. Convention or trade show facilities.
4. Airports, docks, wharves, parking facilities, and so on.
5. Public utility facilities to process sewage or provide electric energy or gas.
6. Air or water pollution control facilities.
7. Facilities for the furnishing of water to the general public.

Only weeks after passing P.L. 90-364, Congress succumbed to various pressures and passed P.L. 90-634. In lieu of the $1 million exemption permitted in P.L. 90-364, the new ruling permitted a $5 million option. This option permitted an issuer to sell up to $5 million in tax-exempt IDBs provided capital expenditures made by the user company within the same city or county in which the project was located did not exceed $5 million during the three years preceding and the three years following the issuance of the bonds. The Revenue Act of 1978 raised the $5 million option to $10 million, effective January 1979. Raising the limit has stimulated a renewed interest in IDBs, but size of issue still seems to be the principal constraint on their use.

To alleviate problems caused by SEC registration, Congress passed provisions in 1970 to exempt IDBs from registration requirements. They are, however, subject to the anti-fraud provisions of the Federal securities laws. The legality of IDBs is now well defined, and the new $10 million limit has made them appealing to more users and investors. But many potential users do not know or fully understand the benefits of IDBs. As a result, the relative importance of the bonds as a means of financing is small but growing rapidly.

Procedure

For a firm considering the use of IDBs, the following steps will serve as a guideline of appropriate procedures. The entire process will normally take ten to twelve weeks.

Step 1: Contact the appropriate state or municipal agency, usually an industrial development board, located in the community of the potential investment. Support from this agency is essential. A proposed project may qualify under federal and state regulations, but the local agency must also desire to have the particular industry. Some communities might look favorably on a brewery; others would not. The agency may also wish to control plant location by insisting on an industrial park site.

The ease of obtaining the support of the local agency will differ from community to community. Some communities are naturally more eager than others to attract new industry. When the board does decide to support a project, it will take some type of formal action indicating its willingness to make financing available. This action normally takes the form of an "inducement agreement" documenting the public purpose for which the bonds are issued. Since the timeliness of this agreement is necessary to preserve the tax-exempt status of the bonds, it is important that this agreement is reached before any construction starts.

Step 2: The municipal agency will issue the bonds, but it is the *firm's* responsibility to market them. The major buyers of IDBs are banks, property, and casualty insurance companies, pension funds, and individual investors.

The agency should be able to provide names of institutions that regularly buy industrial development bonds. If a bank can be located, lawyers representing the firm, the agency, and the bank will draw the necessary documents. If a bank or other investor is not available to buy the entire issue, the firm will usually enlist the aid of a bond broker. Again, the agency can be helpful in supplying names of bond brokers that are active in the community. The remaining steps assume a broker is used.

Step 3: The basic legal documents are typically prepared by legal counsel retained by the municipal agency or the bond broker. These documents include a lease if the firm leases the plant from the board or an installment sale agreement if the plant is purchased from the agency. If a lease arrangement is used, there is normally an option to purchase at a nominal fee or an option to renew the lease at a nominal rent. In either case, the lease or installment payments must be large enough to meet the loan payments. Since leases are sometimes disavowed in bankruptcy proceedings, a separate guaranty agreement from the firm may also be prepared to give additional protection to the ultimate bond buyer. A pledge of personal property may be required. An indenture of trust is prepared between the agency and the bond's trustee (usually a commercial bank). In this agreement the agency pledges all lease or sale receipts it receives from the firm to the trustee. The agency also pledges the project's assets via a first mortgage. The trustee agrees to disburse money to bondholders for interest and principal payments as well as to represent the bondholders in the event of default.

Step 4: An opinion on the tax-exempt status of the bonds should be sought from a law firm whose opinion is recognized in the national tax-exempt bond market. The bond counsel is normally retained by the bond broker; if not, the firm can consult the *Directory of Municipal Bond Dealers*. In a few states (Georgia and Florida) the bond counsel will go through an optional validation procedure where a suit will actually be filed in Superior Court. The court will then rule on the tax exempt status of the bonds.

Step 5: An offering document is prepared by the broker. It includes the description and terms of the bonds and financial statements of the firm. The broker will advise the firm concerning the terms and provisions to be sure that the bonds are marketable. The coupon rate depends on the creditworthiness of the firm. A strong company should be able to sell bonds with a coupon rate ¼ to ½ percent above the conventional municipal bond rate. This premium is normal because of the weaker secondary market for industrial development bonds. Terms such as final maturity date are generally flexible; a ten to twenty-five year maturity is typical. Prepayment is usually restricted, or may even be prohibited, for the first five to ten years. For a strong firm there are usually very few restrictive convenants.

Step 6: The bond broker will either attempt to sell the bonds or actually underwrite the issue. If the broker chooses to underwrite, he must buy the entire issue and attempt to resell it to guarantee a certain proceed for the issuer.

The issue costs will mainly be a function of the size of the issue and the strength of the firm. The stronger the firm, the easier it is to sell the bonds. Typical float costs are 5 to 10 percent for a small issue, 3 percent for a medium size issue of around $2 million, and 2 percent for a large issue of $8 million or more. These costs are higher than for conventional taxable bonds because there is more legal work involved and the tax-exempt bonds are usually harder for the broker to sell.

Advantages and disadvantages

Industrial development bonds offer significant advantages—both monetary and nonmonetary—to a user firm. The monetary advantages are derived from the fact that the bonds are issued by some type of state or municipal agency and the facility being built is technically owned by the agency. The result is a number of tax benefits, the most obvious of which is the IDB's tax-exempt status. This status allows them to sell with a coupon rate of 2 to 2.5 percentage points below the rate on taxable bonds. During 1979 high interest rates and a growing investor interest in IDBs frequently pushed the spread to as much as 3.5 percent.

Because materials used in the construction of a facility are technically purchased by the municipality, they are exempt from sales and use taxes, resulting in a sizable savings. The use tax on any machinery and equipment in a plant can also be saved, as well as ad valorem taxes. This is especially important since ad valorem taxes are paid yearly while sales and use taxes on construction materials and plant machinery and equipment are paid only once. However, the savings in ad valorem taxes may not be possible in all communities. Some communities may require the firm to pay the municipality a yearly fee approximately equal to the entire ad valorem tax, while others may require a yearly fee equal to the school tax portion of the ad valorem tax.

Another possible benefit for an agency-owned facility is that services such as roads and sewerage/water systems may be easier to obtain. Some states make money available for evaluating plant location and site preparation. For example, the state of Alabama allocates funds to counties, municipalities, and Industrial Development Boards organized as public corporations for the preparation of industrial sites, including grading, clearing, and drainage.

It is possible to achieve 100 percent financing with IDBs. Bond proceeds can be used to purchase land, prepare sites, cover construction costs, and even pay the legal expenses of issuing the bonds. Simply avoiding the trouble and high costs of a construction loan can save a firm time and money. While "100 percent" financing is desirable, it is somewhat misleading. IDBs sell on the creditworthiness of the firm, not the municipality. Though the project may appear to be 100 percent financed by the bonds, the bonds cannot be sold without substantial equity in the firm or a pledge of personal collateral.

When comparing industrial development bonds with conventional corporate bonds, it is worthy to note that industrial development bonds are exempt from SEC registration. The accounting and tax treatment of IDB financing is the same as that of conventional bonds. The firm capitalizes the project's cost, depreciates assets under allowable schedules, and treats part of each lease payment as interest. Appropriate investment tax credits are taken by the firm.

A final advantage of IDBs to a firm is increased community interest. This is especially true if the industrial development bonds are sold to citizens in the local community, similar to a bank selling small amounts of stock to local businessmen in an attempt to heighten interest in the bank.

While IDBs have numerous advantages, they also have a few disadvantages. For example, they have been sold under fraudulent conditions and investors have had to accept losses. The Securities Reform Act of 1975 was aimed at eliminating municipal bond sales abuses, but such abuses still occur. Nonetheless, the market for IDBs has gained in depth and breadth.

New or small companies do not have the same access to the IDB market as large, established companies. Investors prefer the security provided by the credit rating of a large company. The owner of a small company could use IDBs, but would first need to locate an investor willing to buy them. The Small Business Administration will guarantee IDBs sold by small business firms for the purpose of satisfying pollution control requirements.

Types of eligible projects

Section 103 of the Internal Revenue Code of 1954, along with its amendments, states that interest on bonds issued by a state or political subdivision are tax-exempt except where the bonds are used for the benefit of a non-exempt user such as a private company. This section of the code does, however, specify circumstances where the interest on these bonds can be tax-exempt. These conditions are based on the dollar size of the bond offering and the ultimate use of the proceeds.

An issue of $1 million or less can qualify if at least 90 percent of the proceeds go to purchase such things as land, buildings, and equipment. This dollar limit is for each firm in each municipality. The firm can use this financing method in as many different municipalities as it has qualifying investments. As previously explained, a firm can select a $10 million option if it adheres to a six-year capital expenditure limit. Under this option, the $10 million limit is reduced by any capital expenditures made by the firm three years before and three years after the bond issue. Three years after the issue, the firm can increase its capital expenditure within that particular municipality as long as there is never more than $10 million in industrial development bonds outstanding at any one time.

There is no limit on the volume of IDBs that can be sold to finance certain types of projects. Bonds used to finance docks, wharves, and related storage or material handling equipment qualify and have no dollar limit if they are used by the public or by a common carrier. Yet it is necessary to be sure that the specific project under consideration qualifies under current Internal Revenue Service regulations. There could be a difference of opinion as to what kinds of projects are *just* for pollution control or docks.

Federal regulations on what can and cannot be financed with IDBs are interpreted differently by the various states. Projects that qualify under the provisions of one state's laws may not qualify under those of another state. Some states require that real property be involved in the project; others do not. For example, Pennsylvania will permit financing of a fast food franchise provided it creates or preserves twenty jobs and has a total cost of at least $200,000. For industrial plants in that state, the requirements are the creation of five jobs and a minimum cost of $100,000. An automobile dealership qualifies in some states but not in others. Projects that are likely to qualify in almost all states are manufacturing or processing plants, warehouses, food processing projects, or pollution control projects. Other projects should be evaluated on a state by state basis.

Despite the numerous advantages of industrial development

bonds, many companies are still reluctant to use them. The reasons for their reluctance are unclear, but a lack of knowledge about IDBs and the $10 million limit for most projects seem to be the most obvious factors. At least 45 states now have laws that permit use of the bonds to finance manufacturing or processing plants, warehouses, and pollution control projects. In addition, tax advantages have made IDBs more attractive as a potential source of funds, while their tax-exempt yields have increased investor interest in their issuance. It seems certain that the use of IDBs will continue to grow.

Industrial Development Bonds: Some Aspects of the Current Controversy

Daniel E. Laufenberg

Tax-exempt securities have been the traditional means by which state and local governmental units have financed the construction of schools, roads, hospitals, and other public improvements. In recent years, another category of these "municipal" securities, generally referred to as industrial development bonds (IDBs), has become important. IDBs are issued by state and local units on behalf of private businesses to finance industrial and commercial projects. The growth of IDB financing has stirred considerable controversy, centering on the appropriate use of implicit federal subsidies and the impact on the borrowing costs of state and local governments. Moreover, concern has arisen about the impact on federal revenues of the tax exemption of interest earned on IDBs; partly for this reason, the Reagan administration has proposed curtailment of IDB issuance as part of its budget program.

Hundreds of state agencies, local development agencies, counties, and cities have issued IDBs in the name of local economic development. But many of the uses to which this financing vehicle has been put have raised doubts about legitimate public purpose. A study by the Congressional Budget Office noted that some less conventional uses of small-issue IDBs have become common, such as commercial real estate development, retail stores, recreational facilities, tourist facilities, and proprietary health facilities.[1] Moreover, small-issue IDB financing is being used extensively by large national retailers and somewhat less extensively by large manufacturing corporations. Such uses seem to contradict the intent of the Revenue and Expenditure Control Act of 1968, which imposed maximum dollar limits on the size of the IDB issue or on the total capital expenditures

Reprinted from the *Federal Reserve Bulletin*, March 1982.

on any one project financed in part or in whole by IDBs, except for special purposes.

This paper reviews the legal definitions of small-issue and selected-purpose IDBs to provide a clearer distinction between IDBs and traditional municipal issues; analyzes the costs and benefits of using tax-exempt financing to promote local development; and discusses the current concerns about IDB issuance.

Background

The use of public tax-exempt credit for private business purposes had its origin in the United States in 1936, when Mississippi authorized cities and counties to incur general-obligation indebtedness to construct industrial buildings for lease to private enterprise. Other states in the South and a few in other regions followed suit after World War II, but through the 1950s the volume of IDBs was relatively small.

In the early 1960s, the total of IDB issuance picked up substantially as more use was made of the revenue version of IDBs, which is secured by the property or receipts of the project financed rather than the full faith and credit of the issuer, and as businesses of all sizes participated in locally sponsored development programs. By 1968, IDBs, most of which were revenue bonds, represented 10 percent of all long-term tax-exempt bond sales.

The growing popularity of such bonds alarmed Treasury Department officials because IDBs threatened sizable losses of tax revenues. As a result, the Treasury ruled in 1967 that IDBs were subject to taxation. This ruling was withdrawn, however, when the Congress enacted the Revenue and Expenditure Control Act of 1968, the statute that still governs IDB issuance. Under this statute, tax-exempt status is denied IDBs except those that are designated as "small issues" or those that finance certain types of facilities.

Legal limits on IDB issuance

Securities issued by state and local governmental units are defined as IDBs in the 1968 legislation if they satisfy two tests. The first is the "trade or business test," which is met if a major portion of bond proceeds are used in business by a nonexempt entity—one other than a state or local government or organization. The second is the "security interest test," which is met if a major portion of the debt service is secured by property used in or payments derived from a business, regardless of whether the bonds are also general obligations of the issuer. IDB issues in recent years have been exclusively revenue bonds, and increasingly have been called industrial revenue bonds (IRBs). For the remainder of this paper, IDB and IRB are used synonymously.

Small issues of industrial development bonds   The Revenue and Expenditure Control Act of 1968 provides a tax exemption for certain small issues of industrial development bonds. Under this exemption, the governmental unit issuing the bonds may select a limit of either $1 million or $10 million. In either case, substantially all of the proceeds from the issues must be used to acquire, construct, or improve depreciable property. An IDB issue is within the $1 million exemption if the sum of the proposed issue and outstanding IDBs, whether or not by the same issuer but used to finance facilities for the principal user in the same jurisdiction, is no greater than $1 million. If the issuer elects the $10 million limit, all capital expenditures incurred by the principal user in the issuing jurisdiction during the six-year period beginning three years before the issuance of the bonds also must be counted against the limit.[2]

In general, capital expenditures must be taken into account if those expenditures are properly chargeable to the capital account of the principal user or a related person. There are, however, exceptions to the "related person" rule when such capital expenditures are made by exempt entities. For example, the IRS has ruled that capital expenditures by the local governmental unit do not count against the $10 million limit unless the expenditures are used to construct facilities that are clearly a part of the project financed with IDBs. On the other hand, capital expenditures by a charitable trust or a nonprofit corporation involved in an IDB financing do not count against the limit even if the expenditures are directly for the financed project.

Exempt facilities   In addition to the small-issue exemption, the Revenue and Expenditure Control Act permits the issuance of IDBs, without limits on the size of the issue or the total capital expenditures on the project being financed, if substantially all of the proceeds are used for selected purposes.[3] Although a few of these purposes are considered to be traditional municipal functions when provided by state and local governments, most of them are not generally viewed as appropriate uses of tax-exempt financing.

The Public Securities Association, the primary source of data on the issuance of tax-exempt securities, reports the volume of all municipal bonds on the basis of the purpose for which they are issued (table 1), but does not provide a breakdown between IDBs and other tax-exempt securities issued for each purpose. Thus the precise relative importance of IDBs in the tax-exempt market is impossible to quantify, but it is clearly greater than that inferred from simply adding the industrial-aid and pollution-control categories in table 1, given the following long list of purposes that are eligible for the special exemption.

Sewage or solid-waste-disposal facilities   Privately owned sewage and solid-waste-disposal facilities qualify for a special-purpose exemption if they are used for the collection, storage, treatment, utilization, processing, or final disposal of sewage and solid waste, and if they are available to the general public. In recent years the separation

Item	1978	1979	1980	1981
	Millions of dollars			
All issues[1]	48,352	43,335	48,368	47,515
Refunding and advance refunding	10,767	1,925	1,768	1,201
New capital	37,585	41,410	46,600	46,314
	Percent			
Use of proceeds				
Education	13.0	12.5	10.0	10.0
Social welfare and public services	6.0	2.0	2.0	3.0
Transportation....................	9.0	6.0	5.5	7.0
Hospitals	6.0	8.0	8.0	12.0
Utilities.............................	24.0	20.5	17.0	22.0
Housing	16.0	29.0	33.0	13.0
Recreation.........................	2.0	1.0	1.0	1.0
Industrial aid[2]	2.0	4.0	4.0	7.0
Industrial pollution control.............................	7.0	5.0	5.0	9.0
Other purposes	15.0	12.0	14.5	16.0

Source: Public Securities Association.
1. Par amounts of long-term issues based on date of sale.
2. The percent of new capital used for industrial aid purposes is based on data from the Public Securities Association, which according to a recent Congressional Budget Office study, substantially understate the volume of small-issue industrial development bonds sold during the past four years. The reason for this discrepancy is that many small issues are privately placed with commercial banks or other lenders and are seldom reported beyond the state level.

Table 1. New security issues of state and local governments, 1978-81.

from garbage of combustible material used as fuel has given this material market value in some areas. As such, it did not qualify as solid waste within the meaning of the Revenue and Expenditure Control Act of 1968. For example, boilers that burned combustible waste no longer qualified as solid waste disposal facilities. To clarify this point, the Windfall Profits Tax Act of 1980 added a section to the Internal Revenue Code that expanded the definition of solid-waste-disposal facilities to include qualified steam-generating facilities and qualified alcohol-producing facilities. At least 90 percent of such fuel must be produced at, or adjacent to, the steam- or alcohol-producing facilities.

Electric energy and gas facilities   The principal factor in determining whether tax-exempt financing is available for privately owned electric energy and gas facilities is the size of the service areas. Only "local furnishing" facilities, which are facilities that service an area no larger than two contiguous counties or a city and a contiguous county, qualify for the exemption. Moreover, the Internal Revenue Service has ruled to allow tax-exempt financing for a privately owned electric generating facility that served a distribution system located entirely within two counties but was owned and operated by a wholly owned subsidiary corporation of a utility that furnished electric energy to the general public in many areas of the state.

Airports, docks, and wharves   Privately owned airports, docks, and wharves are eligible for tax-exempt financing if they satisfy the public-use test. Airports satisfy this test if they are available to the general public or are served by a common or charter carrier that is publicly available. This exemption applies to facilities that are directly related and essential to aircraft landing and takeoff, as well as to those related to servicing aircraft and transferring passengers and cargo. Subordinate facilities that also qualify for the exemption include in-flight meal facilities; commercial space in terminals and hotels to be used by passengers, all of which must be located at the airport; and certain improved or unimproved land adjacent to the airport. Facilities at the airport used to customize new aircraft do not qualify.

Docks and wharves satisfy the public-use test if they are available for use by the general public, are served by a common or charter carrier that is publicly available, or are part of a public port. Functionally related and subordinate facilities include cranes, conveyors, and training and storage facilities. The IRS has ruled that offshore oil ports and onshore oil-storage facilities qualify as exempt facilities but that docks located in a public port to be used for construction of vessels do not qualify.

Polution-control facilities   Facilities for air or water pollution control installed by privately owned companies are considered exempt if they remove, alter, dispose, or store pollutants. In this regard, smokestacks do not qualify because they merely disperse pollutants. Moreover, no part of the cost of a new production facility that avoids the creation of pollutants, rather than treating the pollutants after they are created, qualifies for the exemption.

Facilities for the furnishing of water   An exemption is provided in the tax code for privately owned facilities that furnish water to the general public, and that are operated by a governmental unit or charge rates established or approved by a state or political subdivision, an agency or instrumentality of the United States, or a public utility commission or a similar body of any state or political subdivision.

Sports and convention or trade-show facilities   Privately owned sports facilities that are eligible for tax-exempt financing without limits on the size of the issue include baseball and football stadiums, indoor sports arenas, swimming pools, golf courses, ski slopes, and tennis courts. Facilities directly related to exempt sports facilities, including bathhouses, clubhouses, parking lots, and ski lifts (but not an overnight ski lodge), are also exempt.

For convention or trade-show facilities, only the special-purpose buildings and structures such as meeting halls and display areas qualify under this exemption. To meet the public-use test, the facility must be available for rent by the general public, which means it cannot be leased subject to a long-term contract with one user or group of users. Tax exemption does not apply to bonds issued to finance a hotel, even though most of its clientele are expected to be delegates or participants at conventions and trade shows.

Qualified hydroelectric generating facilities   In 1980, the tax code was amended to permit the issuance of IDBs for qualified hydroelectric generating facilities. Such a facility qualifies if the property is owned for tax purposes by a state or political subdivision, and if the facility generates electricity from the flow or fall of water. The exemption does not apply if debt service is guaranteed, either directly or indirectly, by the federal government pursuant to an energy-production or conservation program.

Industrial parks   IDBs are exempt if they are issued to finance the acquisition or development of land used as building sites by industrial, distribution, or wholesale businesses. These are industrial parks and must be administered by an exempt entity or developed under an overall plan subject to special zoning restrictions to qualify for the exemption. For the purposes of this exemption, development of land includes providing water, sewage, and drainage facilities; road, railroad, docking, and similar transportation facilities; and power or communication facilities. It does not include the construction of buildings or other structures.

Mass commuting facilities   Mass commuting facilities eligible for tax-exempt financing include real property and improvements and personal property including buses, train cars, subway cars, and similar vehicles leased to mass transit systems owned by state or local governments.

Residential mortgage programs   Proceeds of tax-exempt bonds also are used to finance residential mortgages. Single-family mortgage bonds are issued under two general types of programs, mortgage-purchase programs and loan-to-lender programs. Under a mortgage-purchase program, the proceeds are used by the issuer to acquire mortgages that are originated and serviced by participating financial institutions. This type of program has been viewed traditionally by bond counsel as *not* being an IDB-financed project because the mortgages purchased are considered assets of the issuer rather than of the participating financial institutions. Under a loan-to-lender program, the bonds are issued on behalf of participating financial institutions, which in turn use the proceeds to finance mortgages that are held as assets of the financial institutions rather than the governmental authority. This type of program has been viewed by bond counsel as an IDB-financed project.

The marked increase in the issuance of tax-exempt bonds during 1979-80 to finance residential mortgages, mortgages that largely benefited middle-income households, raised doubts about the propriety of this use of tax-exempt financing. This concern and the potential loss of tax revenue to the Treasury were the principal factors behind the passage of the Mortgage Subsidy Bond Tax Act of 1980, which prohibits the issuance of any bonds to subsidize single-family mortgages after December 31, 1983, and places substantial restrictions on the issuance of such bonds in the interim:

1. The residence securing the mortgage must be the principal residence of the borrower.
2. A borrower may not have had an ownership interest in a principal residence during the three-year period before execution of the mortgage.
3. The purchase price of the residence financed may not exceed 90 percent of the average purchase price of single-family residences during the most recent 12-month period for which such information is available in the statistical area in which the residence is located.
4. Each state is limited in the aggregate principal amount of bonds that it and its political subdivisions can issue annually.
5. The arbitrage differential permitted between the effective rate of interest on the mortgages financed by the bond proceeds and the yield on the bonds cannot exceed 1 percent for mortgage-purchase programs and 1½ percent for loan-to-lender programs. The less stringent arbitrage restriction on loan-to-lender programs may explain, in part, why many of the mortgage-subsidy programs in 1981 were of this type.

The Mortgage Subsidy Bond Act also amended the tax code governing IDB issuance to allow tax-exempt financing for multifamily housing only if at least 20 percent of the financed units are occupied by low- or moderate-income tenants, as defined by the Department of Housing and Urban Development. This qualification reportedly deterred some tax-exempt issuers from offering multifamily housing bonds during 1981.

The effects of industrial bonds

IDB issuance, despite the legal restrictions imposed on it in 1968, has once again surfaced as an important topic in the current debate on tax reform. The advantages of IDBs explain why the volume of such bonds has become so great, and the disadvantages of IDBs explain why their purposes have been questioned.

Some advantages Industrial development bond financing is one of a variety of incentives a state or local government can offer business firms to locate or to remain within its jurisdiction.[4] In principle, IDBs can be an effective way to target investment on industries and areas so as to contribute substantially to more balanced national economic growth. However, to the extent that local authorities everywhere use IDB financing to compete against each other, any regional benefits to private businesses are eliminated and such financing functions simply as a conduit to the tax-exempt market.

Like that of any other tax-exempt security, the cost of the IDB subsidy is borne by the federal government but the subsidy is used at the discretion of the local authority. Moreover, in the case of revenue bonds no liability is assigned to the issuing authority for the debt service on the bonds, and few if any limits are placed on the total volume issued.[5] Thus, constituents of the issuing jurisdictions are seldom concerned about the volume or purposes of IDB issues.

Private businesses benefit from the issuance of IDBs because such bonds give them access to the capital market at a rate of interest below market rates on taxable debt obligations. For firms that might otherwise be denied access to capital markets, the relative benefit from IDB financing may be the firm's existence. The opportunity cost to society, in the form of misallocated resources, of providing this subsidy may, however, more than offset any benefit.

If the IDB issue acts solely as a means for a firm to borrow at lower costs in the tax-exempt market, the relative benefit to that firm depends on the ratio of tax-exempt to taxable yields and, because interest expenses are tax deductible, on the marginal tax rate of the borrowing firm.[6]

As table 2 shows, an increase in the ratio of tax-exempt to taxable yields results in a decline in the relative benefit to the firm of IDB financing regardless of the firm's marginal tax rate. Moreover, the higher the tax rate of the firm, the lower the relative benefit of tax-exempt financing.

Because of the tax-exempt nature of municipal securities, investors generally are persons and institutions that are subject to high marginal tax rates. Chief among these are individuals and individual trusts, property and casualty insurance companies, and commercial banks. At present, commercial banks are the primary holders of municipal bonds, but, reportedly, they are relying more often on small-issue IDBs to satisfy their demand for tax shelter. One attrac-

Percent of taxable yield					
	Ratio of tax-exempt to taxable yields (percent)				
Marginal tax rate of the firm (percent)	50	60	70	80	90
26...	37	30	22	15	7
48...	26	21	16	10	5

Table 2. Benefit to the firm of IDB financing.

tive feature that small-issue IDBs offer banks is their resemblance to business loans. Thus the commercial loan departments of banks often assume responsibility for evaluating the risks and negotiating the terms of such IDB issues. Moreover, because these transactions are handled within the commercial loan department, they are often reported as loans rather than tax-exempt securities. By classifying IDBs as loans, banks can avoid the question of whether the obligations are of "investment grade," which is required of securities held by banks.

Some disadvantages   Public programs that offer credit to private business under conditions more favorable than those conventionally offered by the market inevitably involve some element of subsidy. In the case of IDBs, the subsidy is from the federal government, but is triggered by a local authority. Opponents of IDB financing contend that local authorities might dispense a federal subsidy either less carefully than would federal officials or less carefully than a subsidy of local money. They also argue against the use of a federal subsidy to foster new private business that may place established businesses at a competitive disadvantage. Furthermore, they assert that the IDB loses any justification for tax exemption if it is issued for corporations that do not need assistance in financing expansion and in areas where commercial credit is readily available.[7]

Tax-exempt financing entails the loss of tax revenues rather than an increase in actual expenditures. This characteristic of IDBs makes them, in the eyes of critics, an inequitable and inefficient way for the federal government to provide financial assistance to state and local governments.

From the viewpoint of tax equity, the exemption permits individuals and institutions in high tax brackets to avoid the full burden of the progressive federal income tax. While the bondholders could be viewed as paying a "tax" to the state and local governments by accepting lower interest rates on tax-exempt bonds, they are in fact net gainers, because they are willing to engage in the transaction only if the "tax" allows them to avoid a higher federal income tax.

With regard to the cost effectiveness of IDBs as a subsidy, the exemption gives less financial assistance in the form of lower interest rates than it costs the federal government in foregone revenue. Opponents of IDBs contend that, to make the tax exemption attractive to investors in lower tax brackets, the issuance of such bonds pushes yields higher on municipal securities relative to taxable securities. While a relatively higher tax-exempt yield is necessary to attract the marginal, low-bracket investor into the municipal market, the higher yield is available to all who invest in newly issued securities, including those in the higher tax brackets. Moreover, the value of tax-exempt financing to state and local governments declines because they must pay higher relative interest rates on all bond issues regardless of the purpose. The net effect is an increase in the overall cost of tax-exempt financing to the federal government in the form of tax revenue foregone and a smaller relative benefit to municipal issuers. In other words, the efficiency of this type of revenue sharing declines as the ratio of tax-exempt to taxable yields rises.

Current problems

Questions about the public purpose and the inefficiency of IDBs sold during the mid-1960s resulted in the enactment of the Revenue and Expenditure Control Act of 1968, which still governs the issuance of such bonds. Once again, these concerns have surfaced in relation to the reportedly growing volume of small-issue IDBs, but have yet to result in additional legislation. Under current federal law anyone may use small-issue IDBs, and only a few states limit the projects benefiting from tax-exempt financing within their jurisdictions. Thus small-issue IDBs finance a wide variety of business ventures, including projects like private golf courses and fast-food outlets as well as small industrial firms.

Another serious problem with the current use of small-issue IDBs is that many of the bond issues are for business firms that do not need financial assistance to undertake their projects. Critics object to this use of tax-exempt financing because it serves simply as a source of cheap credit at the expense of federal tax revenues.

Addressing these concerns, as well as the federal revenue loss arising from IDBs, the administration has proposed legislation that would limit the use of IDBs to small businesses and bar firms that use IDB financing from also taking accelerated depreciation write-offs for the same projects. Moreover, tax exemption would be limited to IDBs approved before their issuance by state or local elected officials. These restrictions would apply to the issuance of both small-issue and exempt-facility IDBs.

---

1. *Small Issue Industrial Revenue Bonds.* Congress of the United States, Budget Office, September 1981.

For a project that also has financing under the Urban Development Action Grant program, the capital expenditure limit is $20 million, but the tax-exempt issue cannot exceed $10 million.

3. Substantially all of the proceeds, defined as 90 percent of an amount equal to the bond proceeds less the issuance cost and a reasonable debt reserve fund, must be used to purchase land or depreciable property.

4. Other incentives frequently offered by state governments in competing for private business include exemption from state taxes, loan guarantees, and below-cost facilities and services.

5. While the size of any one IDB issue is restricted (except for those whose proceeds finance the exempt facilities discussed above), there are no limits on the number of such issues by any one jurisdiction.

6. The benefit of IDB financing, in this case, is assumed to be the spread between taxable and tax-exempt yields, both of which are adjusted for the tax deductibility of interest costs; that is,

$$B = (Rt - Rte)(1 - t),$$

where B is the benefit, Rt is the taxable interest rate, Rte is the tax-exempt rate, and t is the marginal tax rate of the firm. This expression can be transposed into the following form:

$$B = (1 - r)(1 - t)\, Rt,$$

where r is the ratio of tax-exempt to taxable yields. The percentages reported in table 1 represent the coefficient $(1 - r)(1 - t)$ in the above expression.

7. Advisory Commission on Intergovernmental Relations, *Industrial Development Bond Financing* (ACIR, June 1963), pp. 40–46.

Is There—and Should There Be— a Future for Industrial Revenue Bonds?

Sheryl J. Lincoln

Industrial revenue bonds, the tax-exempt bonds that state and local governments issue to provide below-market financing for private firms, face congressional scrutiny and debate after a decade of relative silence on the subject. The flap over the bonds comes in the wake of a Congressional Budget Office report on the use and abuse of small issue IRBs, and amidst warnings from such sources as *The Wall Street Journal* and *Forbes* that the Reagan Administration's tax bill will place severe hardships on state and local governments, both in the municipal bond market and from revenues lost as a result of tax cuts. Several members of Congress are trying to overturn a ruling by IRS in which "multiple issues" or groupings of the small issue bonds sold on or after August 24, 1981, would no longer qualify for the tax-exemptions available if the issues were sold and marketed as separate issues. President Reagan announced that IRBs would face the loss of their tax exemption in the Administration's second round of budget cuts. At the President's November press conference, he announced he would not be submitting any revenue procedures until after January. Presumably, this will include the Administration's position on IRBs.

While local governments and bond counsels awaited the Treasury Department's official position on the bonds, which had been expected in early October, communities rushed to approve IRB financing in unprecedented amounts. Perhaps the most glaring example was in Baltimore, Maryland, where the city council, fearing a federal cut-off in the tax exemption for industrial revenue bonds, approved, in one day, over $700 million in IRBs. Such actions are in part triggered by memories of last year's Mortgage Subsidy Bond Tax Act, which contained retroactive deadlines on qualifying issues.

Reprinted with permission from *Journal of Housing*, November 1981.

Continued support for continued use of the small issues included an amendment tacked onto the continuing appropriations bill for 1982 funds. When President Reagan vetoed that stop-gap funding measure November 23, the amendment that would have eliminated money for enforcing the IRS regulations for corporations with capital expenditures under $25 million for a three-year period also was eliminated. It is expected, however, that a forthcoming Treasury Department appropriations bill will contain such an amendment.

There have been very mixed reviews on the benefits of the financing technique. Congressional testimony provided [in April 1981] to the House Ways and Means oversight subcommittee both praised and panned the use of tax-exempt bonds, which have been cited for their ability to provide employment and revenue in locally distressed areas as well as for their financing of topless nightclubs, K-Marts, and McDonalds restaurants. Representative Charles Rangel (D-New York), chairman of the oversight subcommittee, submitted a bill that contains specific recommendations for changes in IRB legislation, linking the use of IRB financing for commercial projects to economically distressed areas. These recommendations also include a public hearing requirement prior to approval and issuance of each small issue, a requirement that each state file a report with the Treasury Department on each IRB closing, and that IRB proceeds not be used to finance the purchase of farmland nor to relocate existing activities from one state to another. The bill goes on to require a comprehensive study to be conducted by the Treasury, with analysis of data and recommendations presented to the committee by July 1, 1983. There is a sunset provision effective January 1, 1984.

The eventual fate of the tax exemptions is still unknown. Policy options are being offered from Congress, the Administration, CBO, and the President's Commission on Housing. The options most often mentioned include: (a) targeting the bonds' use to distressed areas; (b) limiting the commercial use of the bonds; (c) complete elimination of IRBs; (d) elimination of the exemption with a compensating federal payment to subsidize taxable bond yields; (e) requiring public accountability of the use, either by the pledging of the full faith and credit of the locality or requiring public hearings and referendums; (f) a local cash match; and (g) choosing between the tax exemption or use of the accelerated depreciation provisions in the Economic Recovery Act. The President's Commission will establish a task force to review use of tax-exempt revenue bonds, whether for housing or other purposes.

Tax-exempt bonds have been used as a tool for economic development by state and local governments since 1936, when Mississippi floated an $85,000 issue to bring a clothing manufacturing company into the state in order to diversify its depressed agricultural economy. Although this particular bond had the backing of the state, industrial revenue bonds do not generally involve the "full faith and credit" of the state or local government: the bond is paid from revenues of the project itself, not from government sources. Until the 1960s, the volume of IRBs was low and mostly used by Southern states. When the volume of IRB sales rose to over $1 billion and the percentage of IRBs in the long-term tax-exempt municipal bonds rose to about 9 percent from 1 percent, with the increase primarily due to the rise in issue size, Congress acted to withdraw the tax exemption except for certain activities—such as residential housing for family units, sports facilities, convention facilities, industrial transportation (including docks, wharves, grain handling and storage, port facilities, and airport facilities), sewage and air or water pollution control facilities, facilities for supplying local gas or electricity, and manufacturers' distribution centers.

Small issues refers to the legislated tax-exempt limit on size and volume enacted in 1968 to allow localities to assist small businesses seeking to locate in their communities while preventing large companies from receiving such subsidies since they are thought to be capable of using other means of financing. Original limits on the small issues, found in the Revenue Expenditure and Control Act of 1968, established a $1 million ceiling on the size of the issuance. A short time later, the legislation was amended to a $5 million cap with an additional limitation that in calculating the $5 million, capital expenditures made by the principal user of the IRB-financed facility three years before and after the bond is issued must be included. Large, high-cost projects were thus precluded from using the issues. A 1978 amendment increased the issue and expenditure limit to $10 million, and granted a special exception for expenditure rules when used in conjunction with urban development action grants. When used with UDAGs, the capital expenditures limit was increased to $20 million, with the bond amount still limited to $10 million. The law currently permits small issues to be used for any private business purpose, subject to the above limitation.

While restrictions curbed the use of IRBs to finance major projects of large corporations, it did not reduce the issues for smaller projects. Most states now issue some kind of tax-exempt bonds to provide below-market financing for private industries. Critics have pointed out the self-defeating nature of so many states trying to attract industries by offering the same incentive.[1]

All but four states—California, Hawaii, Idaho, and Washington—were reported to be actively offering IRBs, according to a 1981 report by the Advisory Commission on Intergovernmental Relations, *The States and Distressed Communities (1980 Annual Report)*. Since that report, California enacted legislation permitting local issuance of small issue IRBs when restricted to industrial facilities. Tax-exempt bond financing for commercial use has, however, been available through local redevelopment authorities. The few states that targeted IRBs to their distressed areas usually limit the restriction only to commercial projects.

These types of restrictions still enable wealthy suburban areas to offer the same tax-exempt financing to an industry that might have otherwise considered the below-market financing an attractive enough incentive to locate in a more distressed area. Without any federal guidance on the use of IRBs, states and localities have the option of making restrictions as lax or as tight as they wish. Many have faced pressure from investment bankers, large corporations needing small plants and interested retail businesses to make the lower cost loans available, leaving regulations as flexible as possible. In addition, bonds raised for industrial development compete with those bond issues that finance more traditional public purpose projects such as mass transit and public school facilities, streets and bridges.

However, now faced with deep cuts in federal assistance for local economic development as a result of reductions in CDBG and UDAG, elimination of CSA and the CETA public service employment program, and the crippling of EDA's programs, communities are left with only 49 percent of the dollar amount of funds they had in 1981. Interest rates remain prohibitively high and Wall Street warns that the municipal bond market is being made less attractive because of lowered tax brackets resulting from the Reagan Administration's Economic Recovery Act and the competition from the tax-exempt "all savers" certificates. The market for bonds is already oversupplied, continually driving up interest rates high enough to attract investors. Credit markets are over-burdened by the huge borrowing needs of the federal government.

Faced with such gloomy economic conditions, state and local governments fear the loss of the one financing technique that allows them to attract capital investment that will in turn provide tax revenues and jobs in their communities. Local tax incentives, particularly as a means of attracting businesses, are viewed skeptically because of the low priority rating businesses give to the importance of taxes as criteria for expansion or relocation, and from the reduction in revenues they create for local and state governments. Capital, especially at its below-market rate, is, for business, a much greater incentive than reduction of taxes. Taking this tool away from distressed communities will only lead to their further deterioration.

In response to a NAHRO [National Association of Housing and Redevelopment Officials] survey, overwhelming sentiment was expressed for targeting use of IRBs to some distress criteria. Officials in Wayne County, Michigan, one of the most economically distressed areas in the country, estimate that IRBs will create or retain over 14,500 jobs. Completion of IRB projects will result in more than $3 million accruing new tax revenues every year for Wayne County. The Economic Development Corporation of Wayne County, which issues the bonds, estimates that, over the next 10 years, employment generated by 30 IRB projects in the pipeline will contribute in excess of $250 million in local, state, and federal tax collections, plus increased corporate and business taxes. Nearly 13,500 construction jobs, or three construction jobs for each permanent job, will be created and $127 million in capital expenditures are expected to result from the new construction. In addition to creating jobs and taxes, the agency sees the bonds as an attempt to diversify an economy that has been totally dependent on the automobile industry. Local officials see IRBs as priming an economic pump, not welfare for business.

One of the more stringent local guidelines is that of Erie County, New York. The Erie County Industrial Development Agency targets IRBs toward distressed areas, and has a strict commercial and recreational use policy. Buffalo has a reputation as an economically declining heavy industrial area. Over 30,000 jobs were lost in the period from 1969 to 1978 as factories closed or reduced their work force. Existing heavy industry facilities are inefficient and obsolete, and have made it difficult for Buffalo firms to compete in its markets.

ECIDA adopted a Buffalo area economic adjustment strategy outlining roles for the major economic development agencies in the area. Companies that retained or expanded were targeted for assistance on the basis of assets to the region as well as growth potential. IRBs have been a primary instrument in local efforts to retain firms. Other federal and local incentives were used also. The Buffalo waterfront village project, which revitalized 66 acres of vacant urban renewal land, could not have moved forward without some incentives to developers. Since the city wished to maintain its tax rolls, it did not offer tax abatement incentives; instead, a payment-in-lieu policy is in effect. However, the lowering of the financing costs through an IRB made the project more attractive to the initial developer, who put $10 million into the project. Eventually, $90 million worth of additional investments plus a UDAG were attracted to the once vacant area.

ECIDA has adopted, effective February 27, 1980, a five-part policy statement on commercial project revenue bonds:

1. The agency would not have financed the particular project except to induce its location or expansion based on a demonstrable need for such project. There must be evidence that the project is integrated with locally-adopted targeted redevelopment areas pursuant to federal development legislation;

2. But for the availability of industrial revenue bond financing and benefits for projects in that area, the project would not be economically feasible;

3. The agency has determined that there is a demonstrable need for services provided by the project and that there will be no substantial disruption of existing employment or facilities of a similar nature in such area;

4. The project will provide substantial employment and substantial capital investment; and

5. The agency will require that a payment in lieu of taxes equivalent to 100 percent of the assessed valuation tax levy be contracted to both the county and the municipality.

Through 1980, the agency closed only one commercial revenue bond. Presently, four issues with a total of $13.6 million are pending. Each of these is an essential component of Buffalo's downtown revitalization program. They are in urban renewal areas and are generally accompanied by UDAGs.

In testimony ECIDA presented before the Ways and Means oversight subcommittee, the agency noted that the IRB process promotes close cooperation between the public and private sectors, in turn creating a positive environment for the incubation of company expansion plans. It also serves to underscore the importance and public purpose of a company's contribution to the community. ECIDA, by actively marketing the IRBs to targeted retention and expansion industries, has been able to avoid many of the abuses the media has noted in other IRB programs.

ECIDA restrictions apply to commercial projects and not industrial projects because of the disparity between the economic benefits of commercial projects as compared to the benefits of industrial projects, in particular, as they relate to the number and quality of jobs created.

The CBO report poses a question for Congress to consider: "Under what circumstances do federal subsidies to lower the borrowing costs of private industry serve a public purpose?" CBO suggests two goals that could be served: (1) stimulating investment and employment, and (2) modifying the market's allocation of credit. The report goes on to state that if the goal of federal interest subsidies is to increase investment and employment, a general business tax cut might be equally effective, if not more so. This report came out before the recent Economic Recovery Act, which did cut business taxes. However, the report states, "If the purpose of the bonds is to stimulate development in economically distressed areas, the Congress may want to consider ways to target IRBs toward specific locations or regions and to coordinate use of the bonds not only with Urban Development Action Grants (UDAG), but also with other federal credit programs."

CBO also finds that IRBs have been to some extent effective in increasing investment among smaller firms, although many large corporations also have benefited from IRBs. As the legislation currently exists, large corporations can use IRB financing to build branch facilities, as long as the capital expenditure is within the $10 million issue limitation.

The CBO report touches on the effects of small issue IRBs as they impact on federal, state and local tax revenues. CBO's revenue loss estimates are based on several economic assumptions that have been contested by other economists. The revenue gains from eliminating small issue IRBs, according to CBO, would be less than the budgetary cost because feedback effects (lower tax collections from reduced economic activity) would offset part of the revenue gain. The assumptions and calculations project a $4.4 billion cost to the federal government in 1986, and a net revenue gain if IRBs had been eliminated in July 1981 would be a slow rise to $.7 billion. Many feel that as a job-generating and revenue-raising tool for the local governments, the value of IRBs is underestimated.

Since recent discussions on development incentives have focused on the urban enterprise zone concept, a number of local and state officials have expressed their preference to see the IRBs targeted to distressed areas rather than use the enterprise zones incentives, or tax abatements that keep taxes off the books. In fact, even as a jobs creation program, IRB financing has been estimated, according to recent testimony, to provide jobs at a cost of $250 per job created or retained in Philadelphia.

Certainly, the abuses of IRBs have been the subject of newspaper and television reports (on the *60 Minutes* program), and congressional hearings. However, an alternative to eliminating them in order to curb abuses is to fine tune IRBs to offer a means of attracting productive investments. As the national economy slips into a recession, there is a need for investment in productive activities. Without restrictions to curb abuses, or targeting requirements to make the financing attractive in under-invested areas, critics of the program have a strong case: it is a costly subsidy to big business. And even though the pendulum is swinging to more local and state control over such programs, many states are constitutionally prohibited from using their general obligation bonding powers to make loans of public funds to private corporations. The bills Congress is considering generally include both public accountability and public purpose (jobs and targeting of use or user).

Because these bonds are widely supported by liberals, conservatives, Democrats and Republicans, their complete elmination is not likely to occur. However, in the upcoming congressional scrutiny and debate—and the concomitant political tradings—the value and potential of IRBs deserve serious recognition.

1.   See "Are Business Incentives Doing
      Their Job?" *Journal of Housing,*
      November 1979, pp. 504–512.

Tax Increment Financing

Richard G. Mitchell

At a time when urban areas throughout the country are beset with the necessity to increase taxes because of rising demands and costs for municipal services, Portland, Oregon, in 1975, achieved a 1 percent decrease in the tax rate and estimates an additional reduction of from .75 to 1 percent this year [1977], with reductions of another .5 to .75 of 1 percent anticipated; the decrease is made possible by the spectacular increase in assessed valuation in the city's South Auditorium renewal project.

William G. Seline, executive director of the Housing and Redevelopment Agency of the City of Sacramento, California, reporting on the Old Sacramento project in that city, stated " ... the area had become a slum of the worst kind. The assessed valuation was approximately $500,000, with the prospect of a steady decline. Now the assessed valuation is 8 million dollars, producing a tax increment of $600,000 annually, and the effect is money to do whatever needs to be done in Old Sacramento. In addition, this 30-million-dollar restoration project is expected to draw a minimum of 2.5 million tourists a year with a spending range of 20 million dollars."

The agricultural community of Tulare, California, with a population of less than 20,000, needed funds to finance a combination industrial/commercial/residential area project if it was to achieve improved housing supply and quality for its residents and create additional needed jobs by providing opportunity for a dairy cooperative expansion. Utilizing meager resources, Executive Director James Smutz turned this problem into the successful Alpine project, with tax revenues from the project area, combined with block grant

Reprinted with permission from *Journal of Housing*, May 1977.

funds, paying the costs of land assembly, relocation, site preparation (street and alley reconstruction, curbs, gutters, sidewalks, water system, storm drainage and sanitary sewer expansion), and land write-down that were needed in order to achieve the improved neighborhood.

In each of these cases and in dozens of similar situations throughout the country (as states adopt the needed enabling legislation), local officials turned to the device of tax increment financing to obtain the funds needed to:

1. Strengthen the tax base and spread the cost of tax services;
2. Salvage a declining area and create a new economic climate; and
3. Improve housing and create new job opportunities.

For example, the Portland (Oregon) Development Commission reports that its South Auditorium project sold 5 million dollars worth of tax allocation bonds in October 1966. The tax increment generated by the project activity that these bond sales helped to make possible was sufficient, by 1974, to permit early retirement of the outstanding bonds; this was done on January 1, 1975. The project produced 15.4 million dollars increased assessed valuation by January 1966; this increased to 30 million dollars assessed valuation annually in January 1973; it is estimated that it will reach 95 million dollars annually this year.

The Los Angeles community redevelopment agency has announced an ambitious program to rehabilitate or construct 6000 dwelling units for low- and moderate-income families throughout the city; the costs of this effort are to be paid from tax increments produced by the Bunker Hill urban renewal project.

In Salem, Oregon, increased tax revenues ($900,000) generated in the 19-block Pringle Creek urban renewal project have been used to assist the housing authority in the construction of a conventional high-rise for the elderly when adequate federal funds were not available. By January 1975, this project had an annual increase in assessed valuation to 10.4 million dollars.

Tulare, California conservatively estimates an anticipated $200,000 increment per year for its Alpine Project; in 1975, the redevelopment agency sold 2 million dollars in tax allocation bonds to finance needed public improvements. The increment generated as the result of this public/private cooperation is already nearly double the amount anticipated and increases annually. The bond issue will be paid off in 10 years, far ahead of schedule.

These are only random examples of the way in which increased property tax revenues generated in redevelopment projects have been used to accelerate the process and progress of redevelopment: cases in point where bootstrap financing solved municipal funding needs.

Tax increment: how does it work?

An awareness is developing around the country that this innovative form of financing—tax increment—provides a new source of funds and the local control and flexibility that have long been needed in funding community development programs.

Tax increment financing has been available as a funding technique in California since 1952 but did not start to be the widely used tool it is in the state today until the mid-1960s, when cities began to perceive its usefulness and flexibility in fostering community programs with a maximum of local control of the process. Now more than 100 cities and counties in California rely on it as one of the principal funding devices in community redevelopment.

The process is amazing in its apparent simplicity yet it contains many pitfalls and cautions, if not understood and used wisely:

1. In a deteriorating area, it is typical to experience a decline in assessed valuation as property values fall, with the costs of needed services shifted to taxpayers in other economically healthier areas of the city. With the adoption of a redevelopment plan for the area, the assessed valuation at the last equalized tax roll is calculated. This becomes the "frozen tax base." There are variations in state laws that permit use of tax increment financing but the basic provision is that each of the taxing jurisdictions continues to receive that share of the taxes collected on the assessed valuation that represents the "frozen tax base," just as if the project had never happened and there had been no change—up or down—in the area assessed valuation (see Chart A).

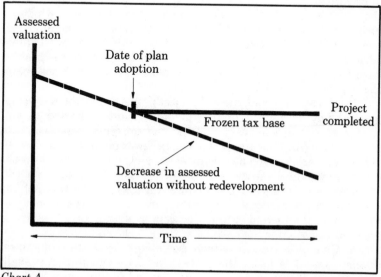

Chart A.

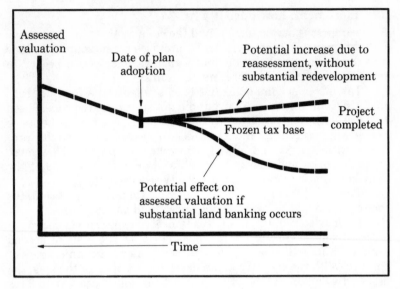

Chart B.

2. Chart B attempts to represent schematically two components of the tax increment process and their impact on taxing agencies:

(a) Preliminary information based on studies now under way in California suggests that adoption of a redevelopment plan and preliminary action to implement it sometimes stimulate a modest surge in private investment in the area even before real redevelopment activity can be noted. This leads to property reassessment, which, in turn, produces increment. While the incidence of this kind of investment interest is limited and is more frequently noted in the areas adjacent to redevelopment projects than in the projects themselves, during the early stages of project implementation it is a possibility that should be noted and;

(b) If there is acquisition of project properties by the redevelopment agency, without accompanying investment in the area to produce increased assessed valuation and, therefore, offset the decline in tax revenues from the area, there will be fewer tax dollars to distribute to the various agencies than they are eligible for, based on the establishment of the frozen tax base. The frozen tax base is the ceiling on assessed valuation that produces the tax revenues to which the agencies are automatically entitled during the time the agency has the right to the increment but that ceiling is attainable only if the assessed valuation is maintained at the base level.

3. Chart C projects the increased assessed valuation due to redevelopment, illustrating the increase in tax increment that is available for project-related activities until project indebtedness has been

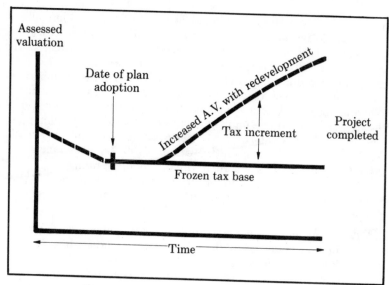

Chart C.

paid off, at which time these increased revenues are distributed to all the taxing jurisdictions in the conventional fashion.

Figuring increment

Much of the confusion that surrounds the subject of tax increment financing stems from a general failure to understand what the "frozen tax base" means and how it is applied. Lack of understanding of this concept generates much of the controversy to which tax increment financing is subject. The basic misconception is the belief that "frozen tax base" means that the tax rate on properties in the project area is held at a constant and that, if tax costs rise, the increased share of the cost project properties would bear is shifted to non-project properties.

"Frozen tax base" does not mean that the tax rate on properties in the project area is set in concrete for the life of the project. Adjustment in the tax rate is applied uniformly to all properties within or outside the project area. What does happen is that the assessed valuation of the project area, as last equalized prior to the adoption of the project plan, is established as the base. For example, if the assessed valuation for the project area at the time of plan adoption was 10 million dollars, that figure is the tax base for the purposes of calculating the floor from which application of the tax increment process starts.

If the assessed valuation remains at 10 million dollars and the tax rate per $100 assessed valuation is $10, this would produce a tax return to be distributed to all taxing jurisdictions of 1 million dollars. There would be no increment available for distribution. If the tax rate were raised to $11 per $100 assessed valuation but the assessed valuation of the area remained at 10 million dollars, this would produce a tax revenue of 1.1 million dollars but since none of this increment is based on new assessed valuation, there would still be no funds available for specific tax increment financing purposes. However, if the assessed valuation after plan adoption increased by 1 million dollars and if the tax rate were $10 per $100, the tax collector would collect 1.1 million dollars. The increase by $100,000 is increment and these funds would be available to the renewal program.

Local agencies may fund improvements from tax increment proceeds in one of two ways but, in either instance, the funds may only be applied against an already existing indebtedness:

1. On a pay-as-you-go basis, utilizing tax increments each year as they are collected by the tax collector and distributed or
2. By issuing tax anticipation notes or tax allocation bonds in advance of the actual collection of the tax revenues so that a larger sum is available for funding up front, thus accelerating the redevelopment process. Tax anticipation notes or tax allocation bonds are tax exempt and require evidence of financial feasibility in order to be marketable. The bond market experience in California has been that each $1 of tax increment will support from $7 to $10 of tax allocation bonds, i.e., $100,000 in increment will support from $700,000 to 1 million dollars (in bonds).

The unique feature of this funding method is that, in effect, the project area generates its own funding. This, in turn, demands that the project management be concerned with the cash flow implications of each of its actions. Considerable sophistication has been developed in this process in recent years as communities have learned to manage their land acquisition and development efforts to maximize the tax increment process. Some of the basic steps in this management process are:

—Minimize land banking (the period of time in which land is in public ownership) so that property remains on the tax rolls until there is a demonstrable need for public action to acquire the site, prepare it for redevelopment, and resell it. This technique of "back-to-back" escrows is based on the principle that the land acquisition action is coupled as closely as possible with the land disposition decision. Land is not stockpiled as was the practice in conventional federally-funded urban renewal projects. Instead, land assembly is a product of market demand. The agency effort is to locate a developer and have an agreement that he will buy the site at an agreed upon price and will commit to develop it in a specified fashion by a certain time.

With these facts understood, the agency can compute its various costs (including land writedown); calculate the approximate amount of tax increment that will be produced by the new development and estimate by what date that increment will become available; and, thus, determine whether the proposed development meets the test of being financially feasible.

—Concentrate on obtaining early development that will result in tax increments that can be plowed back into project development activities, thereby accelerating the rate of progress and shortening the time tax increments need to be utilized for project purposes, thus freeing the proceeds from the new assessed valuation for distribution to all the taxing jurisdictions for their ongoing activities.

Good or bad?

Is this form of community development financing a creative and innovative process or is it a slick way for one arm of local government to pay the costs of neighborhood revitalization at the expense and without the consent of other taxing jurisdictions that, meanwhile, must continue to try to provide the quality and quantity of services their users want and argue they have paid for?

The flood of restrictive language that the California legislature has recently added to its community redevelopment law is an expression of both the confusion surrounding the process and the resentment at the way in which some redevelopment agencies have utilized permissive opportunities in the law to range into areas of community development with, first, hurt and angry taxing jurisdictions protesting what they interpreted as a raid on their treasuries and, second, what the state lawmakers perceived as a need to impose controls and limitations on use of this method of financing.

When some redevelopment agencies, with the approval of their city councils, noted an investor decision to construct an office building or shopping center or institutional facility that would generate large amounts of new tax revenues and capitalized upon this decision as an opportunity to wrap a redevelopment project boundary designation around the site and its surrounding area, thus capturing as tax increment new revenues that would have occurred anyway and were in no way dependent upon the redevelopment process, the hackles of tax collectors could be heard rising for miles around. Proponents argued—often with merit—that such planning was deserved in order to stimulate improvement and enhance the entire area in which the new development was taking place and that their action was timely and proper in exercising the obligation to promote community development when the opportunity was offered. Opponents raged—sometimes with devastating accuracy—that such arguments were specious and that the whole process was nothing more than a rip-off that was cloaked in legally authorized piracy. In either instance, the issue often generated more heat than light.

While the incidence of this exploitation of a loophole in the California law was far less numerous than critics of the process would have us believe, the fact that such acts happened at all provided opponents of the program with the ammunition they needed and they unleashed a steady barrage upon members of the state legislature until it took stringent steps, in 1976, to tighten operations of the community development process.

Use of tax increment funds is sometimes criticized as a form of public subsidy for private benefit. The answer to that has to be that the entire redevelopment process—in which tax increment financing is only an instrument—is premised on the understanding that public action is warranted to correct problems detrimental to the public interest. A hoped-for dividend in this process is renewed interest by private investors in the area. Obviously, if the private investment would have happened anyway, then local public intervention and financial participation was not necessary.

Another—and more realistic—way to look at the use of tax increment and the possible inference that it represents a form of subsidy is to recognize that if government does not utilize the powers and skills it has at its disposal to arrest and reverse the spread of blight and deterioration, it is, by lack of action, adding onto every tax bill a charge for this neglect, which is the product of decreased assessed valuation and demand for increased governmental fire, police, health, and welfare services. The charge will not be identifiable as a separate line item on the tax bill labeled "cost of urban neglect" but it will be there, buried in a whole miscellany of demands on local budgets.

Bringing private investment capital back into the urban core is a role of local government that is every bit as deserving and needed as it is for local government to develop an airport or a harbor or to run a municipal water department. Each of these enterprises is a legitimate extension of the local government's responsibility to see that needed services and facilities are provided by the public sector on a scale and of a quality that would be economically impossible for the individual or company to match. Similarly, providing development space and financing assistance for construction of commercial, residential, or industrial facilities is a partnership role between the public and private sectors. By combining the strengths and resources of these two arms of local enterprise, a community can fashion a development program that benefits all who are touched by it.

Tax increment financing can generally be used to pay for those development and redevelopment activities that benefit the project area: all or part of land acquisition and site preparation costs; relocation expense; and the provision of an extensive range of public improvements. This flexibility in financing equips the local official to provide governmental assistance at the rate and on the scale needed to make the publicly-desired investment proposal realistically possible.

In addition to the obvious increase in assessed valuation in a redevelopment project as it progresses, there are also the less recognized but important increases in sales tax revenues, business licenses, and other evidence of restored economic vitality to an area. These revenues do not become a part of the tax increment pool and, thus, flow directly to the agencies of local government as they are developed.

Local government makes the decision to use tax increment and decides what it shall be used for (within the state statutory enabling legislative authority). This local autonomy makes it possible for local government to move rapidly and precisely to the solution of specific problems, without waiting for external approvals from state or federal officials. This autonomy and flexibility demand a cooperative relationship with other local taxing jurisdictions to calm any apprehensions that money that normally goes to the county or school district or library board or other special taxing bodies is being undermined. It is possible and reasonable for the redevelopment agency to enter into agreements with these other taxing jurisdictions to release portions of the increment realized by project activity so that needed increased services can be provided by them. For example, a residential complex could conceivably increase the demand for educational services. Release of tax increment that is needed by the school district to provide the needed services can be worked out by the appropriate authorities and thus provide funds for the education program required by the project.

Tax increment financing, in its short term effect, can work to the disadvantage of some taxing jurisdictions unless its process is managed with sensitivity and sophistication. Establishing the "frozen tax base" means that each of the taxing bodies receiving revenues from the area will continue to receive those funds *if they are collected*. However, as the local agency acquires sites in the area, they come into public ownership and are removed from the tax roll. Extensive land acquisition and land banking practices can markedly affect the ability of agencies to sustain their ongoing services. It is proper to ask whether the increment generated will offset the losses through the process and to question how long the catch-up process will require. Good public administration dictates that many of these effects be measured against expected benefits in advance and that the undertaking become a shared process among the taxing agencies.

Tulare's executive director, James Smutz, has kept careful records of the consequences of tax increment financing on the various taxing jurisdictions affected and uses the data thus produced to illustrate to the taxing agencies, the city council, and the public at large that the effect is virtually nil. He has itemized that the amount of new property tax income (tax increment) is but a fraction of 1 percent of each of the operating budgets of the nine taxing bodies affected:

County of Tulare	.07 of 1%
Elementary School District	.5 of 1%
High School District	.57 of 1%
Junior College District	.14 of 1%
Hospital District	.12 of 1%
Water Conservation District	.81 of 1%
Mosquito Abatement District	.47 of 1%
Memorial District	.94 of 1%
Cemetery District	.41 of 1%

Use of tax increment should not be considered as the only possible source of local funding for community development and redevelopment. However, it is a valuable financing mechanism where enabling legislation permits its use: it gives local government an additional tool to use in dealing with serious blight problems and it is one more weapon to use in the local government process of finding and using public dollars.

Tax increment financing is no substitute for selection of a feasible project, sound planning, or skilled management.

Conclusion

In the opinion of many, the use of tax increment financing will continue to grow. More and more states will adopt the legislation needed in order to provide local governments with this highly useful tool in financing solutions to urban problems. With this growth in use will come:

1. A greater sophistication in the use of the technique, employing it as a finely tuned, highly flexible instrument for community development and

2. A greater awareness that financing community development should not depend exclusively upon any one method of financing or source of funds.

The combination of these two points will produce a more careful search for and use of the whole range of funding resources that are available for community development activities rather than subjecting any one or two methods—tax increment financing included—to the burden of paying the heavy costs involved and thereby earning, undeservedly, the criticism that such narrow targeting of financing invites.

A Comparison of State Tax Increment Financing Laws

Jack R. Huddleston

Tax increment financing (TIF) has been used by state governments for nearly three decades as a way to finance the redevelopment of blighted areas within cities. Started as tax allocation financing in California, use of tax increment financing laws spread slowly during the 1950s and 1960s, and exploded in the 1970s.[1] Initially used to generate local matching funds for federally funded development projects, TIF has increasingly been adopted by states as the primary financing mechanism for local development efforts.[2]

Unlike development programs that lean heavily on federal or state grants, TIF relies on local property tax revenues and is administered and monitored almost entirely by local government officials. Typically under TIF, cities spend for developments such as land clearance and street improvement within specially created "districts." These expenditures by the city are gradually reimbursed through the payment of "tax increments" from the various local governments having taxing authority over the property located within the TIF district. The increased tax revenues come from increases in property values which result from the expenditures on development. Thus, taxing authorities create development capital by deferring potential revenues. For example, if property values within a TIF district increase by $1 million following a development project by a city, the affected county government that has a property tax rate of 5 mills generates a $5,000 tax increment payment to the city. If the local school district has a property tax rate of 20 mills, the $1 million increase in TIF district property values produces a $20,000 tax increment payment from the school district to the city.[3] This process is continued each year until the original development expenditure by the city is totally recovered. Then the district is dissolved, and the

Reprinted with permission from *State Government*, vol. 55, no. 1.

entire tax base in the district is returned to full use by all local units of government.

In theory, tax increment financing works because several local governments share the same tax base. City, county, school district and other local taxing jurisdictions, for example, all raise revenues from properties located within a city. Without TIF, cities often bear the cost of development alone, while all local taxing jurisdictions share the benefit of an increased local tax base. Tax increment financing provides a way to share the cost of local development among the various taxing jurisdictions which ultimately benefit from an improvement in their collective local tax base.

States currently using TIF and states considering the possible adoption of TIF face several common major issues. The key questions are usually: which projects should be funded, where, and at what scale? The issues arise because tax revenues from several local governments are used to finance projects within particular cities and most state TIF laws give wide discretion to local governments. Equally important are questions concerning which governments should pay tax increments, how much they should pay, and for how long. Protection for local taxpayers, information dissemination, legal considerations and implications for local government planning are also often important.

Each state that has adopted tax increment financing legislation presents a case study in how these common issues can be addressed. This paper compares 14 states, which enacted TIF legislation before 1980.[4] The states were chosen primarily on the basis of availability of public information concerning their TIF laws. For convenience, the comparison is structured into four major categories: nature of enabling legislation; receipt and distribution of tax increments; planning and implementation process; and major TIF project requirements and limitations. The accompanying table [pages 132 and 133] summarizes this comparison for the 14 states.

Nature of enabling legislation

The majority of states included in this study had existing urban renewal laws prior to their use of tax increment financing. For these states, amendments to these laws were the primary vehicle by which tax increment financing was institutionalized. For two of these states, California and Oregon, constitutional amendments were required before adoption of TIF legislation. Free-standing tax increment financing legislation was enacted in states without existing urban renewal laws.

Receipt and distribution of tax increments

The primary local government responsible for implementing TIF projects in all states is the municipality. However, in eight states redevelopment, housing or urban renewal agencies are given authority to use TIF, and in four of these states, the authority to use TIF also rests with county government.

As a general rule, state TIF laws provide for full tax increment payments by local taxing jurisdictions over the life of TIF districts. As described earlier, full tax increments are generated by applying the property tax rate for each unit of government to the growth in property values which occurs within the TIF district. In four of the states surveyed, however, provisions are made to return partial tax increments to affected local taxing jurisdictions. This is done by reimbursing only each year's outstanding indebtedness by tax increments and returning the remainder to each overlying taxing jurisdiction in proportion to their normal share of the total tax levy. Counties, school districts, and other affected taxing jurisdictions (if any) in these states, thus, make only partial tax increment payments during some years. The State of Maine goes further—once a partial increment has been returned, the full tax increment for a TIF project cannot subsequently be collected.[5]

All states allow tax increments to be generated only when district values exceed their level at the time of district creation (or subsequent revaluation). In general, no provision is made for periods in which district property values drop below their original level, which might happen during the land clearance phase of a TIF project, for example. North Dakota, the only exception to this rule, stipulates that all "tax losses" of local taxing jurisdictions which are due to a decrease in property values below original levels be recorded each year. Then, when the district's value begins to increase above the original base, tax increments are first used to repay losses of all affected taxing jurisdictions.

Tax increments are normally generated by all jurisdictions having taxing authority over the property within a TIF district. In five states school districts are exempted from the tax increment process. This can be done by not including the school tax rate in determining each year's tax increment calculation (as in Florida), by returning calculated tax increments directly to school districts (as in South Dakota), or by compensating school districts indirectly through state school aid formulas (as in Wisconsin). The first two approaches have a significant impact on the absolute size of each year's tax increment since school taxes tend to dominate total property tax rates for most areas. The latter approach leaves the size of the tax increment unaffected while introducing an additional contributor, the state, to the TIF process. On the other hand, three states specifically exempt state property tax revenues from tax increments to local governments.

TIF planning and implementation

All states require some determination of blight before a redevelopment district can be created. This is largely done to satisfy constitu-

	Calif.	Fla.	Ill.	Kan.	Me.	Minn.	Mont.	Nev.	N.D.	Ore.	S.D.	Tex.	Utah	Wis.
Nature of enabling legislation														
Constitutional amendment required	1951									1960				
Amendment to urban renewal law	1952	1977				1969			1973	1961		1977	1965	
Original TIF law			1976	1976	1977	1974	1974	1975			1978			1975
Receipt and distribution of tax increments														
Authorized agency:														
Municipality	X	X	X	X	X	X	X	X	X	X	X	X	X	X
Redevelopment, housing or urban renewal agency	X					X		X	X	X			X	
County	X	X						X					X	
Accumulation of tax increments:														
Partial tax increments allowed to be returned to local jurisdictions			X		X	X	X							
"Losses" reimbursed									X					
Overlying taxing jurisdictions														
Exclusion of school districts	X	X	X								X		X	X
Exclusion of state government				X							X			X

Table 1.   Comparison of state tax increment financing laws.

TIF process																
Blight finding required	X	X	X		X		X	X	X	X	X	X	X	X	X	X
Plan requirements:																
Conformance with existing plans	X	X	X	X	X	X	X	X	X	X	X	X	X	X	X	X
Special features	X	X	X	X	X			X			X		X			X
Hearings/resolutions required:																
At plan adoption	X	X	X	X	X	X	X	X	X	X	X	X	X	X	X	X
At district creation		X				X	X				X				X	X
Additional participatory mechanisms	X	X	X	X		X							X	X	X	
Tax increment/allocation bonds allowed	X	X	X	X	X	X	X	X	X	X	X	X	X	X	X	X
Major requirements and limitations																
Areal limits	X		X	X	X	X	X	X				X				X
Property value limits							X					X				X
Time limits		X		X				X				X	X			X
(Re)development projects allowed:																
Residential	X	X	X	X	X	X	X	X	X	X	X	X	X	X	X	X
Industrial	X	X	X		X	X	X	X	X	X	X	X	X	X	X	X
Commercial	X	X	X	X	X	X	X	X	X	X	X	X	X	X	X	X

Table 1, continued.

tional requirements that a "public purpose" be served by the use of TIF.[6] Wisconsin law further specifies that at least 25 percent of the project area be designated as blighted, in need of conservation or rehabilitation, or suitable for industrial development. South Dakota statutes require a similar quantified finding, although only the blighted classification applies.

After the blight criterion has been met, all states require preparation of a district plan describing the proposed projects to be developed. A few states have mandated that special elements be included in the TIF redevelopment plan to guard against local abuses in devising redevelopment projects. Both Minnesota and South Dakota require a fiscal impact analysis for all contributing taxing jurisdictions, while California law necessitates the filing of a neighborhood impact statement for a TIF district and adjacent areas. Illinois and Kansas require all TIF plans to state the specific dates of project initiation, completion and the retirement of all related debt.

In addition, all states require a public hearing to discuss the plan or future plan amendments. Only four states require an additional hearing and local legislative approval for the designation of a TIF district's boundaries. These hearings, in most cases, are the only formal mechanisms provided for participation by local residents and affected overlying jurisdictions in the tax increment financing process. Many states require localities to keep all parties informed of the status of TIF projects through annual reports to affected governments and through published statements in the press.

Four states have included legislative provisions to increase control and provide recourse for parties affected by TIF projects. Maine law requires an advisory board for each development district, and more than half of the members of this board must be property owners and residents of the district or adjacent areas. Municipal residents are also given additional power through a referendum provision for approval of district creation.

Utah requires a referendum when three-fourths of the project area's property owners object to the redevelopment plan, and a majority of local residents must sanction the plan before adoption by the local legislative body. Texas also has a referendum provision by which voters must approve the use of the tax increment financing mechanism before a municipal TIF project plan is begun.[7] In Kansas municipalities cannot proceed with a proposed tax increment financing project if either affected counties or school districts present objecting resolutions (stating expected adverse effects) within 30 days following the TIF project public hearing.

Lastly, state TIF processes vary only slightly in regard to project financing. All states allow general obligation bonds or the general fund of the locality to finance redevelopment projects, pledging the future tax increments to their repayment. Most states surveyed have also legislated the use of tax increment (or allocation) bonds or notes, which are generally excluded from statutory local debt limits and referendum requirements. Most states also allow lease-revenue bonds, industrial revenue bonds, special assessments and municipal improvement bonds to be used as project financing mechanisms.[8]

Project requirements and limitations

The final area of difference in state TIF laws is the controls placed on the TIF process. These controls include project completion time limits, areal or property value constraints on the tax increment financing district and the types of redevelopment projects allowed.

Wisconsin has more constraining requirements than most states surveyed. For example, Wisconsin statutes limit project expenditures to no more than five years after a district's creation and limit the payment of tax increments to no more than 15 years after the last project expenditure. Wisconsin TIF districts must meet the 25 percent blight/conservation/industrial development criterion and must also be contiguous, containing only whole parcels. In addition, the total taxable property value within all municipal TIF districts cannot exceed 5 percent of the municipality's total value at the time a new district is created.

South Dakota, with a law patterned after Wisconsin's, has equally rigorous controls on municipality flexibility. It has similar time limits and a 25 percent blighted area criterion for its TIF districts. In addition, no local district can exceed 5 to 12 percent of the total taxable property value, depending upon community size. (Smaller places can involve a larger proportion of their tax base in tax increment districts.) Tax increment districts in South Dakota must also be contiguous.

Three other states have time limits controlling project completion. Illinois law sets a 23-year limit on the accumulation of tax increments from the date of the ordinance adopting the project area. Kansas requires that development start within one year from the acquisition of property by the municipality and must be completed within five years from the date of the plan adoption. It also stipulates that tax increments can only accrue up to 20 years. Montana law stipulates, in addition, that locally adopted tax increment provisions to redevelopment plans expire within 10 years from plan adoption or when all bonds are repaid, whichever occurs last.

Besides Wisconsin and South Dakota, district areal constraints are included in five additional state TIF statutes. Illinois and Nevada require a minimum district size of one-and-one-half acres and one block, respectively. Illinois further stipulates that each tax increment financing district must contain only contiguous parcels. Although California allows noncontiguous sections to be included within a single district, recent amendments require that each section must be proven individually blighted or necessary for redevelopment.

Other areal and property value controls exist in Minnesota and

Maine TIF laws. Both states' Development District Laws require that a TIF project area be at least 60 percent platted and developed at the time of district creation. This prevents abuses of the major underlying purpose of tax increment financing, which is to eliminate blight. Minnesota law further limits the acreage or property value of each development district and all such districts within a municipality. A Minnesota city can designate a single district with up to six acres, or multiple districts with either 1 percent individually or 3 percent cumulatively of total municipal acreage, or 5 percent individually and 10 percent cumulatively of total municipal property *value*.

Similarly, Minnesota's Port Authority Act, which creates tax increment financed Industrial Development Districts, limits the acreage of each district to 3 percent of the municipality's industrially zoned property and to a 10 percent maximum for all such districts. The State's Industrial Development Act limits project size indirectly by applying a spending limit of $5 million to each participating industrial user or development.

The final common constraint found in the states included in this survey is the type of development or redevelopment activities allowed in each state statute. Eleven states have made provisions to allow residential, commercial or industrial property developments. Kansas and Maine specifically restrict or imply that tax increment financing be used for commercial areas only. South Dakota prohibits the use of tax increment financing for residential development, although it allows the use of TIF for commercial or industrial projects.

Summary
The use of tax increment financing can reasonably be expected to spread to additional states as responsibility for development and redevelopment is increasingly shifted to state and local governments. States considering the adoption of TIF legislation will find that they face issues which are common to most other states and, at the same time, that tax increment financing has proven flexible enough to meet each state's particular goals and circumstances. The comparison of state TIF laws presented here reflects both the common themes and the flexibility of the tax increment financing concept.

1. Two states enacted TIF legislation between 1951 and 1960, four states between 1961 and 1970, 11 states between 1971 and 1975, and 20 states between 1976 and 1980. For a list of states using tax increment financing see *Alternative Sources of Municipal Development Capital: Tax Increment and Industrial Revenue Bond Financing for Cities, Volume I* (Washington, D.C.: National League of Cities, 1979), pp. 7-11.

2. Jonathan Davidson, "Tax Increment Financing as a Tool for Community Development," *University of Detroit Journal of Urban Law 56* (Winter 1979): 406.

3. Tax increment payments are based on the *growth* in TIF district property values. Affected taxing jurisdictions, such as county and school districts, continue to derive their normal tax revenues on the property value as it existed prior to a TIF dis-

trict's creation. Cities also pay tax increments to themselves, applying their general property tax rate to the growth in TIF district property values. See Davidson, "Tax Increment Financing," pp. 408-31 for a description of the typical process involved.

4. The states compared in this study, in order of their appearance in the accompanying table, are: California, Florida, Illinois, Kansas, Maine, Minnesota, Montana, Nevada, North Dakota, Oregon, South Dakota, Texas, Utah and Wisconsin.

5. Once a partial tax increment has been accepted by the municipality, it can only decrease (or remain constant) in percentage of the total tax increment available.

6. Davidson, "Tax Increment Financing," p. 414.

7. This provision is to become void once a constitutional amendment has been passed specifically allowing tax increment financing.

8. Some states specifically prohibit their use in financing tax increment projects. Industrial revenue bonds, for example, cannot be used for TIF projects in Kansas.

Rialto:
A Better Way to
Finance Growth

Walter Pudinski

The summer and fall of 1978 proved to be a time of decision for the City of Rialto [California] on those matters related to growth. Surrounded on all sides by communities and areas that were undergoing heated, hard-fought growth arguments, the City of Rialto analyzed the pros and cons of the prevailing growth issues and after a series of meetings with those portions of the community having strong opinions on either side, the city sought to lay out a growth management plan and a method of financing the attendant infrastructure of the community.

Several important issues, particularly related to who pays for growth, came before the city council and the council essentially adopted a philosophy that new development would pay infrastructure costs and that older, developed portions of the community that have already paid for those facilities presently in place and in operation would be excluded from paying for these new facilities.

Following a review by the city staff, the city council determined that the most urgent and pressing problem in their growth management plan was that of providing adequate sewage capacity for new homes and businesses that would locate in Rialto over the next 10-year period. The city sought the counsel of the active local builders, represented through the Building Industry Association, Baldy View Chapter (BIA). Ultimately a project consultant who developed and supervised the entire project, Don Owen and Associates, Inc., of Orange County, was hired by the city.

Surrounding communities historically had largely relied upon grants through Public Law 92500 for the purpose of financing sewage treatment plant expansion and in each and every case, delays, addi-

Reprinted with permission from the March 1981 issue of *Western City* magazine, the official publication of the League of California Cities.

tional constraints upon the facilities to be constructed and constraints upon future revenue and repayment programs dictated by the state and federal governments had led to costly time delays and actually led to the imposition of moratoriums in the surrounding communities of Rancho Cucamonga, San Bernardino, Redlands, Riverside and Ontario.

Sewer hookup fee

After considerable discussion, the city, in cooperation with the local BIA, undertook a study seeking a better way to finance sewage treatment capacity for growth areas. This effort culminated in a pre-contract report being completed and presented to the city council in March 1979. At the outset of the report activity, the city, recognizing the need for local funds to accomplish the proposed sewage plant expansion fee, established a $700 sewage plant expansion hookup fee which was charged against each and every development of new residences within the city. Surprisingly enough, the local chapter of the BIA and individual builders within the Rialto area welcomed the application of this hookup fee and supported the city's action. This is largely due to the fact that the city showed the "good faith" action by setting aside the funds from this fee to be used for the single and specific purpose of expansion of the sewage facility. This dedication of funds collected from each building permit, created a basis of trust in the city by the city undertaking an ongoing program seeking solutions to their mutual problems.

The report presented to the city in March 1979 called for a financing plan to be developed by the city whereby proposed construction would be entirely paid for by undeveloped property within the city requiring the facilities. In addition, a small portion of the proposed facilities outlined in that report related to improvement of the existing sewage facilities and the report suggested that the city should make a contribution to the construction costs for those improvements which were benefiting existing residences. This basic allocation was established on the theory that new development would pay 100% of the cost (exclusive of the city contribution).

The report outlined the desirability of actually issuing some sort of municipal bond under the name of the city; however, payment of debt service coming from the identifiable revenue sources of either the sale of reclaimed water and/or future hookup fees to be levied on each of the new developments using the facility posed a real dilemma. The problem, of course, was that the city did not have firm contracts, nor could it assure prospective bond underwriters that it would have the flow of money coming each and every year from either the sale of reclaimed water and/or future hookup fees from new development within the city. In essence, the revenue sources recommended for repayment of the proposed expansion were of the type that could not be used as security for municipal bonds. The report went on to suggest an alternative that essentially was the creation of an assessment district under the California statutes commonly referred to as the "1913 Act" and an assessment levy against the undeveloped property so that, in the event that the revenues from hookup fees did not materialize in any given year, the city could assure the underwriter bond repayment through collection of assessments pursuant to the "1915 Act." The municipal bonds issued under this proposed set of conditions (1913/15 Act), would then become a "property secured revenue bond issue."

A detailed investigation of California law did not disclose a specific authorization for this type of issue; however, the review of the "1913/15 Act" disclosed that the city had the opportunity, under the terms of these Acts, to take all necessary actions in order to make the financing program work.

Upon review of the report, the city council authorized a program to undertake the design and construction of the facility, funded by the "property secured revenue bond issue."

For about a year the project proceeded through planning and design phases, satisfying the California Environmental Quality Act through the presentation of an EIR, preparing project plans and specifications, preparing an engineers report, refining the method of assessment and the allocation of costs to each parcel in the assessment district, etc. In March 28, 1980, almost a year to the date of receipt of the original report from the consultants, the City of Rialto City Council confirmed the assessment, ordered the work to commence and sold the bonds to accomplish payment of the work.

Property secured revenue bond issue

A basic understanding of how the "property secured revenue bond issue" functions can best be illustrated by the three pro formas included in the City of Rialto's Official Statement, included herein as Tables 1, 2, and 3. Table 1 shows the total amount of the bond issue (outstanding bonds) at $6,740,000. One should note that because of the imposition of the hookup fee in the fall of 1978, the city had approximately $1.2 million in its sewage plant expansion fund as of the date of the bond issue. The city had a backlog of requests for hookups for 2,325 units at the time, and the Growth Management Plan referred to earlier permits 1,200 hookups per year. If the maximum number of hookups allowed under the Growth Management Plan occurs the hookup fees will have paid for the capacity constructed by the middle of 1988. If at that time the city wants to continue its growth management plan of 1,200 units per year, they can undertake a subsequent expansion of the sewage treatment plant with a similar type of financing program. It should be noted that the financing program was designed to accrue reserve funds at the end of the payoff

Date	Outstanding bonds (000)	Interest (8% est.) (000)	Retirement of principal (000)	Debt service (000)	Sewer expansion fees $ per ESU	Estimated number of hookups (ESU)	Estimated annual fee revenue (000)	Estimated interest on funds (8%) (000)	Est. total reserve funds (000)
5/2/80	$6,740								$1,210[2]
7/2/81	6,060	$629	$ 680	$1,309	756	2,325[1]	1,758	$113	1,772
7/2/82	5,385	485	675	1,106	868	1,200	974	142	1,728
7/2/83	4,710	431	675	1,106	868	1,200	1,042	138	1,802
7/2/84	4,035	377	675	1,052	924	1,200	1,109	144	2,003
7/2/85	3,360	323	675	998	980	1,200	1,176	160[3]	2,341
7/2/86	2,685	269	675	944	1,036	1,200	1,243	160	2,800
7/2/87	2,010	215	675	890	1,092	1,200	1,310	160	3,380
7/2/88	-0-	161	2,077[4]	2,238	1,148	210	241	160	1,543

Source: Don Owen & Associates, Inc., January 1980.

Note: All figures rounded.

Note: Growth Management Policy only includes residential connections—actual annual hookups could exceed 1200.

1. Estimated hookups on equivalent service units (ESU) include 200 authorized in 1979, 1125 authorized in 1980, 600 for special projects and 400 commercial and industrial ESU.

2. Net of Capital Construction Reserve Fund ($1,060,257.00) plus Special Reserve Fund ($15,000.00).

3. 8% of $2,000,000.

4. Includes $1,340,000 par value bonds called prior to their maturity plus 5% call premium plus $670,000 scheduled principal retirement.

Table 1.   City of Rialto wastewater treatment plant expansion debt service/revenue projections maximum connections permitted under growth management policy, current growth trend at $756 fee (+ $56 per year).

period, adequate to provide the city with the necessary money to undertake a new bond issue.

Table 2 depicts the impact of reducing the growth projections to approximately 823 units per year. Under these conditions the financing plan would be completed in the full 10 year period as originally planned. Table 3 illustrates the application of the collection of annual assessments, as included in the issue. In Table 3 it should be noted that moratorium conditions for reasons other than sewage capacity has been assumed. In this case Table 3 shows that the city intends to reduce its reserve fund until such time that the reserve fund is no longer adequate to make annual principal and interest payment on the bonds. If the moratorium were to continue, the city would collect assessments from undeveloped properties still remaining within the assessment district in amounts necessary to make annual debt service payments. As Table 3 shows, upon termination of the moratorium the burden of repayment is once again shifted back to the sewage plant expansion hookup fees. In cases as illustrated in Table 3, the city has elected to provide the vested right to service to those properties that paid under the "1913/15 Act" proceedings. In other words, the payment under the security provisions of the bond issue gives those property owners, having paid their assessment, the right to use that portion of the sewage treatment facility which they have paid for, or, in the event that, in the latter years of the project, the city needs additional capacity and a substantial amount of capacity has been vested under this provision, the city can reimburse those property owners for payments made in the event that they do not wish to use their capacity within the immediate future. It should be noted that the only portion of the debt service repaid by the assessment district's security is that portion necessary to make that annual year's payment and those payments are only applied to the undeveloped property within the assessment district.

The consultant charged with spreading the assessments under the 1913/15 Acts began by exempting all properties of under four acres and included only those properties in excess of four acres to be included within the assessment district. Next, a two-acre exemption was given to each parcel. As each of the undeveloped properties is developed, and a final map is placed upon the property, segregating it into a number of smaller parcels, the lien resulting from the assessment is appropriately subdivided and runs with the new parcels.

In looking at the three charts, it should be noted that the sewage expansion fees start off at $756 per year for each hookup and are escalated by $56 each year through the ten year period of the bond issue. If the property owner chooses to make a cash payment during the cash collection period at the outset of the bond issue, he acquires a certain number of hookup rights. If at a later date he uses those rights, or sells them, the rights automatically escalate by the $56 for

Date	Outstanding bonds (000)	Interest (8% est.) (000)	Retirement of principal (000)	Debt service (000)	Sewer expansion fees $ per ESU	Estimated number of hookups (ESU)	Estimated annual fee revenue (000)	Estimated interest on funds (8%) (000)	Est. total reserve funds (000)
5/2/80	$6,740								$1,210[2]
7/2/81	6,060	$629	$680	$1,309	756	2,325[1]	1,758	$113	1,772
7/2/82	5,385	485	675	1,160	812	823	668	142	1,422
7/2/83	4,710	431	675	1,106	868	823	714	114	1,144
7/2/84	4,035	377	675	1,052	924	823	760	92	944
7/2/85	3,360	323	675	998	980	823	807	76	829
7/2/86	2,685	269	675	944	1,036	823	853	66	804
7/2/87	2,010	215	675	890	1,092	823	899	64	877
7/2/88	1,340	161	670	831	1,148	823	945	70	1,061
7/2/89	670	107	670	777	1,204	823	991	85	1,360
7/2/90	-0-	54	670	724	1,260	823	1,037	109	1,782

Source: Don Owen & Associates, Inc., January 1980.
Note: All figures rounded.
Note: First year hookups (2325) utilize existing capacity.
1. Estimated hookups on equivalent service units (ESU) include 200 authorized in 1979, 1125 authorized in 1980, 600 for special projects and 400 commercial and industrial ESU.
2. Net of Capital Construction Reserve Fund ($1,060,257.00) plus Special Reserve Fund ($150,000.00).

Table 2. *City of Rialto wastewater treatment plant expansion debt service/revenue projections equal annual absorption of expanded capacity, 10 year development rate at $756 fee (+ $56 per year).*

Date	Outstanding bonds (000)	Interest (8% est.) (000)	Retirement of principal (000)	Debt service (000)	Sewer expansion fees $ per ESU	Estimated number of hookups (ESU)	Estimated annual fee revenue (000)	Estimated interest on funds (8%) (000)	Estimated total reserve funds (000)	Capacity in acres	$ of Assessment per acre	Assessment per ESU	$ of Hookup fee credit
5/2/80	$6,740								$1,210[2]	2,470			
7/2/81	6,060	$629	$680	$1,309	756	2,325[1]	1,758	$113	1,772	2,470			
7/2/82	5,385	485	675	1,160	812	1,200	974	142	1,728	2,037			
7/2/83	4,710	431	675	1,106	868	-0-	-0-	138	760	2,037			
7/2/84	4,035	377	675	1,052	924	-0-	-0-	61	(231)	2,037	$113	$38	$ 38
7/2/85	3,360	323	675	998	942	600	565	-0-	(431)	1,837	236	79	117
7/2/86	2,685	269	675	944	919	1,200	1,103	-0-	159	1,437			
7/2/87	2,010	215	675	890	975	1,200	1,170	13	452	1,037			
7/2/88	1,340	161	670	831	1,031	1,200	1,237	36	894	637			
7/2/89	670	107	670	777	1,087	1,200	1,304	72	1,493	237			
7/2/90	-0-	54	670	724	1,143	710	812	119	1,700	-0-			

Source: Don Owen & Associates, Inc., January 1980.

Note: All figures rounded.

1. Estimated hookups or equivalent service units (ESU) include 200 authorized in 1979, 1125 authorized in 1980, 600 for special projects and 400 commercial and industrial ESU.

2. Net of Capital Construction Reserve Fund ($1,060,257.00) plus Special Reserve Fund ($150,000.00).

Table 3.   City of Rialto wastewater treatment plant expansion debt service/revenue projections moratorium condition.

each year that they were held by the property owners. In this way the property owner gets a reasonable return for his investment and has the vested right to service.

Bond performance

The Rialto Assessment District Improvement Bonds went on the market and were sold at the height of high interest rates. Under competitive bids they were purchased by Stone & Youngberg with an 8% coupon value, discounted by 13.50%. It should also be remembered that at the time they went on the market, short-term federal securities were available for the city for short-term investments of the bond proceeds. The interest rates secured on the short-term investments during the construction period are projected to recover over the construction period the full amount of the 13½%. Since this was the first of a kind issue ("property secured revenue bond issue"), it is interesting to note where these bonds rest on today's open market. During the month of September [1980], the Rialto Assessment District Improvement Bonds were available from various security dealers and were currently selling with the 8.00% coupon at a 0.97% discount, yielding an effective interest rate of 8.25%. This resale value and effective yield place the bond in the same general category as the workhorse of historical California municipal financing, the general obligation bond. The issue does well on the resale market because of the double-barreled nature of its repayment capabilities. The bond has essentially the potential of being entirely repaid from the reasonably projected revenue and in the absence of those revenues, the bond can be completely repaid from the collection of assessments pursuant to the 1913/15 Acts. In addition, it should be noted that the backup fund of plant expansion fees plus a $150,000 special reserve fund give additional security to the issue.

The City of Rialto now sits in the center of a large sewage-deficient area with moratoriums geographically surrounding the city on three sides. The city's growth management plan is being implemented, its sewage treatment plant is under construction with its own funds (without financial assistance from the state or federal government), and the new capacity will be available in the spring of next year. In addition, the city's plant expansion fee collected by the City of Rialto is equal to or less than 70% of that of its surrounding neighbors who have constructed sewage capacity under grant programs.

In closing we wonder if the city has found a better way or if they have merely found a Rialto way; we don't know; why don't you be the judge!

PART 5

Increasing the Marketability of Municipal Bonds

Can the Municipal Bond Market Be Broadened to Reach the Average Citizen?

L. Mason Neely

It is my impression that literally millions of individuals have been excluded from the municipal bond market. The people who have been excluded from the municipal bond market are those who have earnings between $12,000 and $30,000 annually. According to the latest Statistics of Income (1976) issued by the Census Bureau, there are 29.9 million Americans who filed income tax returns in year 1976 that had adjusted gross earnings in the bracket of $12,000 to $30,000. These individuals represented 35.5% of all of the income tax returns which were filed in 1976 (84,536,143 returns) and those same individuals paid 48% of the federal income tax which was paid during the year 1976. It is clear to me that these individuals are paying a major portion of the tax burden and at the same time, they have effectively been excluded from the municipal tax exempt bond market. Why have they been excluded? How have they been excluded? What can be done to broaden the bond market so that these individuals can feel comfortable as part of the investing public who will purchase municipal tax exempt issues?

Over the course of the last one hundred years, there have not been significant changes which have occurred in the municipal bond market. The method of selling bonds, the method of distributing and printing bonds, and the method of processing those bonds back through the banks to the issuing agent has experienced little change during a time when America has experienced rapid technological change. The total dollar value of municipal bonds has grown in relation to the total growth of the economy. One can anticipate that during any calendar year, approximately $60 billion worth of municipal issues will be offered for sale. The institutional market is healthy and able to absorb the issues which are being offered throughout the country. This being the case then why would one seek to expand the

Reprinted with permission from *New Jersey Municipalities*, November 1978.

bond market? If the institutional bond market is healthy and if the State, County, and Municipal governments have the ability to go into the marketplace and sell their bonds, then why would anyone consider an expansion of the bond market? Is there a need to be concerned? Are there projected problems with the institutional bond market? All of these thoughts must flash into your mind as you begin to consider the subject of an expansion of the bond market.

Meet Mr. Pennywise

Through the use of a hypothetical example, I hope to demonstrate how individuals have been excluded from the municipal bond market. At the same time, I hope to provide some insight into an effective way that will broaden the bond market for the same individuals. Let me introduce you to Mr. Pennywise. Mr. Pennywise is an average American who lives here in Any Town, U.S.A. Mr. Pennywise is married and has two children. His adjusted gross income is $27,000 a year and with that he is supposed to provide food and clothing for his family, make the monthly mortgage and tax payments and at the same time, be able to squirrel away sufficient savings so that as his children grow older, there will be funds available for their college education. In this current inflationary spiral, Mr. Pennywise is caught! He is finding it extremely difficult to meet all of these requirements. Last year he received a salary increase of 6% but at the same time, he realized that inflation increased by 6.8% and that his net purchasing power has, in fact, decreased over the course of the annual period. Meanwhile, because of the 6% increase in salary, he has now been thrown into a higher income tax bracket and is forced to pay more income tax to both the State government and the Federal government. Mr. Pennywise is feeling the inflationary-tax squeeze.

The squeeze

It is now late Friday afternoon and Mr. Pennywise has cashed his paycheck. He has also paid all of his outstanding bills and he finds that he has $100 which is left. That $100 can be used for some type of savings which hopefully will contribute toward his children's college tuition fund. Mr. Pennywise sits down and begins to analyze all of the investment opportunities that are available to him. He first considers putting it in his commercial bank in a savings account. He discovers that he can receive 5% interest. But if he puts it in a savings bank, he can receive 5¼% interest. Over the course of many years that ¼% interest adds up and so that appears to be a prudent investment. He also looks at the Series "E" and Series "H" bonds which are offered by the Federal government. If he purchases a Series "E" bond, he is committing his money for five years and the interest rate that he will receive is 4½% the first year to 6% in the fifth year. He also looks at the Series "H" bonds which are offered by the Federal government. If he purchases a Series "H" bond, he is committing his money for ten years and the interest rate he will receive is 6%.

Mr. Pennywise begins to search for what other investment opportunities are available. "I have heard of such things as treasury bills, treasury bonds, and treasury notes, and all of these currently pay a higher yield. Possibly, I should purchase a treasury bill." Mr. Pennywise also recognizes that treasury bills, treasury bonds and treasury notes are exempt from State income tax which means that his net earnings would, in fact, be higher than the simple interest rate shown on the face of the instrument. But, as Mr. Pennywise begins to look into the possibility of buying a treasury instrument, he finds that he must have a minimum of $5,000 or $10,000 to even enter the market. One hundred dollars is a long way from $10,000 and, therefore, he is excluded from the treasury instrument market. Those 7% and 8% yields are out of the reach of his $100.

Why not consider the private corporate offerings? Various corporate bonds are for sale and they are paying 8%, 9%, and some 10% interest rates. Those interest rates are very attractive for someone who is trying to save sufficient funds to send his children to college. As he further analyzes the corporate market, he finds that there are no corporate bonds available in $100 denominations. He either will be forced to come up with $5,000 cash plus the commission cost or he cannot invest in the corporate market. Again, Mr. Pennywise is effectively excluded from the high yield corporate bonds. Mr. Pennywise has not given up at this point and he begins to examine what other type of investments may be available to him. He quickly realizes that for every dollar he earns he must pay 28% of that dollar to the Federal government by way of income tax and he must pay 2½% of that dollar to the State by way of State income taxes. Therefore, Mr. Pennywise considers the possibility of buying a municipal tax exempt bond. Mr. Pennywise recognizes that there are a number of municipal bonds offered which pay 6% interest. Six percent (6%) interest on a municipal bond is higher than the 5½% which one would receive from a savings institution and it also is tax exempt. Therefore, the net yield is significantly higher than that paid at a savings institution. But as with the case of the other financial instruments, Mr. Pennywise soon learns that you generally need a minimum of $5,000 if you are going to enter the municipal bond market. There are some towns across the country that offer $1,000 municipal bonds but even $1,000 is a far cry from $100 plus the cost of purchasing the bond which represent commission fees.

The small investor

Mr. Pennywise is certainly becoming depressed. He begins to realize that he is one of many small investors who, because of the small size of the principal which they have to invest, have been effectively ex-

Principal	$100.00	
Savings rate	5.25%	
Earnings	$ 5.25 plus principal	= $105.25
Earnings	$5.25	
State tax rate	2.5%	
State income tax	$ .13	
Earnings	$5.25	
Federal tax rate	28%	
Federal income tax	$1.47	
Earnings	$5.25	
Minus state & federal tax	1.60	
Net earnings before inflation	3.65 plus principal	= $103.65
Principal	$100.00	
Inflation	6.8%	
New principal value	$ 93.02 plus net earnings $3.65	= $96.85
Net loss after one year		$ 3.15

Note: Some savings and loan institutions provide various interest rates. Those interest rates are associated with a minimum deposit and the interest is from the day of deposit to the day of withdrawal. If the interest rate on a 5¼% savings account were compounded quarterly, the net yield at the end of the year would be 5.35%. If the savings account were for 5½% compounded quarterly, the net earnings at the end would be 5.61% yield. Both of these yields require a minimum deposit and if your account drops below the minimum requirement, the interest rate normally drops by 1% to each point.

Table 1.

cluded from many of the high yield financial instruments in the marketplace. Therefore, Mr. Pennywise must use a local savings institution or buy a Series "E" or Series "H" savings bond if he is going to accrue any type of earnings from his $100. At the same time, the interest that Mr. Pennywise earns on those investments is subject to Federal taxes and State taxes. Mr. Pennywise could earn $5.25 interest on his $100 if he left it in a savings bank for a full year. But the Federal government would require him to pay 28% of that $5.25 to them and the State government is going to require that 2½% of it be paid in accordance with the current State law. After all of the taxes are paid and Mr. Pennywise has committed his money for a one year period of time, he will have received $3.65 as his true yield for investing his $100. Meanwhile inflation has increased at the rate of 6.8% and when you take the $103.65 that Mr. Pennywise now has, minus the inflationary factor, his purchasing power is that much less. Mr.

Pennywise has lost $3.15 over the course of the year during which he had his money invested (Table 1).

The problem

Mr. Pennywise has been excluded from the high yield interest-bearing financial market and at the same time, he has in fact lost money as he has attempted to be a good responsible citizen by saving for his children's education.

What can be done?

The Township of East Brunswick recognized this dilemma and it is their feeling that the municipal bond market should be expanded to provide investment opportunities for such people. Many people with the same set of circumstances live in East Brunswick. In fact, there are many such people in the State of New Jersey. The 1976 Statistics of Income reports that New Jersey taxpayers represent 3.5% of those who filed Federal tax returns. The same taxpayers earned 3.9% of the total adjusted gross income as reported but those same New Jersey taxpayers paid 4.13% of the total taxes paid in the United States. The New Jersey taxpayers are paying more than their share of Federal taxes.

The question before the Mayor and Municipal Council was how to expand the bond market to make it available for the individual investor? Why has this not happened before?

Action

Each year, approximately $60 billion worth of municipal bonds are offered for sale. Given the current practice that each bond carries a principal value of $5,000, this means that there are $12 million of municipal bonds that must be sold each year. These bonds carry with them two coupons for each year the bond is in existence. If the bonds simply were sold for a one year period of time, it would represent 24 million coupons. The average life of a municipal bond is some place between 15 and 20 years.

Process

Coupons once turned into a local bank for payment must be manually processed. Someone who owns a municipal bond is responsible for clipping the coupon off the bond. The coupon, once it is clipped off the bond, is placed in a special envelope prepared by the bank. The bank will then take that envelope and process it through its in-house operation on through the banking system until it is returned to the municipality which issued the bond. Municipal coupons that are printed in the traditional format are very small and they provide no source of automation. Therefore, it is a very labor-intensive process and one that requires a great deal of personnel time and cost. If the municipal market were to restructure the issuance of municipal debt in smaller denominations, i.e., smaller than the $5,000 bonds which are common, then the paper flow process may become unbearable. Knowing that $60 million worth of municipal debt translate into 12 million bonds which translate into 24 million coupons each year, just think how much greater ten times the paper flow would be if all of those bonds were issued in the amount of $500. The printing expense, the processing expense and the personnel time required would be tremendous, unless there were developed some method of automating the municipal bond and coupon processing procedures.

Improved handling, i.e., automation, should eliminate some of the concerns that the banking community has with regards to the size of denominations that municipal bonds should carry. East Brunswick Township believes they have found a method to automate the processing of municipal bonds.

The method to be utilized is the very same method that is currently used to route billions of checks all over the country. It is the Magnetic Ink Character Recognition (MICR) encoded documents. This is the black magnetic ink which appears on the bottom of your personal check or your business check. The magnetic ink allows a reader recorder to automatically recognize the characters and to route the instruments throughout the country based on a pre-defined set of numbers. That same system of MICR encoding could be utilized to speed and automate the processing of municipal bonds and interest checks. A review of the technology which is available and based upon an experiment which was conducted in the bond sale of November, 1977, when the Township sold its bonds with check size MICR encoded coupons, the Township thinks a change will work.

Check-size coupons have returned to the bank successfully and the banks have been able to automatically process those coupons.

In the November 3, 1977 Daily Bond Buyer, the Bank of America reported how it lowered per coupon processing time from 15 minutes to one and one-half minutes. Assume a 35 hour work week per employee processing coupons. Such an employee can only process 1,400 coupons per week, if that employee takes no breaks and works 100% of the time. How many employees work like that? Thirty-five hours times sixty minutes per hour equals 2,100 minutes per week divided by 1.5 minutes per coupon is 1,400 coupons per week. Using MICR encoding and the standard reader recorder for any bank, 1,600 check-type coupons can be processed per minute. Compare the cost savings: 1,400 coupons per week compared to one reader recorder processing 1,600 check-type coupons per minute, or 96,000 per hour. That represents a productivity increase through technological change.

Next step

The next logical step is to reduce the principal statement, i.e., the bond, to a check size document and prepare it with MICR encoding.

Maturity date	$100	$200	$500	Interest rate
1979		100	120	4.60%
1980		100	120	4.70%
1981		100	120	4.80%
1982		150	260	4.90%
1983	390	0	180	5.00%

Table 2.

If the bonds and the interest checks (coupons) can be automatically processed, then there should be no objection to reducing the size of the bond from $5,000 per bond to $100, $200, or $500 per bond. When a reduction in the size of the principal required to enter the municipal tax exempt market is undertaken, there will be literally millions of individuals able to take advantage of the tax exempt offerings by municipal governments.

The Township of East Brunswick conducted a bond sale on September 25, 1978. At that time, $529,000 worth of municipal bonds were offered for sale. The bonds were in various denominations, $100, $200, and $500—a total of 1,640 bonds to be sold (see Table 2).

The bonds carried an interest maturity equalled to the current re-offering schedule for Aa bonds. Table 3 will show you the net results if Mr. Pennywise had been able to purchase a one-year $100 municipal bond.

As you can see, the interest which is earned on a municipal bond is exempt from State income taxes and Federal income taxes. Therefore, Mr. Pennywise would have saved $1.29 in Federal taxes and saved $0.11 in State income taxes for every $4.60 worth of interest earned. The total tax savings is $1.40. If you add the $1.40 to the $4.60, you have a true yield of 6% or greater. The purchase of a municipal tax exempt bond is the only instrument in today's marketplace that would provide Mr. Pennywise with that type of yield.

They were available

People purchased East Brunswick bonds in the amounts of $100, $200, or $500. They purchased them at the Revenue Office of the

Principal	$100.00		
Interest	4.60%		
Earnings	$ 4.60 plus principal	=	$104.60
Earnings	$ 4.60		
State tax	—0—		
Federal tax	—0—		
Net earnings	$ 4.60 plus principal	=	$104.60

Table 3.

Municipal Building located at One Jean Walling Civic Center. During the first three days, more than 1,000 bonds were sold to people who lived in the area. The sale was a success.

The bond law

The Local New Jersey Bond Law (N.J.S.A. 40 A:2—et. seq.) requires municipalities and counties to take competitive bids when they sell bonds. If no legally acceptable bids are received at the public offering, such bonds may be sold within 30 days after the advertised date for public bidding. East Brunswick assumed that no bids would be received because a maximum interest rate had been set and a disclosure of principal size and format was made. The institutional market was not prepared to handle small denomination bonds.

At the Council Meeting of September 25, 1978, the Municipal Council passed a resolution authorizing bonds to be sold to individuals who came to the Revenue counter after that date. The bonds could be sold for a period of thirty (30) days or until all were sold. It is the end of the third day as I am writing this report. All bonds will be sold before the thirty (30) day period.

Public acceptance

How did we know that the public would accept bonds which are sold directly over the counter by the municipality? Will the public have confidence in this type of sale as compared to the "mystique" which surrounds the Wall Street banks and the public securities dealers? In October of 1975, the Board of Education for East Islip, New York was faced with a need to raise funds. This was during the height of the New York City fiasco. The lack of disclosure and the lack of adequate controls which resulted in New York City's default caused shock waves. East Islip needed to raise $2½ million and the banking community asked a 14% interest rate. Instead of going through the traditional method and using the banks, East Islip advertised and sold the notes (10% interest) at a public sale to individuals. The principal amounts were $1,000 and $5,000 denominations and the public responded very favorably. All of the notes were sold. In fact, there was greater demand than notes available.

Cooperation required

The State of Pennsylvania most recently had a law on the books which required every government unit to issue a certain percentage of its bonds in $100 denominations. The concept behind the issuance of $100 denominations is the same as that of East Brunswick. Tax exempt bonds should be offered to the small investors as well as to the large investors but the banking community did not find it convenient to market $100 bonds in the State of Pennsylvania. Therefore, the market was not developed and the intentions of the legislation were aborted. The law was finally repealed in 1978. The often used phrase "You can lead a horse to water but you cannot make him drink" has been used. Towns in Pennsylvania were forced to issue $100 in bonds but no one bought them. If you put salt in the oats that you feed the horses, he will drink when you lead him to water. The use of MICR encoding and the ability to automatically process coupons hopefully will serve as salt to the banking community. Now that they will no longer need to manually process coupons or wait for collection and reconciliation, they should be willing to cooperate and assist the small investor.

One of the often heard comments criticizing the use of a check type of coupon is "It will result in duality." Banks will still need to process the old coupons and there will be new coupons which will necessitate two systems. The response to this is: "Henry Ford did not wait for all of the horses to die before he began to build automobiles." Competition is healthy and if the new system is better, cheaper, provides more security and produces a superior audit trail, then the banking community as well as the general public will want to follow the example of East Brunswick, New Jersey.

Municipal Bond Insurance Gaining in Acceptance

Lauren M. Miralia

In a period of high interest rates and great economic uncertainty, it becomes more difficult than ever to select an attractive investment and outperform the market or the competition.

A creation of the 1970s, municipal bond insurance is growing in usage for that very purpose in the tax-exempt segment of the investment market.

A recent survey of the commercial banking industry is highly revealing. The managing agency of the Municipal Bond Insurance Association (MBIA) queried more than 550 portfolio managers and trust officers of a cross section of the nation's commercial banks. We asked them to rate MBIA-insured municipal bonds and their level of acceptance. An impressive 29% of the bankers—from 159 banks of a variety of sizes and locations—responded to a detailed questionnaire.

Highlighting the results was the fact that two-thirds of the responding banks had purchased MBIA-guaranteed bonds. More than a third of that group had also sold them in the secondary market. The marketability of MBIA-backed bonds drew enthusiastic approval. Portfolio and trust officers, by a 10-to-1 ratio, reported that MBIA bonds' acceptability for investment by their investment policy committees, directors, and trust clients was improving.

How it works

Municipal bond insurance provides an issuer that can qualify (but not all borrowers can get coverage) with a guarantee that earns its obligations a higher rating (AAA) by Standard & Poor's than it might otherwise enjoy.

From the investors' point of view, this means that they can buy

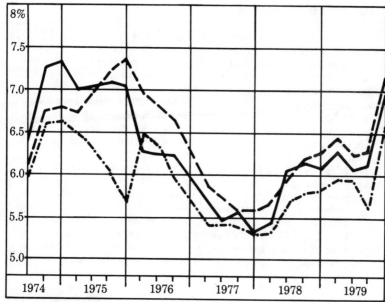

— MBIA-insured
—·—·— Moody's Aa
——— Bond Buyer

*Comparative re-offering yields of 20-year municipal bonds guaranteed by
MBIA vs. Moody's Aa Index and the Bond Buyer Index.*

insured municipals with yields of A- or Aa- rated bonds but with
quality ratings of AAA.

The accompanying chart demonstrates that yields on MBIA-insured bonds, which are rated AAA by S&P, are often 10 to 25 basis
points higher than even Aa rated bonds. The chart goes through the
fourth quarter of 1979. In early January, at this writing, normal 20-
year general obligation bonds rated Aa by Moody's are returning
6.45% while AAA-rated MBIA-insured bonds of the same maturity
yield over 7.20%, a highly significant increase in cash flow and yield
for bank portfolios and trust accounts.

MBIA bonds have other advantages. In deteriorating markets
they, like other AAA and Aaa bonds, tend to hold their value longer.

Background

MBIA was formed in 1973 and now has guaranteed more than 800
bond issues worth over $4 billion in 35 states.

In spite of huge insurance-company resources backing MBIA-
insured bonds, these securities are still considered "story" bonds in
the municipals market—issues whose special characteristics have to

---

Safeguards for muni investors

The big money center banks often say: "We've got plenty of staff to evaluate municipals." So they do. But what about medium and smaller banks that don't? Some lean on their correspondents for buy/sell recommendations. Others opt for reliance on the guarantees of municipal bond insurance.

American Municipal Bond Assurance Corp. (AMBAC), a member of the MGIC group, pioneered the concept in 1971. In 1973, AMBAC expanded the concept to include not only new issues but also existing tax-exempt portfolios held by individual and institutional investors with the investor paying the premium.

More recently, AMBAC set up a major reinsurance program with some of the biggest insurance companies in the country, allowing it to increase vastly the scale of its underwriting. AMBAC reports it now has some $6 billion of insurance in force.

Obviously there are tradeoffs, since insurance costs something. But if medium grade bonds get a higher rating from the rating agencies by virtue of insurance coverage, buyers can often buy higher-yielding paper and still have peace of mind. In such cases, the insurance pays for itself.

---

be explained occasionally. Some buyers' lack of familiarity with such securities, and the fact that many of them do not have Moody ratings, have made MBIA-backed issues the best buy of any top-quality municipal issues in today's market.

While default in payment of principal and interest is a highly unlikely event on the part of the municipalities MBIA insures, wide swings in their individual credit standings are a distinct possibility. MBIA-guaranteed bondholders are protected from adverse economic, legal, political, and social developments which can materially affect municipal governments. Deterioration in a municipality's credit standing will not change Standard & Poor's rating of bonds guaranteed by MBIA.

Unlike most insurance policies, which don't pay a claim until something goes wrong, MBIA's guarantee of payments is readily convertible into increased market value and liquidity. In an era of increasing financial instability, with credit problems abounding, MBIA's guarantee can prevent substantial depreciation in the value of bond investments due to the deterioration of a municipality's credit.

Backers

Four prominent insurance companies comprise MBIA's membership. These, with their share of participation, are:

Aetna Casualty & Surety Co., a subsidiary of Aetna Life & Casualty Co., 40%;

Fireman's Fund Insurance Co., a subsidiary of American Express Co., 30%;

Aetna Insurance Co., a subsidiary of Connecticut General Insurance Co., 15%; and

United States Fire Insurance Co., a subsidiary of Crum & Forster Insurance Cos., 15%.

The MBIA guarantee is an insurance policy obligation. Investors buy MBIA bonds directly from municipal bond dealers, with the policy fully paid in advance and attached to or printed on the bonds. The premium is paid by the municipality, usually 0.75% to 1% of the principal and interest. Timely payment of debt service is guaranteed by MBIA to maturity of the bonds.

Risk lessening

Today, sophisticated bond analysis can project a variety of economic possibilities, providing the basis for contingency planning. While it is true that no technology can guarantee future performance or market price, an MBIA-guaranteed bond is one current investment option that can decrease risk, lessen analytical time, and reduce price volatility.

For this and other reasons, some dealers and other experts in the municipal bond market have commented that "it is easier to trade issues in the MBIA name." Paine Webber Senior Vice President H. Russell Fraser said in a recent interview that "financial guarantees like MBIA are the wave of the future."

And John R. Butler, president of Municipal Issuers Insurance Corp., says: "Insurance throws a security blanket over the issue. It's an unconditional, irrevocable guarantee that we will make payment. There isn't a Proposition 13, a New York City, or any other disaster for a municipal government that isn't covered."

"Co-signer"

MBIA turns down many more prospects for bond insurance than it accepts. MBIA's analytical process is much more comprehensive than most, because we commit capital as a guarantor of the obligation.

Unlike the rating services, which can suspend, reduce or withdraw ratings, we are unconditionally bound to pay—for the life of the bond. In this regard, MBIA is acting as a co-signer of the issuer. As bank officials would not knowingly loan funds to a poor credit risk, MBIA will not guarantee loans which aren't likely to pay off.

However, in contrast to investors in municipal bonds, we do not have to worry about the marketability of the issuer's bonds or any deterioration of ratings or quality other than outright default. Clearly, this gives us the advantage of being able to take a wide range of market-price risks (as opposed to default risks) which most investors are unwilling or unable to accept.

Aside from the present yield advantages of MBIA-insured bonds, there are sound technical, legal, and operating advantages for fiduciaries. Our commitment to research, credit analysis, and follow-up surveillance is total. When MBIA reviews, analyzes, and approves an issue, the bank officers' usual geographic and technical policy restrictions should be eliminated. For example, a trust officer in Indiana can invest in lesser known Florida, Pennsylvania, or California issues that carry MBIA insurance, and get an AAA rating at an A or Aa yield level. Investment policy committees of many institutions have added MBIA-backed bonds, as a class, to their approved lists.

Each issue analyzed by the managing agency of MBIA is subject to further analysis by the analytical staff of each MBIA-member insurance company. Ultimately, the member companies must either approve or turn down every issue submitted.

The accuracy of our initial credit-quality assessment is monitored and utilized for further development of our analytical techniques. Additionally, credit surveillance provides us the opportunity to give notice to the municipalities if their credit is deteriorating or bond covenants are not being met.

Municipal Bond Banking: The Diffusion of a Public-Finance Innovation

Martin T. Katzman

I. Introduction

Vermont and Maine established municipal bond banks in 1970 and 1972, respectively, to deal with the difficulties their constituent municipalities have had in floating debt. These are the high transactions costs and risk premiums inherent in floating large numbers of small, heterogeneous, and infrequent issues. While there have been several descriptions of bond banks in the literature [7; 8], there has been little quantitative analysis of their benefits, with the exception of a cursory examination of the first Vermont issue [2].

The purpose of this paper is to examine the factors affecting the diffusion of this innovation. There is considerable evidence that the rate of financial innovation varies directly with net benefits [13]. A methodology is described here that permits the quantification of benefits of participation and identification of the type of issuers that receive the greatest net gains. A logit analysis confirms that the actual likelihood of municipal participation varies with these estimated benefits. Potential "private" municipal gains are insufficient to account for the creation of the municipal bond bank, a public good, in the first instance. Because of the necessity for collective action in establishing a bond bank, the distribution of benefits among communities is important as well. These factors are illustrated by an analysis of the distribution of benefits from a potential Massachusetts Bond Bank. The likelihood of the diffusion of bond banks to other states is discussed.

II. The operation of a municipal bond bank

A municipal bond bank is an arrangement for pooling general obligations of localities and special districts within a state. By pooling such

Reprinted with permission from *National Tax Journal*, vol. 33, no. 2. Published by the Tax Institute of America.

issues, a bond bank can offer larger issues that attract more bidders, reduce the cost of underwriting and marketing which are subject to economies of scale, and, more important, effectively reduce the risk of holding debt of small, and often unrated, issuers.

The existing bond banks operate in the following manner:[1]

1. To participate in a Bank issue, a municipality (or special district with taxing power) must first undertake its normal constitutional obligations in floating debt, such as holding an election if necessary, as verified in the opinion of its own bond counsel. The town then submits an application to the bond bank providing the type of information normally used by credit rating agencies, such as anticipated tax collections, assessed valuation per capita, overlapping debt per assessed valuation, and percentage tax delinquencies.

2. The Bond Bank collects a list of municipalities desiring to issue general obligations bonds through the bank as well as the amount needed by each municipality. Local participation in the Bank is optional, and several towns with ratings higher than that of the Bank have occasionally, but not always, declined to participate.

3. The Bank has the formal power to decide which of these municipalities can participate in an issue on the basis of the information in the application, which is analyzed by its financial adviser. A town can be excluded from an issue if, in the opinion of the Bank's financial adviser, such a town would significantly detract from the marketability of the Bank's bonds. While the possibility of politically-motivated exclusion exists, only financial criteria influenced the few cases of actual exclusion in Maine [5], none before 1976.

4. When at least $6 million[2] in prospective local debt has been aggregated, the Bank issues bonds for a sum equal to the total amount borrowed by the municipalities plus approximately 10 percent for a reserve fund, which equals or exceeds the maximum annual debt service. The term structure of the Bank's bonds are determined by the aggregated term structure of the underlying issues, plus the schedule for retirement of the reserve fund.

5. Proceeds of the Bank's issue are used to purchase the general obligations of the participating municipalities, and the remainder, the reserve fund, is invested in U.S. Treasury securities. The term structure of interest rates on the debt of the towns is equivalent to that of the Bank's consolidated issue.

6. Marketing and operating expenses thus far have been covered by profits of the reserve fund, which result from the differential between the state's tax-exempt borrowing cost and the returns on taxable Treasury securities. Were these net revenues

insufficient, municipalities would be billed on a *pro rata* basis. The state incurs no out-of-pocket costs from the operations of the Bank.

The security behind the Bank bonds are first the reserve fund, then the full faith and credit of the municipality, next a lien on state grants-in-aid to the municipality, and finally a moral obligation of the state to replenish the reserve fund in case of depletion. Because of the moral rather than general obligation of the state, Bond Banks have generally received a rating one notch lower than that of the corresponding states.[3]

III. Potential savings of a municipal bond bank

The municipal bond bank can reduce the cost of borrowing to municipalities by means of pooling risks and spreading the fixed transactions costs of issuing bonds. These savings operate through several channels: reoffering yields, underwriting spreads, and other marketing costs.

Both reoffering yields and underwriting spreads depend upon many characteristics of debt issues that are unaltered by bond banking, such as the term structure of the bonds, callability, average market interest rates, and outstanding debt of borrowers. Bond banking alters two crucial aspects of debt issues: their average size and their credit ratings. In general, the higher the rating of the debt, the greater the number of bidders and hence the lower reoffering yields and underwriting spreads.

The savings are calculated here on the assumption that in the absence of a municipal bond bank, each municipality would issue debt whose reoffering yields, underwriting spreads, and other marketing costs would be equal to those of the average issue of equivalent size and rating.

Reoffering yields   Prior to the establishment of the Bond Banks, only about five percent of the towns in Vermont and nine percent of those in Maine were rated. Fragmentary evidence suggests that unrated issues generally enjoy reoffering yields similar to those of Baa-rated issues [10, table 10]. While a rating can be obtained for a fee, the infrequency with which these towns entered the market, the high fee, and the low likelihood of their receiving ratings above Baa dissuaded many towns from doing so. As indicated, one impact of the municipal bond banks has been to raise the effective ratings of participating towns to Aa.

In the period 1959-1967, the spread in 20-year reoffering yields between Aa and Baa-rated issues was at least 46 basis points, *ceteris paribus*. Because higher rated issues attract more bidders, the spread in reoffering yields increased by another 3 basis points, for a total of 49 basis points. Since there has been a secular decline in spreads be-

Size of issue	Rating		
($1000s)	Unrated	Average	Aa
0 - 249	38	24	-27
250 - 499	27	15	-27
500 - 999	22	3	-33
1,000 - 4,999	23	- 2	-35
5,000 - 19,999	21	-13	-37
20,000+	—	-27	-39

Source: Petersen [p. 134].

Table 1.   Reoffering yields by size of issues and rating, deviation from bond buyer 20 index, general obligation bonds of average terms of 11-15 years, 1967-1971.

tween ratings, this spread overestimates the effect of ratings arbitrage in the 1970s [4, tables 9 and 10; 10, table 13].

A quantitatively less important impact of the Bond Bank operates through an increase in issue size. Because institutional investors prefer to deal with larger issues in order to minimize their own transactions costs, reoffering yields tend to vary inversely with size of issue.

In both Vermont and Maine, the median size of local issues has tended to be less than $500,000; the mean, less than $1 million. In contrast, Bank issues have been on the order of $10 million. The quantitative impact of this scale factor on reoffering yields is somewhat difficult to estimate since Kessel's [4] study excludes issues of less than $1 million. If one is willing to extrapolate downward, Kessel's regression coefficients imply that for the size of issues that have been consolidated by the Banks, savings were only about one or two basis points. An analysis of the files of the Securities Industry Association by Petersen [8] suggests that the spread in yields between issues in the $500-999 thousand range and those in the $5-20 million range is approximately one to four basis points, depending upon rating (Table 1). While this study held ratings and average term roughly constant, other features of the issues, such as callability were not. Nevertheless, this study suggests that the reoffering yield spread between an unrated issue in the $500-999 thousand range and an Aa-rated issue in the $5-20 million range is about 59 basis points. This is somewhat higher than the (49 + 2 =) 51 basis points derived from Kessel's study, but is of the same order of magnitude.

An empirical estimation of the effects of consolidating local issues should ideally take into account the maturity structure of the serial bonds and should compare issues which differ only in size and rating. Because the rating variable seems to have the greatest impact on reoffering yields, the effect of the bond bank on reoffering yields is estimated here by the observed differentials, as reported in *Moody's Bond Record*, in bond averages for issues of different ratings, for the weeks during which the Bond Banks floated their issues. Since these averages take no account of the differences in term structure and issue sizes of the differently rated bonds, and since higher rated bonds tend to have a longer maturity structure and larger issue size, this method underestimates savings in reoffering yields. Yield differentials estimated by this method are roughly 10 basis points lower than those generated by Kessel's equations.

The credit rating of each participating governmental unit was derived from *Moody's Bond Record* for the month in which a municipality participated in the Bank. In the absence of the bond bank, we assumed that each town would pay the interest equal to Moody's bond average for its rating class; and that the interest rate of all state issues would have been the average of these interest rates, weighted by the relative size of each municipality's issue. Likewise, the Bond Bank is imputed the interest rate of its rating class, to wit, Aa, although the Banks have actually performed slightly worse than the class average [5].

The present value of the interest savings can be approximated by either of two methods. Both assume that bonds are liquidated with a constant annual debt service, whether or not issued through the Bank. Method A assumes that the municipal demand for capital expenditures is completely interest inelastic. Therefore, the value of the bonds issued through the Bank would have been identical to the value issued in the absence of the Banks, despite the higher interest rate and higher annual amortization payments. The hypothetical, higher amortization payments are then capitalized at the actual, lower, Bond Bank interest rate. The difference between the resulting higher capitalized payments and the actual value of the issue equals the interest savings. To the extent that the interest-elasticity of demand for municipal infrastructure is less than zero, this method overestimates the consumer surplus from the interest savings.

Method B assumes a unitary interest-elasticity of demand for capital expenditures. Therefore, in the absence of a bond bank, amortization payments would have been the same, but the value of the capital financed would have been less. The resulting difference underestimates the capital gain from interest savings, especially since the elasticity of demand for municipal infrastructure is closer to zero than to unity [11]. In practice, the two methods produce savings estimates which differ only on the order of about two percent.

Underwriting spreads   In addition to savings on reoffering yields to investors, the bond bank narrows the underwriting spread that bridges the gap to the real interest cost to municipalities.

Underwriting costs per thousand vary with the size of issue, rating, and the number of bidders per issue, which itself is a function of

	A	B
Rating	Unadjusted differences ($)	Differences adjusted for bids ($)
Aaa - Aa	-1.30	-1.35
Aa - A	-0.84	-1.06
A - Baa	-0.96	-1.19

Source: Column A: Kessel [table 5]; Column B: Petersen [table 13].

Table 2.   Differences in underwriting spread (per $1000 bond) between credit ratings, unadjusted and adjusted for number of bidders.

issue size and rating. As computed by Kessel, the difference in underwriting costs between an issue of $850 thousand (the mean size of a participating issue) and $46 million (the size of the first Vermont Bond Bank issue) is about $1 per thousand. Total underwriting cost savings per thousand were computed as the product of Kessel's regression coefficient for issue size in thousands (-2.4×10^{-5}) and the difference between the mean size of each issue and the consolidated issue.

The difference in costs of underwriting Aa and Baa (or unrated) bonds is about $2.25 per thousand. About $0.45 of this difference results from the greater number of bidders the more highly rated issue attracts (Table 2). Kessel found that the differences in underwriting

Size of issue ($1000s)	Finan. advis.	Bond notice	Bond prospts.	Bond printing	Bond rating	Sub-total
0-499	$9.09	$ .62	$ .95	$1.02	$2.01	$13.69
500-999	6.86	.45	.71	.71	1.16	9.89
1,000-1,999	4.69	.26	.76	.64	.65	7.00
2,000-2,999	3.70	.13	.59	.34	.46	5.22
3,000-4,999	2.40	.13	.26	.24	.29	3.32
5,000-9,999	2.68	.10	.15	.28	.16	3.37
10,000-24,999	1.45	.05	.07	.17	.09	1.83
25,000 and over	.20	.04	.05	.16	.03	.48

Source: Municipal Finance Officers Association, *MFOA Special Bulletin*, "Subject: Costs Involved in Marketing State/Local Bonds," no date. This survey of January 1973 resulted in 481 responses from localities in 44 states. It is not clear whether the sample or the respondents were randomly selected.
Note: Includes only costs that are pooled by a municipal bond bank.

Table 3.   Costs of marketing general obligation bonds by cost category and issue size (per $1000 of bonds).

Issue	Principal*	Savings on interest		Under-writing savings by		Other marketing costs avoided					Total savings	% of issue**
		A	B	Size	Rating	Fin. adv.	Bond not.	Bond pro.	Bond prnt.	Rating		
8/73	$ 9,225	233	239	2	15	52	3	7	7	9	328-335	3.6
4/74	$10,900	228	233	2	15	49	3	7	6	8	318-323	2.9
10/74	$ 8,590	403	423	2	18	50	3	7	6	8	497-517	5.8
3/75	$12,125	562	584	3	22	59	3	6	7	9	671-693	5.5
Total	$40,840	1,426	1,479	9	70	210	12	27	26	36	1,814-1,868	4.4
% Distribution		78.7	—	0.5	3.8	11.6	0.6	1.5	1.4	1.9	100%	
				4.3		17.0						

*Excludes reserve funds.
**Calculated using Interest Savings Method A.
Method A assumes that participating governmental units pay the same amortization payment with or without the bond bank. They borrow more by participating in the bank because of lower interest rates.
Method B assumes that the savings caused by the bond bank's lower interest rate are used to reduce the annual amortization payments of the governmental units. Thus, each unit borrows the same amount of capital with or without the bond bank.

Table 4a. Savings by issue, Maine Municipal Bond Bank ($000s).

Issue	Principal*	Savings on interest		Under-writing savings by		Other marketing costs avoided					Total savings	% of issue**
		A	B	Size	Rating	Fin. adv.	Bond not.	Bond pro.	Bond prnt.	Rating		
1/71	$41,230	1,249	1,289	39	85	218	13	27	24	36	1,691-1,731	4.1
3/72	$18,205	195	197	7	18	98	6	12	11	16	363-365	2.0
12/72	$ 7,300	115	116	1	8	51	3	8	6	9	201-202	2.8
1/74	$10,380	565	598	2	11	60	4	6	6	11	665-698	6.4
Total	$77,115	2,124	2,200	49	122	427	26	53	47	72	2,920-2,986	3.8
% Distribution		71.2	—	1.7	4.1	14.3	0.9	1.8	1.6	2.4	100%	

*Excludes reserve funds.
**Calculated using Interest Savings Method A.

Table 4b. Savings by issue, Vermont Municipal Bond Bank ($000s).

spreads between rating classes have decreased over time; therefore, these underwriting spreads may overestimate the experience of the 1970s.

Other marketing costs The major marketing costs which can be pooled through the bond bank include financial advice; the printing of the notice, prospectus, and the bond itself; and the rating. All of these are subject to economies of scale (Table 3). While not all towns would have utilized financial advisers, the calculations below assume they did.

It should be noted that marketing costs which are not pooled by the bond bank, including special elections, local attorney, and outside bond counsel, account for about one-half of the marketing costs which municipalities have experienced in recent years. Combined, these latter marketing costs were as large as those which can be pooled through the bond bank.

Magnitude of savings   The total cost savings of the municipal bond bank are estimated by comparing the reoffering yields, underwriting spreads, and other marketing costs of all eight consolidated issues as of January 1976, of the Vermont and Maine Municipal Bond Banks with eight hypothetical yields, spreads, and marketing costs of their components if issued separately. All cost estimates are based upon the assumptions described above, rather than upon the observed costs *ex-post*. The reason for this approach is that it provides a method of estimating the ex-ante advantage to a town of issuing through a bond bank or to a state of adopting a municipal bond bank.

Savings as a percent of issue size varied by series but averaged 4.4 percent in Maine and 3.8 percent in Vermont (see Tables 4a and 4b). Interest savings comprised the great majority of savings in both states (78 percent in Maine and 71 percent in Vermont). Variations in interest savings, due to variations in spreads between ratings classes, were responsible for the variations in total savings from issue to issue.

It should be noted that despite the crude manner in which interest savings were computed, they result in estimates of the same order of magnitude of another study of the Vermont Bank. Forbes and Renshaw [2] computed the net interest cost savings of the first Vermont Bond Bank issue by matching issues in that state with other issues of similar maturity and issue size. While their estimated interest saving was about 50 basis points, ours was 38.

Savings by characteristics of the issuer   Because the major impact of the bond bank operates through lowering interest rates through ratings arbitrage, it is not surprising that the savings to participants in the bond bank are greatest for the lower rated municipalities (Table 5). While unrated or Baa-rated towns saved about six percent of the principal in Maine and four percent in Vermont, savings dropped to less than three percent for A-rated towns, and about one percent for Aa-rated towns. For towns rated Aa, the same as the bond banks, there are of course no interest savings according to our methodology, only those reflecting economies of scale.

Savings in transactions costs amounted to 1.4 percent of the face

| Rating/ state | Interest | Underwriting | | Other marketing costs | | | | | Total savings as percent of issue |
		Size	Rating	Fin. adv.	Bond not.	Bond pro.	Bond prnt.	Rating	
Aaa									
Vermont	−150	2	−10	37	3	4	4	8	−2.4
Maine	—	—	—	—	—	—	—	—	—
Aa									
Vermont	0	3	0	66	4	7	7	13	1.1
Maine	0	2	0	62	4	9	8	10	0.9
A									
Vermont	56	4	5	20	1	2	6	3	2.4
Maine	71	1	4	16	1	2	2	2	2.8
Baa/ Unrated									
Vermont	73	2	4	13	1	2	1	2	4.2
Maine	81	0	4	10	1	1	1	2	5.7

Table 5.   Savings by credit rating (item as percent of total savings).

value for issuers of debt amounting to less than $0.5 million, falling to 0.7 percent for issues in the range $1-2 million, and 0.3 percent for issues over $3 million.

Characteristics of participants: a logit analysis   The majority of participants in the issues of the bond banks were either unrated or rated Baa: 72 percent in Maine and 89 percent in Vermont. As mentioned above, the majority of issues were below $1 million: 65 percent in Maine and 79 percent in Vermont. About 40 percent of the participants in the banks were both unrated/Baa-rated and issued debt of less than $500 thousand.

The pattern of participation is more easily appreciated by computing the probability of participation in the bond bank by rating and size of issue. All municipal issues for a period commencing three months before the first issue of each bond bank and ending January 1976 are examined from the *Monthly Bond Buyer*.[4] While this publication excludes private placements, it lists all public issues. Municipals issued through the Bond Banks are identified on the prospectuses.

A discrete multivariate analysis (identical to logit analysis with dummy variables) is undertaken for the pooled sample of 162 Vermont and Maine issues in the 1970-76 period (Table 6). As indicated by the signs of the coefficients in columns I and II, the odds of participating in a bond bank are inversely proportional to ratings and to size. As indicated by the magnitudes of the Pearson chi-squares (χ^2), the strength of these relationships is rather weak.[5] The ratings effect is far more powerful than the size effect, as the chi-square for a model

		I	II	III
Ratings				
Aaa		−2.20		−2.22
Aa		−1.32		−1.13
A		.50		.52
Baa/unrated		3.02		3.02
Size				
< $0.5 million			.56	.66
$0.5–1.0 million			.12	−.08
> $1.0 million			−.64	−.56
	X²	24.8	262.7	22.2
	d.f.	12	16	10
	p	.006	<.0001	.007
	no. issues	162	162	162

Table 6.   Log-odds of participation in a bond bank: Vermont and Maine, 1970–1976.

with ratings alone is smaller than the chi-square for size alone. A comparison of the chi-square statistics in columns I and III indicates that the addition of the size factor to the ratings factor improves the goodness-of-fit insignificantly. Despite their tenuousness, these relationships are consistent with the computations above that identify ratings arbitrage as the major channel of cost savings.

Hidden costs to the state's taxpayers   While the out-of-pocket costs for the operations of the Maine and Vermont Bond Banks have been borne by net revenues from reserve fund investments, a bond bank may impose hidden opportunity costs on the state's taxpayers. To the extent that the market perceives the bank's securities as general obligations of the state, an increase in the volume of outstanding low-quality debt may adversely affect the state's cost of borrowing. Any such impact would adversely affect taxpayers from nonparticipating municipalities, who derive no direct benefits from the bank.

The evidence on such impacts is far from compelling. Interviews with underwriters suggest that the debt of the two bond banks is not perceived by the market as general obligations of the state and has not adversely affected the states' credit ratings [5]. Furthermore, econometric evidence about the effect of added indebtedness on credit ratings and the cost of borrowing is ambiguous. Kessel finds that holding ratings constant, issuers with larger amounts of outstanding debt face an increased number of bidders and *lower* underwriting spreads and reoffering yields. This somewhat paradoxical result suggests that, at a given rating, larger and more frequent issue provides the market more information and hence reduces risk. Ratings and outstanding debt may be collinear; however, Rubinfeld [12] finds that indebtedness has insignificant effects on credit ratings of New England municipalities. On the other hand, Petersen [10, chap. 7] cites several studies with contrary evidence. Maine and Vermont have issued too few in the 1970s general obligations to test the hidden cost hypothesis directly. The verdict is Scotch.

IV. Potential benefits of innovation diffusion

In order to decide whether a particular state would benefit from establishing a bond bank, one must know the credit rating of the constituent municipalities and the credit rating of the state, for ratings arbitrage contributes the bulk of the potential savings. Since a bond bank generally receives a rating one grade lower than that of the state's general obligations, a state with a rating of Aa or less would provide relatively little benefit to its subdivisions. In January 1976, eighteen states had ratings of Aaa, and thus enjoyed one of the prerequisites for potential savings. Within these states, only about one or two percent of the municipalities have ratings of Aa or better, with Virginia having the highest (5 percent). Of bonds issued in these states during the late 1960s, the percent rated Aa or better ranged from less than ten percent in Tennessee to more than fifty percent in Utah [8].

Even in states with ratings lower than Aaa there are some positive benefits to a bond bank. To illustrate, we apply our methodology to computing the value of a potential bond bank in Massachusetts. While general obligations of Vermont and Maine have consistently enjoyed Aaa ratings, those of Massachusetts have recently fallen from Aa to A1. Second, while only eight and five percent of the localities were rated A or above in Maine and Vermont, respectively, fully 58 percent of Massachusetts localities have such ratings [9].

To estimate the savings of a hypothetical Massachusetts Bond Bank, we identified all the 1975 issues of Massachusetts cities, towns, and districts, which were listed in the *Monthly Bond Buyer* and which had terms of at least five years. Savings were calculated under two alternative conditions: (A) that the state has an Aa rating, the bond bank has an A rating, and hence participants have ratings of A or below; or (B) that the state's rating rises to Aaa, the bank's to Aa, and localities with ratings of Aa or below participate.

The absolute savings to a bond bank under Condition A is about $1 million a year. In absolute value, this exceeds the savings from the existing bond bank issues. For purposes of eliciting support for a bond bank, relative savings of potential beneficiaries would seem more relevant. Under condition A, total savings would be only 0.8 percent of the total value of issues of participating towns; under condition B, 1.5 percent. Even under the most optimistic assumptions

Bond bank rating	Value of par- ticipat- ing issues	Interest savings	Underwriting savings Size	Underwriting savings Rating	Other market- ing savings	Total savings % of issue Total size	Total savings Num- ber of units
(A) A	135,610	113	421	15	546	1,095 0.81	43
% of Total		10.3	38.5	1.4	49.8	100.0	
(B) Aa	547,005	2,598	4,523	158	1,018	8,296 1.52	63
% of Total		31.3	54.5	1.9	12.3	100.0	

Table 7. Hypothetical Massachusetts Municipal Bond Bank savings summary, 1975 ($000s).

about the state's credit rating, these relative savings are far below those experienced by bond banks in Maine and Vermont.

Since only those localities with ratings equal to or less than that of the bond bank were included, why were the savings so low? First, almost all the towns which issued debt in 1975 were rated Aa or A, which means that the possibilities for ratings arbitrage to provide interest savings were limited. Second, whereas 65 and 79 percent of the participants in Maine and Vermont, respectively, issued debt of less than $1 million, about 90 percent of the issues in Massachusetts were over this figure.

As a result of these characteristics, the benefits of a municipal bond bank would accrue to a smaller percentage of jurisdictions in Massachusetts than in Vermont and Maine. Consequently, the base of political support for such a bank would be narrower in the Bay State than in northern New England.

Because the benefits of a bond bank accrue to low-rated towns, while costs are spread to all residents in a state through its moral obligation to replenish the reserve fund, there is a substantial group of citizens, particularly living in large, well-rated cities, who risk losses from the establishment of a bond bank. Indeed, bond bank legislation has been introduced into at least eleven states during the 1970s, eight of which enjoyed Aaa ratings. Only five adopted the innovation: Vermont (1970), Maine (1972), Alaska (1975), North Dakota (1975), and New Hampshire (1978) [5]. Since these states are not unusual with respect to their percentage of low-rated towns and low-rated debt issues, and hence potential for gains, it is possible that this innovation may diffuse to some of the remaining AAA-rated states.[6]

The actual diffusion of municipal bond banking appears to be slower than implied by the analysis. Perhaps the slowness can be explained by the appearance of alternative mechanisms for risk pooling that impose less risk upon the state's taxpayers. First, debt advisory agencies can improve the financial planning and reporting capabilities of localities, at a small financial outlay and no risk to the state. North Carolina's venerable Local Government Commission has apparently reduced the interest costs of the state's municipalities by about 40 basis points, nearly as much as a bond bank [3, chap. 8]. Second, private municipal bond insurance has in effect provided municipalities an opportunity to purchase AA and AAA ratings, since the early 1970s. Bond insurance may lower net interest costs by 40-60 basis points, gross of insurance premiums. These premiums may add back the equivalent of 20-30 basis points to the total net interest cost [6]. On balance, municipal bond insurance provides less of a benefit to issuers than debt advisory commissions or bond banks. Policies, moreover, are generally unavailable for issues of less than $300 thousand. Third, the Tax Reform Act of 1976 permitted mutual funds to pass the tax-exempt status of interest payments on municipals to shareholders. While these three alternatives are risk-reducing devices for holders of municipals (and thus indirectly to the municipalities), they do little to reduce the flotation costs of small issuers. Since the bulk of the benefits of bond banks to municipalities are interest savings, this deficiency of the alternatives is relatively inconsequential.

The fact that bond banks may be only marginally superior risk-pooling devices to debt advisory commissions and bond insurance, at the same time they may place the credit rating of the state in some jeopardy, may hinder the further diffusion of this innovation. One method of reducing any risk to the state is the elimination of the moral obligation, thereby transforming issues of the bank into revenue bonds. While this proviso might result in slightly lower interest savings to participants, it can reduce the opposition of well-rated, large issuers in a state.

V. Conclusion

The bond bank is an institution that can lower the costs of issuing small debts by poorly rated municipalities in states with high credit ratings. The major mechanism of cost reduction is ratings arbitrage, while economies of scale in flotation costs are a minor mechanism. The success of this innovation in terms of its survival and in the savings enjoyed by participants suggests that there are profitable opportunities for risk pooling in the municipal bond market. These risk-pooling benefits are independent of the fate of the tax-exempt status of municipals. The slowness of the diffusion of this innovation among potential adopting states may reflect the rise of alternatives which impose less perceived risks on taxpayers of municipalities unlikely to participate. Elimination of the state's moral obligation might reduce opposition to bond banks and accelerate their diffusion.

This research was begun under a contract for the New England Regional Commission and completed under a small grant from the First National Bank of Boston. The author is indebted to Judith Payne and Fu Brice Ai for assembling the data, Peter Fortune for comments, and Stephen E. Fienberg for counsel on the logit analysis.

1. A formal description of the procedures of the Bond Banks can be found in *Prospectus for Maine Municipal Bond Banks*, 1975 Series A, B, C and D Bonds; or *Prospectus for Vermont Municipal Bond Bank*, 1972 Series A, prepared by Goldman, Sachs and Co.

2. As shown below in Tables 1 and 3, the economies of scale in flotation costs and underwriting spreads continue beyond $6 million. On the one hand, the aggregation of larger issues, would reduce the frequency of issue and entail greater delays for participating municipalities. On the other hand, more frequent but smaller bond issues, of say $1 million, would result in only slight increases in costs. The selection of $6 million as the minimum issue size is an apparent compromise between considerations of delay and cost.

3. When the Bond Banks were established in the early 1970s, Vermont and Maine had ratings of Aaa, and the Banks received ratings of Aa.

Subsequently, the ratings of these states fell to Aa, but that of the Bond Banks remained at Aa. Prospective issues of the Maine Municipal Bond Bank have been suspended as of summer 1976, pending settlement of a Federal suit over Indian land claims.

4. The analysis ends in 1976, when an Indian land claim suit in Maine temporarily suspended the national marketing of municipals.

5. Discrete multivariate analysis is undertaken with LOGLIN 1.0, a computer algorithm from the Harvard School of Public Health. The coefficients in Table 6 are the natural logs of the odds of participating in the bond banks; i.e., $\ln (p_{ij}/(1 - p_{ij}))$, where p is the proportion participating of those with characteristics i and j. For example, the coefficients in column II indicate that the odds of a small, unrated issue participating equals (anti-log $3.02 + .66 =$) 40-to-1.

6. In 1973, Puerto Rico established a Municipal Finance Agency which functions like a Bond Bank. While Puerto Rico's rating is only A1 and that of the Agency is only A, only 9 of the 78 municipalities in the Commonwealth are rated, all at A rating. This suggests that small risk-arbitrage gains may provide inducements to innovate in certain circumstances.

References

1. Fienberg, Stephen E., *The Analysis of Cross-Classified Categorical Data* (Cambridge: MIT Press, 1977).

2. Forbes, Ronald and Renshaw, Edward, "Vermont Municipal Bond Bank—A Promising Innovation," *Daily Bond Buyer*, Feb. 2, 1971.

3. Forbes, Ronald and Petersen, John, "Background Paper," in *Building a Broader Market* (New York: McGraw Hill, 1976).

4. Kessel, Reuben, "A Study of the Effects of Competition in the Tax-Exempt Bond Market," *Journal of Po-litical Economy*, 79 (July/Aug. 1971): 706-738.

5. Jarrett, James E. and Hicks, Jimmy E., *The Bond Bank Innovation: Maine's Experience* (Lexington, KY: Council of State Governments, 1977).

6. Joehnk, Michael D., "Determining the Advantages and Disadvantages of Private Municipal Bond Guarantees," *Governmental Finance*, 7 (Feb. 1978): 30-36.

7. May, Eleanor G., *Bond Banks* (Charlottesville, VA: University of Vir-

ginia Graduate School of Business Administration, 1973).

8. Municipal Finance Officers Association (MFOA), "State Bond Banks," *MFOA Special Bulletin*, E (Sept. 1, 1972).

9. New England Regional Commission, *Report of the New England Regional Commission Task Force on Capital and Labor Markets* (Nov. 12, 1975).

10. Petersen, John E., "Background Paper," in *The Rating Game* (New York: The Twentieth Century Fund, 1974).

11. Phelps, Charlotte, "The Impact of Tightening Credit on Municipal Capital Expenditures in the United States," *Yale Economic Essays*, 1 (Fall 1961): 275-321.

12. Rubinfeld, Daniel, "Credit Ratings and the Market for General Obligation Municipal Bonds," *National Tax Journal*, 26 (March 1973): 17-27.

13. Silber, William (ed.), *Financial Innovation* (Lexington, MA: D.C. Heath, 1975).

Evaluating Your City's Credit Position

———————— Martha S. Wall

Having the flexibility to borrow monies when they are needed and for the purposes they are needed is a critical issue for city managers. Investors will not lend funds to a city if the city is considered a bad risk. Without investors the city will not have the flexibility to make capital improvements at the time they are needed. Instead, the city will have to take funds from current revenues and build up a sinking fund until it can afford to pay for the improvements.

Besides the need for flexibility in borrowing, city managers need to be able to incur debt with the least possible future costs. City managers sometimes find that debt service costs are rising and the amount of funds available for direct services to citizens is decreasing. The costs of borrowing can be related to investor confidence in the city. If investors have doubts about the city's ability to pay for debt, they will expect a higher return on their investment to compensate for the risk they are taking. The higher the return to the investor, the higher the interest costs the city must pay.

This report is designed to help city managers evaluate the credit position of their city through the eyes of the investor and the credit analyst. It contains a checklist of issues that city managers and staff can use to analyze the risk to investors in lending funds to their city. The ultimate goal of this report is to increase the flexibility of the city in borrowing and to decrease the cost of issuing debt. The process of internally evaluating the credit position of a city and thereby improving its attractiveness to investors follows.

———————

Reprinted with permission from Management Information Service Reports, vol. 12, no. 6 (Washington, D.C.: International City Management Association, June 1980). This report resulted from a finance management project funded by the National Science Foundation.

Factors in evaluating risk

Credit analysts Credit analysts measure risk by evaluating a city's financial condition.[1] A checklist of pertinent issues is described later in the section, "How Cities Can Rate Themselves." From these categories analysts can examine a city's resources (population size, incomes, property, employment, business and industry), its ability to pay debt, and the responsiveness of the mayor, council, and city manager to citizen needs and problems.

The total resources a city can tap to pay for debt depends on the:

1. Present and expected level of resources available to the city;
2. Present level and type of citizen demands for services;
3. Degree of local autonomy; and
4. Spending philosophies of citizens and elected officials.

A city's willingness to tap its resources and its ability to effectively manage them are seen in its:

1. Past record of revenue raising and expected future performance;
2. Past, present, and expected level of service delivery;
3. Management of debt structure, particularly with respect to debt service;
4. Other legal claims on taxing ability such as pensions;
5. Management of cash flow fund balances; and
6. Level of deterioration and obsolescence in the capital plant.

Finally, the future responsiveness of elected officials and managers to community needs and the symptoms of fiscal problems are gleaned from the level of officials' involvement and understanding of financial policy development and the types of existing tools, practices, and policies.

City managers From the point-of-view of the city manager, borrowing is a risk for several reasons. If the city cannot repay the principal and interest on the debt obligations, future credit lines will be either nonexistent or very costly. If the value of bond instruments decreases due to national economic circumstances, competition between cities for investors will increase. To make an obligation look relatively more attractive, the city might have to offer higher yields or profits to investors. If the city does not plan for increases in inflation during the budget year or does not receive adequate revenues, paying for debt may cause other programs and services to suffer.

Investors Investors are diverse in their economic status and location. The majority of holders of municipal bonds are commercial banks, fire and casualty companies, municipal bond investment funds, and individual persons. Other investors in municipal bonds are state and local retirement funds, mutual savings banks, life insurance companies, state and local governments, and other miscellaneous financial institutions.[2] These bond holders can be either located in your community or anywhere throughout the country. In general, the smaller the bond issue, the less likely it is that you'll have investors from all over.

The reasons why investors buy municipal bonds are decisive.[3] The security of such bonds is considered by some analysts to be second to only U.S. government securities. Their diversity enables investors to obtain bonds that are issued in the geographical area of their preference and that mature at the time they wish, whether for a short-, medium-, or long-term investment program. They are marketable and can be resold or used as collateral for a loan. Most important in investors' decisions is that the municipal bond interest income is exempt from all federal income tax.

Bond ratings

How investors use bond ratings   Many investors do not have the time, money, or inclination to perform a thorough analysis of the financial condition of all the cities which issue bonds. Yet they need such information to be able to make a decision on which city (or cities) to invest in.[4] That's where the credit analysts come in.

According to Fitch Investors Service, the aim of credit analysis is to:

1. Evaluate the *ability* of the issuer to pay its debts;
2. Evaluate the *willingness* of the issuer to pay its debts;
3. Determine whether there are *significant features of weakness* that may lead to trouble in the future; and
4. Assist in comparison of one issuer with another, or *categorize the credit by level of quality.*

Credit analysts fill the need for investors to have the financial information of cities analyzed and summarized so that the risk of investing in one city over others is reasonably measured. The result of the credit analyst's evaluation is a rating of the quality of the bond issue.

Investors use bond ratings to measure credit worthiness and the return on the investment relative to the security's credit quality. The bond market is so large—over 120,000 issues are sold and resold each year—that investors need a shorthand way of comparing one bond issue with another. For the large investor who has credit analysts on his staff, the bond rating is only one factor taken into account (in its own internal review of the city's financial condition). The small investor relies more heavily on the bond rating. He uses the rating as a screening device to limit the number of securities eligible for investment, or he may only invest in those securities that are conservatively acceptable.

Banks have regulations that determine which types of rated securities they may invest in. Because of these regulations, banks have reduced in-house evaluation of municipal securities options, deferring to the opinion of credit rating agencies. Underwriters who trade in municipal bonds must know the differences between bonds, since their business is highly competitive. They use bond ratings to match borrowers with investors.

Technically, bond ratings only measure the probability that the municipality will pay back the principal and interest on securities. They are not designed to measure investor returns or the amount of interest the municipality must pay. Bond ratings influence investor yields and interest rates by measuring the degree of risk of the bond issue. To summarize the investor's viewpoint, the higher the rating the greater the marketability of the bond issue, the lower the yield or return on the issue, the easier it is to find a market, the less exposure to a downrating, and the less exposure to market reversals.

What bond ratings measure   Credit analysts such as Moody's Investors Service, Standard & Poor's Corporation, and Fitch Investors Service analyze the components of financial condition (described earlier in terms of a city's resources, ability to pay debt, and leaders' responsiveness). The result of the analysis is a rating of the city's bond issue.

Moody's and Standard & Poor's employ essentially the same symbols and definitions for their bond ratings. Table 1 shows the symbols and shorthand definitions for each grade or rating.

The narrow definition of a credit rating is a judgment of the relative degree of probability of the repayment when due—in other words, the probability of default. Some analysts believe that this definition is too narrow and maintain that ratings measure credit risk, which is the risk of future developments adverse to the interest of the creditor. Two risks that are adverse to the creditor are the risk that bond quality will be diluted by an inordinate increase in debt, and that the ability to meet maturing bond principal and interest may be impaired under depressed conditions.

What bond ratings do not measure   Bond ratings do not measure the yield or return to the investor. Ratings influence the return because of their acceptance by investors and others as a measure of the credit worthiness of the municipality. The ratings also do not measure the interest rate to the issuer. Generally, the higher the rating the lower the cost of borrowing. This condition is again due to the acceptance of the rating.

Further, the ratings do not attempt to measure the performance of the issue as it enters the bond market. The bond rating is one fac-

Moody's	Standard & Poor's
Aaa—Best quality; interest payments are protected by a large and stable margin and principal is secure.	AAA—Capacity to pay interest and principal is extremely strong.
	AA—Strong capacity to repay, but differs from AAA in a small degree.
Aa—High quality; margins of protection may not be as strong as Aaa securities.	A—More susceptible to adverse changes in circumstances and economic conditions than higher rated categories.
A—Elements exist which suggest a susceptibility to impairment in the future.	
Baa—Protective elements bond holders desire may be lacking, and susceptible to changes in economic conditions.	BBB—Adverse economic conditions or changing circumstances are more likely to weaken capacity to repay principal and interest.
Ba—Future cannot be well assured, therefore is a speculative rating.	BB—Predominately speculative with respect to capacity to repay obligations.
B—Lacks characteristics of a desirable investment.	B and CC—Highest levels of speculation.
A1 and Baa1—Designates within the A and Baa categories bonds which have maximum security, may be upgraded, and are relatively more attractive than others in the A or Baa categories.	Plus (+) and Minus (−)—Can be added to AA through BB category to show the relative standing within these categories.

Table 1. Rating symbols and definitions.

tor used to influence market performance. Others are the decision of the investor to buy or not to buy the bonds at the credit quality suggested by the rating, and the decision of the investor either to buy the bonds at the yields offered, or to put his or her money in alternative investments.[5]

The ratings are not objective judgments of the financial solvency of the city. Many objective measures are used, but the weight or importance attached to the measures are essentially subjective judgments of the credit analysts. Some nonqualifiable factors are taken into consideration. So, ratings are judgments or opinions that are given great weight in investor decisions.

The relationship between bond ratings and interest rates There is some controversy between credit analysts and finance researchers on how much the bond rating affects interest costs. Some believe that the bond rating has a minimal impact on borrowing costs. They believe that the bond market will anticipate when a community is of better or worse investment quality and that the bond raters merely catch up with changes that have already been made in the market. Others believe that the bond rating has a major impact on investors' decisions and therefore affects costs to the city.

Although there have been many studies made on how much the bond rating affects interest costs, no definitive answer or set of data exists to support either argument. A cautious summation: bond ratings influence, not measure, issuer interest rates.

Which cities need a rating   The issuer of bonds uses a bond rating to enhance the marketability of the bonds and thereby to lower the cost of borrowing. For cities that go to market often and have sizeable bond offerings and a national market, it is better to have a Baa or BBB rating than none at all. Under certain circumstances below a Baa or BBB it would be best not to apply for a rating because they are published nationally. (As seen below, under other circumstances it is better to have a low rating than none at all.)

The bond issues that enter a market without a credit rating usually are small and oriented to a local market. If a city does not enter a bond market often, its issues are consistently small, and it has had a history of local investor interest, it does not need a bond rating. Bond ratings are optional, and carry a cost to the city to pay the firm which conducts an evaluation for the rating. A city must evaluate its circumstances to decide whether it wants a bond rating.

An unrated bond issue can carry some problems. First, because investors may not evaluate the worth of a bond issue other than by looking at the rating, the city may not have much of a choice other than local investors. If local investors lose confidence in the city's ability to pay back the debt, the city may have no investors. At times it is better to have a low bond rating than none at all, because some investors will buy an issue with such a rating, even if local investors will not lend the funds. Second, the unrated bond issue will have higher interest costs due to its lack of marketability. Since the issue may be limited to a local market, the municipality may not get the preferred bid (lowest net interest costs possible).[6]

How credit analysts rate bond issues   As will be seen in the final section of the report, the key to enticing investors is knowing what looks good and bad to the credit analysts and improving on the bad. Before a city can assess its credit rating as the credit analyst does, it should be familiar with the sequence leading to a city receiving a bond rating.[7]

1. The municipality applies for a rating, sends all pertinent information regarding the bond issue, and pays a fee.
2. If the city has not been rated before, it is requested to send as

much information as possible in the categories of debt, socioeconomic characteristics, administration, and current account characteristics.

3. Researchers check all the data for accuracy, completeness, and trends.
4. This information is given to one or two analysts, who are assigned to a specific geographic area by the credit firm.
5. Sometimes the analyst visits the city to talk to governmental personnel and business and civil leaders.
6. The analyst evaluates the data using correlations, comparisons, and benchmarks. The key feature is how the issue in question compares with similarly rated credits.
7. The analyst recommends a rating and presents his findings to a rating committee of senior analysts. The analysts discuss the quantitative and qualitative factors used in making the rating recommendation. The committee assigns a rating based on a compromise of various viewpoints of the committee members.
8. The rating is published in either Standard & Poor's *Bond Outlook* and *Bond Guide* or Moody's *Bond Survey*.
9. Municipalities can appeal their rating to the major credit rating agencies. Those that do are given a full hearing, and, occasionally, the firm reverses itself. When it does, the usual reason is that information not previously submitted or known has been disclosed.
10. Standard & Poor's has a policy that all ratings are reviewed 17 months from the date the financial information in the last statement was furnished to them.

How cities can rate themselves

As stated earlier, credit analysts measure risk by evaluating a city's financial condition, focusing ultimately on its resources and ability and willingness to repay debt. They move from various categories of financial condition (e.g., external influences, legislative and management policies, finance management factors, and level and quality of service delivery) to the analysis of the city's ability and willingness to repay debt. To get a bigger picture, the city can do the same thing by focusing on the areas of concern to credit analysts.

These concerns can be broken down into *environmental influences*, which include economic and demographic characteristics of the city, external legal (intergovernmental) constraints, and external economic conditions; *legislative/management policies and practices*; and *finance management*, which consists of revenues, expenditures, debt structure, operating position, unfunded liabilities, and condition of capital plant. Some of these issues may be measured; but in some cities data cannot be obtained or are too expensive.

Below are questions which management may pose to itself; where appropriate, measurements are suggested in the form of questions. These are provided as tools to help a city evaluate its own credit position and, to the extent possible, identify historical trends. There is no set rule for how long the historical trend should be, but three to five years is probably sufficient. The historical period should be long enough to show consistent changes.

With this data the city can get a feel for its credit rating (much as the credit analysts would) and begin to anticipate what the response of the credit analysts might be. This data should provide a starting point in continuing discussions on problems and strengths and on how to solve the problems while maintaining the stronger aspects of financial management.

Environmental influences

Economic and demographic characteristics

1. Is the tax base diverse? What are the types of revenue bases and the percent difference in revenues from bases?[8]
2. Is the property tax base strong? Are values declining? Is the housing stock deteriorating? What is the strength of other tax bases? What is the per capita market value of property? What are the trends in retail sales and personal income on a per capita basis? What is the growth rate of assessed value of real property?[9]
3. Are employment opportunities numerous and diverse? Is the employment base stable? What is the nature of employment? How does it compare with surrounding areas? What is the rate of unemployment? What is the percentage and percent change of employment in each industrial sector? Which are the 10 to 20 largest employers? What is their position in the regional and national economy? What is the percentage of manufacturing in durable goods industries?
4. Where do people live and work? What is the income of the citizens? How is it derived by employment source, occupation, and location of employer? What is the percentage of income from employment or from transfer payments? What is the total income by occupation, industrial sector, and location and percent differences?
5. What are the kinds of manufacturing, wholesale and retail trade, and services located in the municipality? To what extent does each of these contribute to the tax base? Has the movement of industries been into or out of the locality, or has industry been stable?
6. What is the rate of increase or decrease in population? How is the community characterized by age, sex and race? What is the percentage increase or decline in population? the percentage of population under 18 and over 65 years of age?
7. What are the geographic characteristics of the community?

Have there been or will there be any annexations? Does the municipality have any natural assets such as harbors, scenic attractions, or natural resources? What is the condition of its transportation facilities?
8. Are there educational, cultural, and recreational opportunities? What is the median education completed?

External legal (intergovernmental) constraints

1. What are the debt legal limitations? Does any law forbid the issuer from selling additional bonds without the approval of the voters? Does the state impose a limit on the amount of debt the issuer may incur? If so, what is this limit? How close is the issuer to the limit?
2. What are the limitations on the tax rate? How close are the tax rates to the legal limits?
3. What is the nature of limitations on any future bond issuance?

External economic conditions

1. How has the budget fared with respect to inflation? How does the current budget growth rate compare to the real growth rate as adjusted for inflation by using a consumer or municipal price index?
2. How has the budget fared with respect to infla-periods of economic growth or decline? What is the percentage change of unemployment rates for the Standard Metropolitan Statistical Area or county?

Legislative/management policies and practices

1. What is the form of government involved? Does it have wide-ranging authority and responsibility? Can it impose taxes without voter and/or state approval? How professional is management? What is its background and training? What is the government's administrative reputation? Is the structure and form of the financial administration such as to encourage cohesive direction and supervision? Does the community have sound budgetary practices?
2. What are the locality's future capital plans? Is the capital improvement program fiscally realistic, politically accepted, and efficiently administered?
3. For capital projects, what are the spending priorities for maintenance costs, debt service, reserve fund, renewal, and replacement?
4. Will management and elected officials raise rates if they have to?

5. Are the municipality's accounts subject to compulsory annual audit?
6. Does the municipality engage in any unprofessional financial practices (such as the movement of funds without the knowledge of the mayor and council, or cash management practices designed to deceive independent auditors)?

Finance management

Revenues

1. Are revenues increasing, decreasing, or stable? What revenues are increasing or decreasing? What is the amount and growth of state and federal aid?
2. What is the trend in tax rate collection and delinquencies? Is there prompt enforcement in the collection of delinquencies?
3. Does a project have any outstanding liens on its revenues?
4. If the city does its own assessments, do the assessments keep pace with market values? How often is property reassessed?
5. Is the revenue calendar such that cash is received when needed?
6. For capital projects, are gross or net revenues pledged? (Credit analysts prefer net revenues.)

Expenditures

1. How much of the city's expenditures are financed by intergovernmental aid? What percentage of direct general expenditures, general revenues, and own source general revenues is intergovernmental aid?
2. What are the city's expenditures per person and per household?
3. How rapidly did the budget increase (or decrease) in size?

Debt structure

1. What is the nature of the security behind the city's bonds? Is it full-faith-and-credit, nonguaranteed, or some other combination or form?
2. Has a city ever defaulted on principal or interest? Has such a default occurred in the past two decades?
3. How does the amount of currently outstanding debt compare with what will be retired? What is the average life of tax-supported debt outstanding? What is the general obligation debt service maturing in the next five years? (The usual rate of debt retirement is 15-25 years. The point is not to have too much principal and interest coming due in any one year.)
4. How much needs to be borrowed? How does the amount to be

borrowed compare with debt already outstanding? What percentage of the full value of assessed property is the total general obligation debt? What is the growth rate of the total debt compared to the growth rate of the full value of assessed property? (The majority of debt as a percent of property assessed valuation is in the 5-10 percent range. Less than 5 percent is low, greater than 10 percent is high. Per capita net debt of $400 is considered low. Debt of $900-$1,000 is considered high. Over $1,000 will constitute a negative factor in a bond rating except when there is high per capita income or high per capita market valuations on property. Per capita debt less than 10 percent of per capita income is good, 10-15 percent so-so. Per capita debt in excess of 15 percent of per capita income is considered high. A two- or three-fold increase in the ratio of per capita debt to either per capita income or property market valuations is high. A decrease in the trend is favorable.)

5. Is there a balance in the debt structure so that large amounts do not come due in any one year? What is the ratio of debt service to total expenditures? (A ratio of debt service to gross revenues less than 10 percent is comfortable. In the 20-25 percent range you are running a risk. When short-term debt is added, the ratio should be less than 40 percent.)

6. What is the level of short-term debt? For what purposes is such debt used?[10] What percentage of total expenditures are short-term indebtedness and unpaid invoices at year end? (A two-year trend of increasing short-term debt may be considered a sign of problems.)

Operating position

1. Did the operating account end the fiscal year with a surplus in balance or a deficit? What has been the trend in operating accounts?[11]

2. Does the city have sufficient liquidity to pay its bills?

3. Does the city have sufficient reserves in case of emergencies?

Unfunded liabilities

What is the policy regarding funding pension liabilities? Is the policy being followed? Is the pension funding a funded reserve system or is it paid out of current revenues each year? Is the ratio of pension fund receipts to disbursements low or about one to one?

Condition of capital plant

What is the condition of the capital plant? At what rate is it deteriorating? When were the most recent repairs made?

What looks good
- Balanced budgets
- Revenue bases with steady growth patterns
- Diversity of revenue bases
- Liquidity to pay current liabilities
- Steady employment growth rates
- Low outstanding debt at time new debt is incurred
- Even debt schedule

What looks bad
- Deficits for more than one fiscal year
- Short-term debt not retired at end of fiscal year
- Shrinking revenue bases
- Lack of revenue diversity
- Sudden large increases or decreases in population, particularly if the income of the majority of new or remaining residents is lower than necessary to support services
- Tax rates and debt amounts close to or at legal limits, particularly with shrinking revenue bases
- Large amounts of outstanding debt at time of new borrowing
- Lay-offs and/or strikes in either the public or private sector
- History of defaults or financial gimmickry

Table 2.   Factors that might make an analyst improve/downgrade a rating.

What looks good and what looks bad to credit analysts

Along with evaluating credit position through these questions, a city can gain a sense of what factors might make an analyst improve or downgrade its credit rating. Table 2 lists these factors, and Table 3 lists suggested actions for maintaining a positive relationship with credit analysts.

Enticing investors

After identifying fiscal problems from the above evaluation, the next step is to determine what areas the city can improve and what areas it cannot do much about. Then, the city should choose what procedures to develop and implement in order to bring about improvement in these areas.

1. Provide all financial information (see the section, "Enticing Investors").
2. Apply for a rating early, and give at least one month for the analyst to evaluate the issue.
3. Invite the credit analyst to visit the city, or meet at his or her office. It is usually better to show the credit analyst around the city, identifying progress and problems. Regardless of where the meeting occurs, discuss with the representatives of the rating firm all issues and questions openly and frankly. Credit analysts will become skeptical of a picture of the city that is too rosy.

Table 3.   Maintaining a positive relationship with credit analysts.

City managers can take financial action in various areas to entice investors. What follows are components of recommended action plans, all of which involve the coordinated efforts of the city manager and staff. Tables 4 and 5 break down one of these areas of financial action to be taken: the disclosure of financial information to credit analysts[12] and to investors in the bond prospectus,[13] respectively. Implementation of the following action plans will not guarantee a higher bond rating or greater investor interest. But it will show that city management is forward-looking, skilled in analysis, and anxious to please.

Debt administration

When to incur debt.   Local governments can borrow when cash flow is such that the amount of current revenues does not equal current expenses. This type of short-term borrowing is in the form of Tax or Revenue Anticipation Notes. It is permissible as long as the lack of current revenues is temporary and expected future revenue flows are more than sufficient to repay the loan within a few months. Local governments use long-term debt to finance capital assets such as land, facilities, or equipment, which have a long life span. In general, the useful life period should be no less than five years, and the period

---

a. Annual financial reports for five years
b. Budget for current year
c. Trend of revenues and expenditures for five years
d. Capital improvements program, capital budget, and sources of funds
e. Interim financial statement
f. List of all long-term debt descriptions
g. List of all short-term debt with descriptions
h. A comparison of outstanding debt for past ten years
i. Schedule of bond maturities by class of bonds
j. Identification of overlapping debt
k. Schedule of debt retirement
l. Comparative trends of debt service in past and planned for future
m. Schedule of principal maturities on outstanding debt by category
n. Full text of bond resolution or ordinance
o. Legal tax limitations
p. Assessed valuations of real estate and personal property ten years to present
q. Ratio of assessed valuation of market value
r. Tax rates, fees, and charges
s. Tax collection record for five years
t. Details on public utilities—physical facilities, consumption of utility services, and rate schedules
u. Economic and demographic data

Table 4.   Information to be disclosed to credit analysts.

a. Total principal amount of securities, name of issuer, date of obligations' principal and interest, denominations of securities, redemption features, maturity schedule, statement of tax status of interest, ratings, statement of authority for issue, summary statement of security or source of payment.

b. Description of securities (besides those covered in *a*); provisions of state constitutions and other statutes regarding debt; purposes for which proceeds of offering are going to be used; provisions relating to security and sources of payment; provisions regarding enterprise revenues, maintenance of reserves, and maintenance of insurance of properties; purposes and provisions for which additional debt may be issued; and terms of securities including modifications of bondholders' remedies.

c. Description of issuer—year in which established and form of government, elected officials, principal services performed, revenue sources for services, intergovernmental service agreements, condition and character of facilities of issuer, historical and current data on population, employment, income and industrial base, and customers and consumption of enterprises.

d. Debt structure—category of indebtedness, amount authorized, amount outstanding as of date, amount to be outstanding, debt service schedule, indebtedness of overlapping governments, historical and current information regarding per capita debt, debt to assessed valuation, debt to market value of property, debt per capita to income per capita, long-term and short-term indebtedness for past five years, debt limitations, and whether municipality has ever defaulted.

e. Financial information—summary of operations for the fund/account groups related to securities being offered, combined information regarding the general fund, description of accounting practices and budgetary process, source of payment for nonguaranteed securities, tax collection procedures and levy for past five years, description of any circumstances where proceeds of bonds were used for operating expenses, description of any circumstances where loans have been used to meet principal and interest payments, and description of pension fund liabilities and assets. In footnotes provide a summary of significant accounting policies, bond indenture provisions, long-term debt provisions, leases, provisions of pension fund, and contingencies.

f. Legal matters—describe any pending legal proceedings that may alter issuer's ability to meet debt obligations, including bond counsel's legal opinion, and state that at closing a certificate of no litigation will be provided.

Table 5.   Information to be disclosed to investors in the bond prospectus.

for repayment of the debt should be no longer than the useful life of the asset.

How much debt.   The amount of debt a locality can incur is related to its level of economic resources (i.e., the community's ability to pay now and in the future). Many states have debt limitations. It is advisable for each city to set its own limits. Here are some examples: (a) debt service on general obligations in any fiscal year should not exceed 15-35 percent of operating budget; (b) at least 10 percent of the cost of capital assets should be paid from current revenues each fiscal year; (c) at least 25 percent of the total principal payments outstanding should be retired within five years after the debt is issued; and (d) outstanding debt should not be greater than 10-15 percent of the total taxable property valuation.

What types of debt.   There are several ways to classify long-term debt. The most typical means is by the security that is pledged. The Bureau of the Census classified debt in the following way.

Full-faith-and-credit debt is long-term debt for which the taxing power of the government is unconditionally pledged. This type of debt includes debt payable from fees or charges of an enterprise. If these are insufficient, the full taxing ability of the government backs the debt. There are several advantages of full-faith-and-credit debt: it is the strongest pledge available to local government, special reserves need not be created, and it has a simple debt service structure.

Nonguaranteed debt consists of debt payable solely from earnings of revenue-producing activities, special assessments, or specific non-property taxes. A typical form of nonguaranteed debt is revenue bonds. The advantages of revenue bonds are that: they will conserve general obligation debt for nonrevenue bonds producing projects; they avoid dilution of full-faith-and-credit debt which helps maintain a higher rating for such debt; repayment of debt is distributed to users, not to the community as a whole; they can usually be issued without electoral approval; and they broaden the borrowing capacity of the government.

Preparing the bond issue.   Preparation of a bond issue entails enacting a bond ordinance, planning the size and maturity schedule of the issue, preparing a bond prospectus, and selling the bonds. To help with these efforts the city can employ various professionals. A bond attorney can review the legality of the bond issue and give an opinion on it. An official statement or bond prospectus cannot be published without this opinion. Engineers can be employed, if needed, to make estimates of the costs of the capital assets to be funded by the bonds. These estimates would be included in the prospectus.

If the city does not have the staff capabilities, consultants can be employed to perform economic analyses, to sell market potential of the bonds, and/or to prepare the bond prospectus. Finally, a certified public accountant can be employed to audit and give an opinion on the financial statements and financial information in the prospectus.

Management of debt service.   Each bond issue should have a separate financial account. The accounts should show at any time the amount outstanding, the amount of principal, and interest paid. A debt service schedule should be established for the payment of principal and interest by maturity date. Funds from the operating budget should be set aside to meet these expenses.

Operations budgeting[14]

Budget control. A budget control system should contain the following: (a) an accounting system which follows generally accepted accounting principles (GAAP), as recommended by the National Council of Governmental Accounting and the Municipal Finance Officers Association, and endorsed with interpretations by the American Institute of Certified Public Accountants; (b) a budgetary accounting system which reserves funds prior to the issuance of purchase orders; (c) a reporting system which provides for periodic reports of revenues and appropriations; (d) purchasing and personnel procedures which provide for orderly expenditure of personnel and other expense funds; and (e) continual budget review to relate spending to revenue sources.

Examples of practices that impair budgetary control include excessive use of confirming and emergency purchases for which purchase orders have not been issued, abuse of emergency appropriations, and abuse of budget transfers.

Cash management[15]

Administrative framework. A framework should be set up for establishing and maintaining policies to perform the cash management program, establishing annual objectives for the program, and evaluating the ongoing performance of the program.

Cash budget. This is a monthly estimation of receipts and disbursements which determines cash availability and develops an investment strategy. The cash budget should be prepared using historical information and knowledge of future events, updated on a regular basis, and should be used to make investment decisions.

Cash information and control systems. A formal system should provide information for cash accounting, cash budget status reporting, investment status and earnings reporting, reconciliation of cash accounts with bank records, and performance reporting. The system consists of computer-based or manual systems producing daily or periodic reports on cash received, committed cash, and cash disbursed.

Collection, deposit and disbursement practices. Revenue collection policies should be developed for each revenue source. Special deposit procedures should be implemented to handle major processing problems such as the property tax, and should be established for each type of revenue and collection location. And disbursement policies should be established for each type of expenditure and category of vendor.

Borrowing. Borrowing should be conducted within federal arbitrage regulations. Revenues from bonds should be invested immediately. Short-term borrowing should be limited and repayment related to the future receipt of a specific revenue.

Banking cash. The locality should know the banking services available. It should know the bank's cost of providing each service. There should be periodic competition among banks for the locality's deposits, daily competition among banks to get the best values for making investments, and periodic review of banking relationships.

Investing cash. The cash manager should know the different characteristics of securities, the yields of different securities, the securities that the locality is permitted to invest, and the mechanics of security transactions. The locality should have an investment strategy to govern actions to be taken on a day-to-day basis to achieve the maximum yield on cash for investment.

Conclusion

Investors and credit analysts are becoming more and more sophisticated in their analysis of municipal bonds. They are using computer-based systems, financial consultants, and certified public accountants to evaluate the financial condition of local governments. Increasingly, they will be more demanding of local governments to supply them with financial information and to adopt accepted standards for financial management. To attract investors, city management has to be one step ahead of them in assessing the city's financial condition.

With inflation ever increasing, local governments will be issuing debt in greater amounts as paying for capital items from current revenues becomes more unfeasible. Local governments will have greater competition from other local governments for funds to support capital improvements. So, city managers must be kept apprised of developments in the bond market, changes in old procedures or developments of new ones in the areas of financial and debt management, and changes in the socioeconomic and physical characteristics of the community.

Finally, departments should be informed of those things that might alter investor interest and credit ratings, and they should be responsible for keeping the city manager informed about these developments. Periodic analyses of the city's financial condition and the progress of its action plans, described above, should be undertaken.

For a more detailed discussion of most of the issues covered in this report, see the footnotes and references below.

1. U.S. Congress, House, Committee on Interstate and Foreign Commerce, *Municipal Bonds Rating Regulation*, 94th Congress, second session, on H.R. 675 (Washington, D.C.: U.S. Government Printing Office, 1976), pp. 76-77.
2. Alan Rabinowitz, *Municipal Bond Finance and Administration* (New York: John Wiley and Sons, 1969), p. 61.
3. Investment Bankers Association of America, *Fundamentals of Municipal Bonds*, 6th ed. (Washington, D.C.: Investment Bankers Association of America), pp. 27-28.
4. Twentieth Century Fund Task Force on Municipal Bond Credit Ratings, *The Rating Game*, with Background Paper by John Peterson (New York: The Twentieth Century Fund, 1974), p. 5.
5. Lennox Moak, *Administration of Local Governmental Debt* (Chicago: Municipal Finance Officers Association, 1970), pp. 169-170.
6. Hyman Grossman, "The S & P Municipal Bond Rating Process," Presentation to the Annual Conference of the North Carolina Public Finance Officers' Association, Institute of Government, The University of North Carolina at Chapel Hill, 1978, p. 7.
7. Hugh Sherwood, *How Corporate and Municipal Debt is Rated: An Inside Look at Standard & Poor's Rating System* (New York: John Wiley & Sons, 1976), pp. 21-26.
8. Elizabeth Dickson, "Fiscal Trends: Local Revenue Bases, Expenditures, and Tax Burdens," Working Paper No. 09-0251-08 (Washington, D.C.: The Urban Institute, January 1978), p. 13.
9. Lennox Moak and Albert Hillhouse, *Concepts and Practices in Local Governmental Finance* (Chicago: Municipal Finance Officers Association, 1975), p. 396; Moak, op. cit., p. 106; Sherwood, op. cit., p. 120.
10. Richard Aronson and Eli Schwartz, "Determining Debt's Danger Signals," *Management Information Service Report*, Vol. 8, No. 12 (Washington, D.C.: International City Management Association, December 1976), p. 14.
11. Brian Cooper, "Short-Term Warning Signals—Deficits, Liquidity, and Cash Flow," Working Paper No. 09-0251-02 (Washington, D.C.: The Urban Institute, January 1978), p. 3.
12. Moody's Investors Service, Inc., *Pitfalls in Issuing Municipal Bonds* (New York: Moody's Investors Service, Inc., 1974), pp. 35-36.
13. Municipal Finance Officers Association, *Disclosure Guidelines for Offerings of Securities by State and Local Governments* (Chicago: Municipal Finance Officers Association, 1976).
14. Arthur Mohor, *Budget Preparation and Control* (Athens: University of Georgia, Institute of Government), pp. 43-77.
15. Frank Patitucci and Michael Lichtenstein, *Improving Cash Management in Local Government: A Comprehensive Approach* (Chicago: Municipal Finance Officers Association, 1977), pp. 7-10.

Additional readings

Aronson, J. Richard and Schwartz, Eli. "Determining Debt's Danger Signals." *Management Information Service Report.* Vol. 8, No. 12. International City Management Association. December 1976. A broad statistical picture of what is happening in the municipal bond market. Includes a checklist and two hypothetical case studies showing how to measure your community's debt burden to protect your bond rating and maintain your fiscal health.

Moak, Lennox. *Administration of Local Government Debt.* Municipal Finance Officers Association. 1970. Presents an overview of the forces in the municipal bond market and the influence of various interested parties on the availability and cost of municipal bonds. Describes procedures for planning debt, determining debt policy, securing specialized services, scheduling debt issuance, determining bond features, determining the interest cost and best bid, and marketing the bonds.

Moody's Investors Service, Inc. *Pitfalls in Issuing Municipal Bonds.* 1974. Discusses what a bond rating is and why it is important to local governments. Describes some of the mistakes local administrators make under the topic headings: inadequate legal advice, incomplete or unfavorable financial history, inconveniences for the investor, faulty timing on the way to market, failure to advertise the issue the right way, and poor public relations.

Smith, Wade S. *The Appraisal of Municipal Credit Risk.* Moody's Investors Service, Inc. New York, New York. 1979. A "how-to" manual about learning to form sound credit judgments. Describes the concepts and procedures actually used by professionals in forming credit judgments on state and local borrowers, and in setting municipal bond and note ratings.

Twentieth Century Fund Task Force on Municipal Bond Credit Ratings, with background paper by Peterson, John E. *The Rating Game.* The Twentieth Century Fund. New York, New York. 1974. Evaluates the rating system in view of the changed nature of the market and the increased demands with which it has had to cope. Considers such questions as whether the current practice of having communities pay to be rated is fair and appropriate, whether the criteria for ratings are clear and equitable, whether the ratings are adjusted in timely fashion, and what changes, if any, should be undertaken to make ratings more accurate and sensitive.

The Battle to Advise Municipalities

Diane Hal Gropper

When the finance director of a large East Coast county needed to arrange some short-term financing in the spring of 1980, he turned as a matter of course to the county's traditional financial adviser, a well-known "independent"—or non-underwriting—counselor. The advice seemed perfectly sound, and the finance director duly adopted it. But no sooner had he done so than county officials were taken aback by a visit from some eager emissaries of an investment bank—who "took it upon themselves to second-guess and strongly criticize" the independent's advice. The finance director shakes his head: "That investment bank tried to cloak it 'in the best interests of the county,' but the reality is that they wanted our advisory business."

The head of debt finance for another large municipal issuer recalls a similar story, where the tables were turned. This time an independent adviser, in the course of making a pitch for the issuer's business, learned that an investment banking firm was after the same account—whereupon he launched into a scathing attack on the competing firm, accusing it of having an "underhanded relationship" with the issuer's lead underwriter and being incapable of delivering unbiased counsel.

While their tactics may be more brazen than most, that adviser and banker are hardly unique in pursuing an increasingly remunerative business: advising the nation's tax-exempt issuers on how to raise money and solve other financial problems. Today, the competition among independents, big investment banking firms and commercial banks for that advisory dollar is plainly picking up. And while few believe it has reached the pitch of the scramble for tax-exempt underwriting business (*Institutional Investor*, June 1981),

Reprinted with permission from *Institutional Investor*, January 1982.

the field is getting sufficiently crowded that finance directors of major issuers can virtually count on being courted—probably aggressively—by would-be advisers.

The business of tendering advice to tax-exempt clients is, of course, not new. What *is* new is the phenomenal growth in demand for such services. "The biggest change in this business," says Jean Rousseau, managing director of Merrill Lynch's public finance group, "is that advising has come to be a significant part of the overall financial exercise in recent years." Five years ago, adds Samuel Katz, president of Public Financial Management, an independent firm, "it was tough to convince issuers they needed an adviser. That's not a problem anymore."

There are good reasons why even large, well-known issuers boasting sophisticated in-house staffs increasingly turn to financial advisers:

1. Growing financial woes. Many public issuers are in dire financial straits as a result of years of overall financial and debt mismanagement, and are burdened with declining credit ratings. More are enlisting the aid of financial advisers to bring order to their financial houses.
2. High interest rates. High and volatile interest rates have made it tougher to bring badly needed financing to market and so have spawned new kinds of deals such as option bonds or bonds with warrants. Complex and difficult to structure, price and manage, they frequently demand the expertise of a financial adviser.
3. More negotiated deals. More issuers are going the negotiated route, in part because of volatile markets. Then, too, Proposition 13 fever has curtailed the issuance of tax revenue-backed general obligation bonds and given rise to more revenue bond issues. Because of their complexity, these deals are usually brought on a negotiated basis. Many issuers understandably feel more comfortable these days with a financial adviser at their side when they sit down to bargain with a syndicate of underwriters.

New entries

Not surprisingly, supply has responded quickly to this burgeoning demand. A whole new crop of independent advisers has sprung up since the mid-1970s, joining the numerous large and regional independents that constitute the industry's "old guard." Of the new firms, three have been particularly impressive in wooing new clients. New York's James J. Lowrey & Co. has about 50 clients and was founded in 1979, as was Government Finance Associates, with 25 clients. Public Financial Management in Philadelphia is three years older and has about 40 clients. All three firms offer advice on long-term financial strategies as well as more immediate recommendations on the timing, structure and pricing of deals.

It is in the latter area that these independents have caused no small amount of grief for investment bankers, many of whom claim that, as lead underwriters in negotiated deals, they provide all the financial advice an issuer could possibly need. As a result, underwriters have increasingly resisted the hiring of independent advisers because it can drive a wedge between them and their clients. "Certain firms have voiced very negative reactions to our clients when we're hired as financial advisers," gripes Chester Johnson, president of Government Finance Associates. But then he wryly adds, "After all, the more folks there are in the kitchen, the greater chance they'll bump into one another."

The investment banks' discomfiture is not altogether pitiable; many of the larger ones are competing more aggressively with the independents by undertaking more pure advisory work themselves instead of simply rendering advice as lead underwriters. And the zeal with which they pursue the business varies widely. Blyth Eastman Paine Webber, for instance, has been doing advisory work for more than two decades and boasts a roster of more than 50 clients. Lazard Frères currently serves about 25 clients and, since senior partner Felix Rohatyn spearheaded the New York City bailout, has become even more aggressive in the advisory field. Although Lehman Brothers Kuhn Loeb has only been at advisory work for about four years, the firm already caters to twenty clients. By contrast, Goldman Sachs, First Boston, John Nuveen & Co., Dillon Read and Smith Barney, Harris Upham have moved into advisory work on a more limited scale, and Merrill Lynch and Salomon Brothers have shied away from the field almost completely.

In their case, abstinence may be the wiser policy. They and other investment banks that have hesitated to plunge headlong into pure financial advisory work are mindful of the fact that, in many instances, it can preclude them from the much more profitable activity of underwriting for a particular client. The Municipal Securities Rulemaking Board's rule G-23 specifies that an underwriter can act simultaneously as financial adviser to an issuer and bid competitively for the issuer's bonds, provided the issuer has no objections. But in a negotiated deal, an underwriter can only participate in the syndicate if it first obtains the issuer's permission to end its formal advisory role.

Underwriters with large distribution networks and a high overhead, such as Blyth Eastman, have thus found advising in competitive deals the more attractive option. "We can't assure our system a product, so we feel more free to enter an advisory relationship," explains Blyth's Stanley Pardo, head of public finance. But in negotiated deals where underwriting is so much more lucrative, big underwriters prefer to offer advice as lead underwriters and not as pure financial advisers, since the latter course "would deny merchandise to their sales forces," explains John Noonan, managing director of public finance at John Nuveen. Conversely, although Lazard Frères has built up its distribution network considerably in recent years, the firm's municipal underwriting capability is still relatively modest—which explains its predilection for advising issuers that customarily go the negotiated route. As John Tamagni, partner in charge of municipal finance concedes, "We are making a virtue out of a necessity."

Foot in the door

That may be so, but the big investment banks have found advisory slots in negotiated deals alluring for other reasons. Blyth's Pardo cites one: For large issuers where "the underwriting relationships have already been determined," advising can be a profitable alternative because fees are often set on a per-bond-issued basis; larger issuers can also better afford fixed or hourly rate fees. John Nuveen's Noonan is equally enthusiastic. "Advising can add a lot to the bottom line," he points out, adding that it is virtually risk-free compared to underwriting in volatile markets. And not to be overlooked as a motive is the decline in overall municipal financing last year, with the resultant squeeze on some firms' underwriting revenues. Lazard's Tamagni suspects that these firms may be trying to refashion their surplus underwriting personnel into "advisers," at least "to the extent that they are able to in order to cover overhead and keep incomes up." Especially inclined toward such activity, he says, are those banks that "built their nightclubs for New Year's Eve."

Still, the real reason for the heightened interest in advisory work may be more subtle—but also much more significant for the investment banks' long-term strategy. Many plainly view an advisory role as a foot in the door for future underwriting. "The banks aren't blatant about wanting to do underwriting later, but the motivation is definitely there," says one large, sought-after issuer. "[Advisory work] enables them to get to know about an issuer's operations and needs and gives them a real advantage relative to other firms." Salomon Brothers' head of public finance, Gedale Horowitz agrees that the prospect of future underwriting business has been "one of the main considerations for investment bankers in taking on advisory work."

An investment banker-adviser that holds out the hope of becoming a client's underwriter is not entertaining an unreasonable expectation. After having advised the Maryland Health and Higher Educational Facilities Authority for about five years, Smith Barney decided that "for the long haul we'd prefer underwriting," says vice president Louis Hauptfleisch. So the firm resigned—and, barely six months later, co-managed a bond issue for the authority.

Waiting in the wings

Clearly, there's plenty to tempt an investment bank into biding its time (profitably) as an adviser until it can be rewarded with an underwriting role. But what about commercial banks, which by law cannot underwrite most municipal revenue bonds? What accounts for their seemingly even greater enthusiasm for advising? For example, Bank of America, in the business for a decade, counsels some 50 clients; Morgan Guaranty Trust has steadily expanded its advisory capacity since the mid-1970s and now dispenses advice to about 40 clients; Chemical Bank, having launched its advisory service in 1981, already numbers twelve clients; and Bank of New York, Chase Manhattan and several other banks are proving equally eager to peddle their advice.

The overriding explanation appears to be that the commercial banks fancy themselves investment banks-in-waiting; they look forward to the day—perhaps not so far off—when the Glass-Steagall Act will be modified (or dropped) and they can underwrite cities' and counties' revenue bonds along with investment banks. So advisory positions "afford opportunities for exposure in all facets of the market and development of reasonable ties with issuers," explains John Olds, head of public finance at Morgan Guaranty. Moreover, advising tends to be relatively more profitable for commercial banks than for investment banks, simply because the commercial banks' underwriting is currently restricted to general obligation and only certain revenue bonds.

As more independents and underwriters have crowded into the advisory market, the competition has tended to center around a touchy question: Who is better suited to counsel tax-exempt issuers? The independents have two aces: specialization in one activity and the fact that they don't underwrite, which frees them from conflicts of interest that can arise for an investment or commercial bank adviser. "All the independents sell is knowledge and total objectivity," says an approving Randolf Rosencrantz, director of finance for Baltimore County. Chester Johnson, president of Government Finance Associates, which advises Baltimore County, sees the "Who's best" issue in terms of focus. "Either you're structured intellectually and organizationally to be an underwriter or an adviser," he declares. "You can't be both." (Although James Lowrey recently became the only major independent with an underwriting operation, he claims he won't be underwriting for advisory clients.)

Johnson and the other independents are quick to contend that an investment or commercial bank's underwriting activities can color its financial advice all too easily. Take the case, says Public Financial Management's Katz, of one of the largest regional issuers in the country, whose financial adviser happens to be an investment bank. Considering that many major investment banks underwrite this issuer's bonds, and that its investment bank adviser routinely underwrites other unrelated deals with these same banks, well, "aren't there opportunities for conscious or unconscious cooperation?" Katz asks. Elaborating on his implied conspiracy theory, he notes that the adviser could conceivably tread softly in its negotiations with the agency's lead underwriter in order to maintain good relations with that investment bank—with which it might be co-managing an unrelated deal. No one can prove these things happen, Katz allows, but "because the same parties are dealing with each other all the time, the potential for collusion is there and the appearance of a conflict of interest is strong."

GFA's Johnson tells of an instance where a major investment bank, acting as financial adviser to an agency, allegedly went along with an overly generous fee structure proposed by the agency's syndicate of underwriters. The financial adviser failed to deliver an "arm's-length opinion" on the fee structure, he claims, because it found that structure attractive in its own underwriting deals. And Johnson is even more critical of firms that plan to move from the advisory to the underwriting side and of lead underwriters that give financial advice. In those cases, he feels, there is great temptation for the underwriter to recommend the kinds of securities or issue structure it would find easiest to sell. As a case in point, he cites one senior manager who counseled an issuer to establish a special reserve fund against a debt issue, which probably would have made the issue easier to sell. But GFA counseled the client against the special fund because its establishment would imply that the issuers' debt structure wasn't sound, invariably increasing its long-term interest costs.

Toothless wonder?

The MSRB's rule G-23 does afford issuers some protection in theory by requiring that a financial adviser who moves over to underwriting disclose this potential conflict of interest to the issuer. But Johnson charges that G-23 is just a "toothless wonder," because it doesn't deal with the potential problem of collusion. And as to the disclosure provision, he scoffs, "anyone who thinks that solves the conflict of interest problem needs to have his head checked." Mere disclosure of a potential conflict doesn't eliminate the potential, he argues. And G-23's supposed toothlessness may be reflected in the fact that some underwriters apparently don't even bother to "resign and disclose." One regional investment banker openly admits his firm acts both as formal financial adviser to some clients and underwriter of their issues in negotiated arrangements, so long as it is not the sole underwriter. "It all depends on how you interpret G-23," he explains.

At least one investment banker, Salomon's Horowitz, finds G-23's purported loopholes regrettable. As chairman of the MSRB when G-23 was passed in 1979, he voted against it, and would have preferred that bankers be barred from underwriting when they're also advising. Says Horowitz, "I've seen too many cases in which firms advise right up until the deal comes, and then waive their fee and get permission to move over and underwrite. To me, that's not what a financial adviser should do because there's an absolute conflict of interest." Yet, even though he personally doesn't like the idea of switching over, Salomon is considering doing more advisory work (it only has about five clients) with an eye to moving over to underwriting. Switching over has become so commonplace, concedes Horowitz, that "we're losing opportunities for underwriting business."

A yellow flag

Not surprisingly, other investment and commercial bankers don't concur with his assessment of the conflict of interest potential. Many bankers say they write a clause into their advisory contracts stipulating that they will not underwrite for the issuer while they are an adviser if the issuer requests such protection. Still other bankers— Blyth's Pardo, for example—claim that many issuers are not the least bit concerned that switching over poses the risk of a serious conflict of interest. "Some of our clients don't want us to do it, some don't care and some actually want us to eventually underwrite," says Pardo. In fact, adds Christopher Taylor, executive director of the MSRB, rule G-23 is designed to allow each issuer to make its own judgment on the conflict of interest issue; the disclosure process "raises a yellow flag, asks the issuer to think, and then make its own decision," he explains.

Issuer sentiment on the subject does indeed vary. The executive director of the State Bond Advisory Division in Mississippi, Grover Allen, believes issuers are becoming increasingly averse to advisers switching over; he pledges to do everything in his power to prevent it in Mississippi. "It just doesn't look good to the public," he explains. "I don't blame the banks for trying to do it, but if I let them get by with it I have to sleep with it at night." On the other hand, the treasurer of the Washington Public Power Supply System, James Perko, didn't think there was any conflict of interest when Blyth moved over from WPPSS' financial adviser to co-manager early last year. "We don't allow switching back and forth," he says, but in that case the switch made sense because of Blyth's large underwriting capability.

Needless to say, many bankers also dispute the independents' charge that they are incapable of giving unbiased counsel. No bank can get away with giving bad or self-serving advice as either an adviser or lead underwriter, insists Richard Tauber, vice president in charge of marketing in the public finance department at Morgan Guaranty. "This is as competitive a piece of turf as you can find," he says. "If you give bad advice, you'll find you are replaced."

In justifying their role, bankers also take the offensive. Underwriters are simply better suited to dispense advice than independents, they reason, because they make markets. The independents have to garner their market information secondhand from a variety of underwriters. Stanley Pardo of Blyth puts it plainly: "There's no way you can be in touch with the market if you don't have money and deals at risk on a daily basis." The head of public finance at a commercial bank picks up this theme: The "secondhand information" independents collect from underwriters can easily be off the mark in volatile markets. He says he has seen several instances where independent advisers brought competitive deals to market for their clients and didn't receive a single bid because they'd misjudged current market conditions.

A bogus issue?

Not all issuers buy the "market maker" thesis. Boston's treasurer, Lowell Richards, says the fact that independents don't underwrite doesn't worry him at all. Any good independent—including Boston's adviser, GFA—has former "investment bankers on staff and good relations with many houses," he notes. And James Lowrey thinks it's all a bogus issue. "The markets are no different than putting on your shoes in the morning," he says. "They can tell you there's a bogeyman in the closet, but if you know the market, you know it no matter what."

Nonetheless, a number of issuers prefer to have an investment or commercial bank for an adviser because of their direct involvement in the markets. The Alaska Housing Finance Corp., for example, has traditionally leaned toward investment bankers as advisers; John Nuveen is its current financial adviser. They have a better feel for who's buying securities and how best to get a deal done, explains Harry Goldbar, executive director. "They're just better versed and better informed on market conditions on a daily basis."

The MSRB's Taylor makes a related point that echoes a grievance of many bankers: "Anyone can go out and hang up a shingle as an independent because there are no regulations or minimum requirements." He has proposed to Congress that the MSRB also regulate the independents. Cautions Taylor, "Being an independent doesn't necessarily mean that you're all clean and going to provide good advice."

Despite the sometimes nasty squabbling between independents and banks over customers, the market for their services appears to be fast growing and diverse enough to allow for prosperous coexistence. After all, notes Herman Charbonneau of Chemical Bank, between the drying up of institutional demand for municipal securities, tax law changes and the volatile markets, issuers in the future are "going to need all the good financial advice they can get." Edward DeSeve, director of finance for the city of Philadelphia, estimates that the independents have tapped only about 10 per cent of the potential market and the banks another 10 per cent, leaving 80 per cent up for grabs. Offhand, that suggests a competitive free-for-all. Yet that prospect in part depends on how vigorously each group pursues new business and what kinds of clients are deemed most attractive.

Optimum target

One pattern is firmly established, however: The optimum target is the large, frequent issuer whose size alone makes the adviser's labor worthwhile. Almost two-thirds of Lowrey's work, for instance, is in the public power area, where issuers tend to be Brobdingnagian. And the other independents are concentrating on large cities, states and counties as well. Moreover, commercial bankers seem especially committed to big issuers. Bank of America, for example, is establishing a "coast-to-coast posture," reveals head of public finance, Merrill Ring, with special emphasis on "states and state agencies, not local issuers, which sell securities the bank can't underwrite." B of A's preference for sticking to areas where it has had direct underwriting experience explains why the bank tends to offer counsel to water, sewer and housing bond issuers and not public power or health care entities. "It just wouldn't be fair to the client," says Ring.

Morgan Guaranty, by contrast, is unfazed by the current underwriting constraints and is expanding its advisory work in a broad but selective fashion, emphasizing large investment-grade or better issuers in many areas, including public power. Richard Tauber explains: "There's nothing mystical about this business. If we don't have immediate expertise in a given area, we can learn pretty quickly." He adds that "expertise from the lending side helps us rapidly move up the learning curve."

Investment banks—even those that don't plan to greatly boost their advisory work—tend to be enamored of large clients as well. Although Blyth Eastman has found "a fairly comfortable balance between advisory work and underwriting," says Pardo, the firm will still take on advisory "projects of sufficient size and significance"— especially when a negotiated underwriting is out of the question. Robert Downey, head of the municipal bond department at Goldman Sachs, admits that "if we can't be an investment banker, we're happy to be a financial adviser," particularly to large and complicated issuers. Likewise, reports Tamagni, Lazard Frères is on the lookout for "large issuers with large visible problems" of the kind experienced by decaying cities, troubled utilities and collapsing transportation systems. And Lehman Brothers is "aggressively and selectively pursuing" housing, health care and public power business, according to managing director Austin Koenen.

If the really intense competition is to be over big-ticket issuers— as is clearly the case—investment bankers may have the real edge: their greater underwriting and market expertise, compared to independents and even commercial banks. Boston's Richards, for example, believes that large issuers that have "big problems and need some overkill" might be better off with an investment banker adviser. "Inherently," he notes, "the resources available to an investment bank are much greater." Significantly, one major issuer, the Washington Public Power Supply System, glanced over some independents when it was seeking a financial adviser last year but chose not to interview any of them. In the end, says WPPSS' Perko, the utility selected Lazard Frères, because of its "demonstrated experience of dealing with large, complex financial problems in the past."

Tough sledding

Many independents and investment bankers alike think the commercial banks will find it very tough to make headway with large issuers in areas—like public power—where they have not been able to underwrite. Indeed, Bank of America's Ring fears commercial banks "have a long way to go" on this score. However, at least one commercial banker, Morgan Guaranty's Tauber, strongly disagrees. Morgan, he points out, recently bested a major investment bank and an independent in winning its first joint-action public power agency advisory position (Indiana Municipal Power). He expects more of the same. Commercial banks offer large issuers a "broader range of understanding of total financing needs" as well as more services than investment banks, Tauber boasts. Goldman Sachs' Downey does not deny that investment bankers feel some trepidation about the kind of competitive threat commercial banks can pose, given their package of banking services.

The independents, for their part, seem unworried by the prospect of greater competition—and certainly don't fret that they will be locked out of the big-issuer market. James J. Lowrey & Co. already advises three major joint-action public power agencies and numerous large cities. And Public Financial Management's Katz touts the independents' ability to undercut banks' fees, thanks to lower overhead, as the key to big-ticket business. Presumably, both competitive fees *and* ability were important factors when PFM and GFA one-upped a number of investment banks for the advisory business of several large issuers last year.

Apart from attractive fees, the independents are, of course, counting on their freedom from potential conflicts to win them a big share of the future advisory business. And the bankers will be just as aggressively pushing *their* market experience as well. But in the end, the key to tax-exempt issuers' hearts may lie in a subtle quality where no one has a clear or quantifiable edge: creativity. "The market is growing," concludes James Lowrey. "And if you've got good ideas, it's all yours."

For Further Reference

Part 1: The Municipal Borrowing Crisis

Bagwell, M. N.; Evans, M. W.; and Nielsen, M. F. "The Municipal Bond Market: An Analysis and Suggested Reform." *Harvard Journal on Legislation* 16, no. 1 (1979): 211-67.

Peirce, Neal, and Chodos, Shelby. "New Tax Law Adds to Cities' Woes By Putting Squeeze on Municipal Bonds." *National Journal*, September 5, 1981, pp. 1592-94.

Weberman, Ben. "An Irresistible Investment." *Forbes*, October 12, 1981, pp. 151-58.

Part 2: Innovative Financing Techniques

Bettner, Jill. "Once-Stodgy Municipal Bonds, Going Modern, Now Offer Flexible Yields, Shorter Maturities." *The Wall Street Journal*, December 8, 1980, p. 48.

Greenebaum, Mary. "Innovations in Tax Exempts." *Fortune*, January 25, 1982, pp. 99-100.

Gunn, G. "Unusual Lures Attached to Tax Exempts." *Barrons*, April 13, 1981, p. 70.

Stern, Richard. "Will Alter to Fit." *Forbes*, March 29, 1982, pp. 89-90.

Part 3: Leasing: An Alternative to Borrowing

Glenn, Nichols. "Debt Limitations and the Bona Fide Long Term Lease with an Option to Purchase: Another Look at Lord Coke." *The Urban Lawyer*, spring 1977, pp. 403-20.

Greene, Richard. "The Joys of Leasing." *Forbes*, November 24, 1980, p. 59.

Harrell, Rhett, Jr. "Governmental Leasing Techniques." *Governmental Finance*, March 1980, pp. 15-18.

Harris, William. "Wanna Buy the Brooklyn Bridge?" *Forbes*, March 15, 1982, pp. 59-60.

"Lease Your Way to Up-to-Date Capital Investments," *American City & County*, October 1982, pp. 43-44.

Mentz, Roger; Menaker, Mitchell; and Pesiri, Emil. "Leveraged Leasing and Tax Exempt Financing of Major U.S. Projects." *Taxes*, August 1980, pp. 553-60.

Parry, Robert W., Jr., and Webster, Stuart K. "City Leases: Up Front, Out Back, in the Closet." *Financial Analysts Journal*, September-October 1980, pp. 41-47.

Schnellenback, Peter, and Weber, James. "Leasing: An Alternative Approach to Providing Governmental Services and Facilities." *Governmental Finance*, November 1978, pp. 23-27.

Part 4: Economic Development and Redevelopment Financing Techniques

Alternative Sources of Municipal Devel-

opment Capital: Tax Increment and Industrial Revenue Bond Financing for Cities. Volume 1: Description of Financing Tools. Washington, D.C.: National League of Cities, 1979.

Ballard, Frederic, Jr., and Currier, Thomas. Industrial Development Financing. New York: Practising Law Institute, 1981.

Davidson, Jonathan M. "Tax Increment Financing as a Tool for Community Redevelopment." Journal of Urban Law 56 (1979): 405-44.

Edmonds, Charles, and Lloyd, William. "Industrial Development Bonds Find Commercial Uses." Real Estate Review, summer 1981, pp. 103-106.

Gray, Gary, and Woolridge, J. "Industrial Development Bonds—Opportunities and Challenges." The Bankers Magazine, July-August 1981, pp. 82-87.

Melvin, Donald. "Another Look by Washington at Industrial Revenue Bonds." The Journal of Commercial Bank Lending, August 1981, pp. 59-64.

Mitchell, Richard. "Tax Increment Financing for Redevelopment: Is it as Bad as Its Critics Say? Is it as Good as Its Proponents Claim?" Journal of Housing, May 1977, pp. 226-29.

Richardson, Pearl. Small Issue Industrial Revenue Bonds. Washington, D.C.: Congressional Budget Office, 1981.

Stanfield, Rochelle. "States, Cities Can't Agree on the Need for Tax-Exempt Development Bonds." National Journal, May 15, 1982, pp. 870-72.

Part 5: Increasing the Marketability of Municipal Bonds

Benson, Earl. "Municipal Bond Interest Cost, Issue Purpose and Proposition 13." Governmental Finance, September 1980, pp. 15-19.

Cole, Charles, and Millar, J. A. The Impact of State Bond Banking on Municipal Interest Costs. Department of Finance and Accounting, West Virginia University, February 1980.

Cole, Charles, and Officer, Dennis. "The Interest Cost Effect of Private Municipal Bond Insurance." The Journal of Risk and Insurance, September 1981, pp. 435-49.

Famham, Paul, and Cluff, George. The Municipal Bond Rating Process: Implications for Local Government Decisions. Atlanta: Georgia State University, 1981.

Fischer, Philip J.; Forbes, Ronald W.; and Petersen, John E. "Risk and Return in the Choice of Revenue Bond Financing." Governmental Finance, September 1980, pp. 9-13.

Joehnk, Michael, and Kidwell, David. "A Look at Competitive and Negotiated Underwriting Costs in the Municipal Bond Market." Public Administration Review, May-June 1980, pp. 222-25.

_____. "Determining the Advantages and Disadvantages of Private Municipal Bond Guarantees." Governmental Finance, February 1978, pp. 30-36.

Kelly, Peter. Municipal Bond Insurance: An Evaluation. New York: Merrill Lynch, Pierce, Fenner and Smith, Fixed Income Research Department, January 1980.

Kidwell, David. "Call Provisions and Their Effect On Municipal Bond Issues." Governmental Finance, August 1975, pp. 28-32.

Lehan, Edward Anthony. "The Case for Directly Marketed Small-Denomination Bonds." Governmental Finance, September 1980, pp. 3-7.

Raman, R. "Financial Reporting and Municipal Bond Rating Changes." The Accounting Review, October 1981, pp. 910-25.

Rousmaniere, Peter. "How Can Localities Influence Their Credit Rating?" Massachusetts Advocate, March 20, 1979.

Stock, D., and Robertson, T. "Improved Techniques for Predicting Municipal Bond Ratings." Journal of Bank Research, Autumn 1981, pp. 153-60.

Weberman, Ben. "Both a Belt and Suspenders." Forbes, November 9, 1981, p. 261.